JAWS 2

THE MAKING
OF THE HOLLYWOOD SEQUEL

UPDATED AND EXPANDED EDITION

BY MICHAEL A. SMITH

WITH LOUIS R. PISANO

FOREWORD BY CARL GOTTLIEB

BearManor
Media

Albany, Georgia

Published in the USA by
BearManor Media
P.O. Box 71426
Albany, GA 31708
www.BearManorMedia.com

Hardcover Edition
ISBN-10: 1-62933-329-8
ISBN-13: 978-1-62933-329-8

Foreword copyright ©2015 Carl Gottlieb
Cover design by Phil Heeks
Printed in the United States of America

TABLE OF CONTENTS

PREFACE

THE AUTHORS WOULD like to thank, collectively: The writers and editors of The Destin *Log* and The Martha's Vineyard *Gazette* for allowing us to access their archives, Alfa-Betty Olsen, Jim Beller, Matt Taylor, John Konrardy, Eddie McCormack, Dana Goudreault, Chris Kiszka, Roni Lubliner, Jessica Taylor and Diedre Thieman at Universal Studios, David Holcomb, Joyce Brown Cox, Kevin Pike, Frank Sparks, George Demmy, Dan Arbieter at ABC, helicopter pilot extraordinaire Johnny Rowlands, Dana Street and Nathaniel Janick at the Martha's Vineyard Museum, Janet McArdle, Greg Van Cott, Kyle Bowe at Dreyfuss/James Productions, Dominic Mancini, Melanie Chapman at The Bubble Factory, Julianna Jenkins and the staff of the Special Collections Library at UCLA, everyone on the Navarre Beach – Holiday Inn Facebook page, Kinkos in Lee's Summit, Missouri, Chad Godfrey and the staff at Home Video Gallery in Lee's Summit, Missouri.

They would also like to give their sincere thanks to the cast and crew of *Jaws 2* who shared their stories. Special thanks to Tom Dunlop, Carl Gottlieb, Jeff Kramer and Billy Van Zandt, who went above and beyond in their assistance on this project.

Louis R. Pisano would like to thank: Jim Beller, Edith Blake, John Campopiano, Tom Dunlop, Ronald and Patricia Goulet, John Konrardy, Richard and Virginia Pisano, Dianna L. Pisano, Alyssa Preston, Peter Spadetti, Justin White and all of the Amity Kids.

Michael A. Smith would like to thank: Jim Beller, for his friendship and encouragement; Edith Blake, for her kindness; Nolan B. Canova, for making me a writer; Will Moriaty and ED Tucker, for making me a better writer; Mike and Patty Gencarelli, our other kids; Mike G, Lauren Damon, Adam Lawton and everyone that picked up the slack at Media Mikes; my Podcast partners Brett Alan Coker and Jeremy Werner; my former educators Richard Daiberl, Ken Otero and Dr. Robert McGinnis; Matthew John Drinnenberg, my best friend in *Jaws* and everything else; Steven Awalt, for his advice and assistance; John Konrardy, whose enthusiasm for this project knew no bounds – thanks for everything "Ski"; Tom Dunlop, Carl Gottlieb, Jeff Kramer, Billy Van Zandt and the rest of the cast and crew of *Jaws 2;* John Hancock and Dorothy Tristan, for opening their home to me (thank you again for the cookies); my father, Floyd, for making me take typing in 10th grade; my mother and step-father, Rose and Rick Parrish, for always supporting my dreams; all of the "parents" who helped mold me as a person, including Louis and Margie Drinnenberg, Leo and Barbara Castellano, Jim and Janetta Gilbert, Mary Gregory, and Al and Dolores List; my brothers and sisters – I love you all; my son, Phillip, for making me a better Dad and, finally, my wife Juanita, who is simply my reason for being. She's been patient with me for the past four years and now the next four are going to be devoted exclusively to her. I love you, honey!

PHOTOGRAPHS

The photos in this book were acquired from members of the cast and crew, their families or friends. The majority of our photos came from three people:

EDITH BLAKE: A long time photo-journalist for the Martha's Vineyard *Gazette* and the author of the best-selling book, *On Location – On Martha's Vineyard: The Making of the Movie JAWS*. Ms. Blake's photos are among the only photographic record of the John Hancock—era on Martha's Vineyard.

BOBBIE CHASARIK: Bobbie's father, Charles, was a crewmember on *Jaws 2* and she has very graciously allowed us to reproduce them here. We asked Bobbie to write something about her dad that we could share with our readers:

'Charles Chasarik, a welder in Pensacola, felt honored when Universal Studios hired him to work on the set of Jaws 2. Charles carried a camera in the front pocket of his shirt to capture his experience behind the scenes. The pictures he took have been tucked away in a family album, all except for the one taken of Jaws and Charles together. This photo always hung on a wall in his home reminiscent of his days working on the set. Charles would have been proud to share his photographs for this special commemoration of the film today.'

TOM RICE: Tom first contacted us when an article about the book ran in the Destin *Log*. He sent us an email that read:

Fresh out of the Army and back home in Ft. Walton Beach, Florida, I worked at an Italian restaurant named Perri's. We were very popular with, as its chef/owner Vic Perri called them, "show folks." Cast and crew would crowd the place and order things we had never offered. One dish was cooked spaghetti tossed in sautéed onions and ketchup—kind of a BBQ taste, and popular with Roy Scheider and company. I recall being surprised at how short Mr. Scheider was, after seeing him on the big screen in Jaws.

Mr. Rice went on to mention that he had some items from the filming, including a script and an album of photos. Many of those photos appear in this book. Mr. Rice is the proprietor of The Magnolia

Grill in Ft. Walton Beach. If you're ever in the area, we recommend the meatloaf!

We'd also like to thank the following individuals for allowing us to reproduce their photographs and illustrations:

Captain Jerry Baxter, Jim Beller, Richard Boluk, Karen Corboy, George Demmy, Gary Dubin, Ann Dusenberry, David Hamilton, Chris Kiszka, John Konrardy, David Leckey, Lenora May, Susan McMillan, Sol Negrin, David Owsley, Edmund Papp, Joel Salsbury, Nancy Sawyer, Debbie Singleton, Skip Singleton, Alan Stock, Martha Swatek, Bryan Utman, Billy Van Zandt, Andy Vasiloff and Tegan West.

FOREWORD

IN LITERATURE AND FILM, a sequel rewards an engaged and enthusiastic audience that wants to hear, read, or see more of whatever it was that appealed to them in the original: wonderful characters like Sherlock Holmes; continuing adventures (Holmes again, the Corleone Family, James Bond, and Jason Voorhees), and of course, The Fish—the Great White Shark from *Jaws*.

Two dedicated followers of that movie, Lou Pisano and Mike Smith, have made it their grand passion, and written a book that one might consider a sequel to my own (*The Jaws Log*)[1]. While I was limited to immediate memory, still fresh from the long summer of production of the first film, Mike and Lou had the advantage of the Internet. Couple

[1] *The Jaws Log*, by Carl Gottlieb, introduction by Peter Benchley, © 1975 & 2001, Newmarket Press for It Books, HarperCollins, New York, 217 pp, 2012. Available online wherever books are sold, in a variety of editions.

that formidable resource with their own passion, dedication, and meticulous research, and the result is this book, four years in the making: a chronicle of the production of *Jaws 2*, which was the most successful sequel of all time, in its time.

They've interviewed everyone involved, reunited the cast, and explored the location, even though decades of wind and weather have completely changed the landscape and seashore. The big Holiday Inn that housed the cast and crew, in Navarre Beach, Florida, is gone, a hurricane victim like most of the Gulf Coast from Florida to Texas. The scattered vacation homes on the sugary white-sand beach have been supplanted by condos and developments of what some might call "The Redneck Riviera." But like all memorable adventures, *Jaws 2* left a footprint bigger than Godzilla's, and these two authors have talked to everyone involved who's still alive to tell the tale. They've also exhumed archival material and memories of those who've passed, so their journal is as complete as they could make it.

I have mixed and scrambled memories of that production; I was called in at the last minute to replace a failed rewrite and a director who wasn't up to the studio's expectations. There was a huge cast and crew on a mandatory hiatus, waiting for new pages to shoot, and I was living among them at the Holiday Inn, living in one room and writing in the adjacent space in which the beds had been replaced with a desk, an office chair, a hot plate, and with hotel "art" replaced by bulletin boards filled with storyboard sketches, 3 x 5 note cards, and (gulp) the production schedule.

For about ten days, I was in close consultation with producers Richard Zanuck and David Brown, and the replacement director, Jeannot Sczwarc. While everyone else waited, we were working. Whatever we did was going to be filmed, and there would be no second chances or additional rewrites. It was a tense situation, exacerbated by the well-meaning inquiries of *everyone* staying at the hotel: more than a hundred cast and crew. Whenever I left my rooms to get a meal or clear my head or just breathe some fresh air, every person I met would nod and smile and say the same thing: "How's it going?"

That doesn't make it go any easier, I can tell you.

After dark, a band called "Brandy" played in the hotel's cocktail lounge, frequently repeating the song of the same title that was their theme. I grew to hate the music, and the inevitable inquiry from whichever attractive young server was working: "How's it going?" I couldn't even get a beer in peace.

But eventually, we all bonded, as crews on distant locations often do. The many "kids" in the film shared the same sensibilities, and I got to know them all. The authors got their stories, as well as the recollections of the other actors, the below-the-line crew members, and the rest of the creative team marooned on Navarre Beach. I'm sure everyone remembers it slightly differently, and tells it as it was in his or her own perspective, through the prism of their personal experience. Believe 'em all—there's some truth in everyone's memory. Doubt them all—nobody's got a lock on "The Truth."

Count on one thing, though: Mike and Lou have done everything in their power to bring you the story, and if you have any questions, ask them; I don't remember a thing except that hotel room and the tune of "Brandy." There's a bound copy of the script and storyboards in my library, and a DVD on a shelf near the television. I can always look at them for more memories.

Carl Gottlieb
Los Angeles, 2015

PROLOGUE

"The iron law of sequels is 'only the last one loses money.'"

THESE ARE THE WORDS of Carl Gottlieb, co-writer of the screenplay for *Jaws* (1975) as well as *Jaws 2* (1978), and *Jaws 3-D* (1983), addressing the subject of film sequels during the outstanding *Jaws* documentary *The Shark Is Still Working* (2007). A wise man, Carl had nothing to do with *Jaws: the Revenge* (1987) which was, thankfully, the LAST sequel. But what about the FIRST one?

History tells us that the very first film sequel was *Fall of a Nation* (1916) a follow-up to D.W. Griffith's classic 1915 film *The Birth of a Nation*. But before we get into understanding the power of the sequel let's make sure we agree on what a sequel is. The dictionary tells us that the word "sequel" is a noun and that it means *a literary work, movie, etc. that is complete in itself but continues the narrative of a preceding work*. The James Bond films, while featuring the same main character, are not sequels. You don't have to see *From Russia with Love* (1963) to understand *Skyfall* (2012). Same with the Dean Martin *Matt Helms* films or the popular *Flint* series that starred James Coburn. Same characters, but you could walk into any of them at any time and not need to know what had happened in previous films to follow the storyline.

As the popularity of movies grew, occasionally the audience response would be so great that a follow-up film was soon in theatres. *The Bride of Frankenstein (1935), Edison the Man (1940), Men of Boys Town (1941), and Father's Little Dividend (1951)* were true sequels, picking up the story after the original film (in case you're curious: *Frankenstein (1931), Young Tom Edison (1940), Boys Town (1938), and Father of the Bride (1950)* – the Spencer Tracy/Joan Bennett/Elizabeth Taylor version – not the Steve Martin/Diane Keaton version which inspired its own sequel). In 1968, 20th Century Fox released *Planet of the Apes*. In the next five years, they would release four more *Apes* films, each progressing the original story. After Paramount saw their 1972 film, *The Godfather*, become the highest grossing film of the year, they urged director Francis Ford Coppola to do a follow-up film. Teaming with the book's author, Mario Puzo, Coppola helped change Hollywood by being the first to put the words "Part II" after a title.

As this book is being written, here are the top ten highest grossing films of all time according to the Internet site *BoxOfficeMojo.com*:

1. *Avatar (2009)*
2. *Titanic (1997)*
3. *The Avengers (2012)*
4. *Harry Potter and the Deathly Hallows - Part 2 (2011)*
5. *Frozen (2013)*
6. *Iron Man 3 (2013)*
7. *Transformers: Dark Side of the Moon (2011)*
8. *The Lord of the Rings: The Return of the King (2003)*
9. *Skyfall*
10. *The Dark Knight Rises (2012)*

Notice a trend?

Of these ten films, six of them are sequels; one is part of a continuing series; director James Cameron has promised not ONE but TWO *Avatar* sequels and, if we know the good people at the Walt Disney Company, it's only a matter of time before we see *Frozen 2*. Heck, if the damn boat hadn't sunk (spoiler alert!) at the end of the film I'm sure some studio would be trying to hatch a *Titanic* sequel. What happened? What caused Hollywood to go sequel crazy? Of the next forty highest-grossing films on the list, twenty-five of them are sequels; three are prequels *(Star Wars: Episodes I (1999) III (2005)* and *"The Hobbit: An Unexpected Journey (2012)* and five actually spawned sequels. Where did this "sequelization" of Hollywood begin?

Following the enormous success of *The Godfather Part II (1974)* the studios looked to some of their recent successes, slapped a Roman numeral on the title, and took their chances. In 1975 20th Century Fox' *French Connection II* allowed Gene Hackman's Popeye Doyle to travel to France to find Frog One. Nobody cared. Two years later, Warner Bros. got fancy, releasing *Exorcist II: the Heretic (1977)*. The latter film was so bad that the story goes it was literally laughed off screen at its premiere. The film was so unloved that, twice after it had opened, the film was removed from theatres and replaced with a new version. Though destroyed by critics (the film maintains a 22% approval rating on RottenTomatoes. com, with fourteen of the eighteen published reviews being negative) the film did make a little money. 1977 also saw the release of *The Bad News Bears in Breaking Training"* (sequel) and *Airport '77* (no).

June 9, 1978 saw the release of the 20th Century Fox feature *Damien: Omen II* while June 23rd brought us Paramount's third installment of Kelly Leak and his teammates, *The Bad News Bears Go to Japan*. But it was the film released between them, opening on June 16, 1978 on 640 theatre screens that gave sequels the reputation they still carry today.

That film was *Jaws 2*.

MORE JAWS

On June 20, 1975, Universal Pictures released the film *Jaws* on 409 screens across North America and, literally, changed the way the nearly eight-decade old industry did business. Thanks to an amazingly popular advertising campaign—*Jaws* was one of the first films to saturate television with commercials—the public's appetite was whetted. There were more than 200 extra screens available on which to play the film but MCA/ Universal Chairman and CEO Lew Wasserman had a plan. Wanting to see "lines around the block all summer," Wasserman limited the initial release of the film. In doing so, he got his wish. According to the *Internet Movie Data Base*, *Jaws* earned an amazing $7,061,513.00 dollars in its opening weekend. With the average ticket price in 1975 being $2.05 that means that over three-and-a-half million people saw the film that weekend, averaging more than $17,000.00 per screen. In

1

comparison, *Avatar* opened on 3,452 screens, grossing $77,025,481, for a per-screen average of a little over $22,000.00 on a 2009-era average ticket price of $7.52. The biggest difference? *Jaws* cost $8 million to make while *Avatar* cost an estimated $237 million. That's right. *Jaws* almost paid for itself in its first three days of release. *Avatar* needed three weeks.

In August 1975, *Jaws* became the first film in history to surpass over $100 million in film rentals. Universal's President, Sid Sheinberg, made an inquiry of producers Richard D. Zanuck and David Brown—when are you doing the sequel? The filmmakers were apprehensive. How do you follow up the most successful motion picture ever made without looking like you were just chasing a buck? But they agreed. "We knew others would produce *Jaws 2* if we didn't," Brown would later say.(2) Hoping to find a writer familiar with the idea, the team contacted Carl Gottlieb, who had co-written the original film with the book's author, Peter Benchley. Unhappy with the money being offered, Gottlieb said no. Not dissuaded, the producers contacted Howard Sackler. Sackler, a playwright whose works include *The Great White Hope,* winner of both the Pulitzer Prize and the Tony Award for Best Play.

A friend of Browns', as a favor Sackler had done a re-write on Benchley's original script for *Jaws* and was familiar with the material. It was Sackler who suggested that the character of Quint's hatred toward sharks stemmed from him being a survivor of the attack on, and sinking of, the U.S.S. Indianapolis towards the end of World War II. The scene where Quint recalls the event, later re-written, in part, by Gottlieb and actor Robert Shaw, remains one of the most memorable in film history.

Keen on the idea, Sackler met with Zanuck and Brown and suggested, not a sequel but a prequel. What if the film detailed the mission of the U.S.S. Indianapolis, following the ship as it delivers its top-secret cargo and ending, tragically, with the doomed sailors being picked off, one by one, by sharks after the ship has been sunk. The producers liked the idea and the three men met with Sheinberg to discuss it. But it wasn't to be. After considering the pitch Sheinberg shook his head and told the trio, "That's a different shirt then we want to wear."(3) Sheinberg wanted more of the familiar formula: everyday people in danger. Preferably young people. From Amity. While Sackler wrote, *Jaws* continued to make money.

Having increased its run to almost 700 screens, the film was still averaging a box office revenue of $6 million each weekend. *Jaws* remained the #1 film at the box office for 14 straight weeks and became the first film to gross $7 million or more in a weekend three times in a row. Again, an amazing statistic considering the price of tickets and the number of screens. In comparison, *Star Wars* (1977) was only #1 at the box office for three weeks in a row when it opened (it would later lead for another 5 weeks later in the year). *Avatar* only led the box office race for 7 weeks. *Jaws* created a history in Hollywood that other films are still trying to achieve.

With the script being written the producers turned to the task of finding a director. Steven Spielberg had been in talks to helm the baseball comedy *The Bingo Long Traveling All Stars and Motor Kings* (1976) after he finished *Jaws*. However, thanks to the success of *Jaws*, Spielberg was now planning to film a science-fiction project he had conceived, to be titled *Watch the Skies* (now known, of course, as *Close Encounters of the Third Kind* (1977). *Bingo Long* was turned over to Spielberg's former office-mate at Universal, John Badham. With Spielberg unavailable, the producers began their search.

Howard Sackler recommended a young director he had worked with in the theater, John Hancock. Nominated for an Academy Award for his short film *Sticky My Fingers . . . Fleet My Feet* (1970), Hancock had written and directed the horror classic *Let's Scare Jessica to Death* (1971), directed Vincent Gardenia to an Oscar nomination opposite Michael Moriarty and Robert DeNiro in the baseball drama *Bang the Drum Slowly* (1973) and had just finished *Baby Blue Marine* (1976), which starred Jan Michael Vincent. Having gambled on the unknown Spielberg, Zanuck and Brown offered Hancock the job. With a script in the works and a director on board, the next step was casting.

With the idea of the film taking place in Amity, it would seem pertinent to bring back as many familiar characters as possible. Obviously Robert Shaw wouldn't be back, but Sackler did create a mysterious young man, nicknamed Sideburns, who is later revealed to be Quint's son.

Sideburns has come to the island to get his father's reward money. Of course, by the time the filming began, that character was renamed Bob Burnsides by Carl Gottlieb; Burnsides as a play on "Sideburns" and Bob because his character was to face a grisly death which left him legless and the upper half of his torso "bobbing" on the water. Murray Hamilton agreed to return as Mayor Vaughn, as did Jeffrey Kramer, who had played Deputy Hendricks.

However, there were TWO deputies in Sackler's script; Hendricks and Batliner. Even though he was a new character, Batliner had the majority of the lines, with Hendricks there to throw in the occasional one line joke. Unhappy with the direction of the role, Kramer withdrew from the project. Lorraine Gary also returned as Ellen Brody. That still left two familiar characters to entice back. Richard Dreyfuss (Matt Hooper) was locked into what is now regarded as another Spielberg masterpiece, *Close Encounters of the 3rd Kind*. Hoping to still include the character of Hooper in the story, the producers offered the role to Swedish actor Erland Josephson. The veteran of many of director Ingmar Bergman's greatest films turned the role down.

If the film was going to have a firm link to the original it was important to get Roy Scheider on board. Since *Jaws*, Scheider had been on screen as a closeted hit man opposite Dustin Hoffman and Laurence Olivier in *Marathon Man* (1977) and was currently working on the William Friedkin version of *Wages of Fear* (1953) entitled *Sorcerer* (1977). Next on his schedule was the role of Merle (later Michael) in the Vietnam War film *The Deer Hunter* (1978). However, during pre-production, a major plot point was altered. In the original script, Merle/Michael was the character that stayed behind in Vietnam, playing Russian roulette for money and sending it back home to another soldier. When that plot point was changed (it was decided that another soldier, Nick, would stay behind), Scheider left the project. It should be noted that the actor that played Nick, Christopher Walken, would go on to win the Academy Award as Best Supporting Actor for his work in *The Deer Hunter*. This left Scheider in a contractual bind.

After *Jaws*, Scheider had signed a three picture deal with Universal. The first film on that contract was *Sorcerer*. *The Deer Hunter* was due to be the second. But when Scheider quit, the studio had him where they needed him. They repeatedly offered him roles they knew he would turn down. Finally, they offered him *Jaws 2* with a little sweetener. If he would agree to do the film they would count it as two, thereby completing his contract. Though he had reservations, Scheider took the job. He knew they were going to make the film with or without him and he didn't like the idea of seeing the film and watching another actor playing the role.

With the main players attached, Universal quickly printed up posters which were displayed around the studio heralding the upcoming production. Casting turned to filling the various teenage roles in the script, which are highlighted in later chapters. With the cast and crew nearly set it was time for the Universal onslaught to return again to Martha's Vineyard.

MARTHA'S VINEYARD

Rumors began to swirl as early as 1976 on Martha's Vineyard that *Jaws 2* would be, at least partially, shot there. Islanders were buzzing about the sequel. There was little doubt whether *Jaws 2* would be made though, because Publisher's Weekly reported that the author for the Putnam Books novelization of *Jaws 2*, Hank Searles, had been selected. The question among islanders was is the film really being shot in part on Martha's Vineyard?

It was rumored that Tom Joyner, Assistant Director on *Jaws*, and who was rumored early to possibly be the sequel's director, was on island in the spring of 1976 and visited once again after that. It was rumored that Shari Rhodes, Casting Director on *Jaws*, was also on island and tried to reach out to her former assistant, islander Jini Poole, who was off-island at the time. The biggest rumor and probably the rumor that really peaked the anticipation with residents was that Producer David Brown was on island inquiring about renting islander Captain Roy W. Campbell's tugboat "Whitefoot" for two months.

Excitement was building but it would be over two months before rumors that Martha's Vineyard would once again become Amity Island were confirmed.

It was February 1977 when the residents of Martha's Vineyard knew for certain that, to use the phrase that was heard around the island that month, "*Jaws* is back!" In late February, Shari Rhodes was on-island and staying with West Tisbury resident Mrs. Daniel Hull. The first order of *Jaws 2* business for Rhodes was to attempt to round up as many locals who appeared in *Jaws* to reprise their roles in *Jaws 2*, no matter how small that role may have been. Seeing as the Hollywood sequel was a new venture, this was obviously the most logical endeavor for Rhodes to undertake first.

It was Mrs. Henry Scott, who played Miss Polly, Chief Brody's secretary from *Jaws*, who was the first islander approached for role reprisal. When asked to once again play Miss Polly, Mrs. Scott enthusiastically accepted the offer; quite possibly because she was well aware that only she can legibly print the new beach closed signs for the sequel. This process of contacting previous players from *Jaws* continued and it wasn't long before Rhodes realized her task at hand was complicated immensely by one particular casting requirement she had to adhere to, an impediment that was difficult to overcome.

Pensacola, Florida was where a great majority of *Jaws 2* was to be shot. It was this aspect of the production that complicated Rhodes casting search on Martha's Vineyard. She found very few islanders who would be able to fly to Florida on short notice. Popular islander Dr. Robert Nevin, who played the Medical Inspector in *Jaws*, was approached to reprise his role. He declined because he would be unable to fly to Florida for an undetermined length of time and leave his medical practice and patients.

One fortunate fact for Rhodes was that her primary duty at this time was to cast a group of teenagers aged thirteen to nineteen years old. Simple enough, just visit the island schools and listen to some of the teens read some lines. In theory, yes, however that particular week the island schools were closed and once again Mrs. Hull assisted and arranged for Rhodes to meet some island teenagers at the Kelly House, an establishment tucked neatly on a side street in the middle of Edgartown that was also the unofficial headquarters on the original *Jaws* set three years before. Rhodes would also visit Boston to meet more teens but it was the islander teens that really impressed Rhodes. She planned to have director Hancock come listen to the teens read lines in early March 1977.

Everything seemed to be falling into place in terms of casting. Roy Scheider was secured as Amity Police Chief Martin Brody. Scheider was very reluctant to partake in the *Jaws* sequel. A sequel was a risky venture for everyone's career as we've mentioned. However, Scheider was bribed by Universal to return. The studio agreed to take the two remaining films Scheider was under contract with them for and allow him to satisfy that contract with one film, *Jaws 2*. Lorraine Gary was returning as the Brody matriarch as was Murray Hamilton as the shrewd Amity Mayor Vaughn. The early buzz on the film was that it was to be more action-packed and more exciting than the original film. Amity was to be still recovering from the shark scare three years earlier in much the way the islanders were still recovering from the "Jaws" invasion three years earlier. Life mirrors art.

Shooting on *Jaws 2* was scheduled to begin in Pensacola, Florida on May 6, 1977. It was planned that later, in June 1977, that a 2nd Unit crew would start shooting on Martha's Vineyard in what was scheduled to be a 22-day shoot. During the second week of May 1977, *Jaws 2* Production Manager Tom Joyner and Art Director Gene Johnson advised the town fathers that shooting for *Jaws 2* would officially begin June 6, 1977 and that they planned to have finished shooting by July 1, 1977.

The idea was that, since most of this film was being shot in Florida that it was in the island's and productions best interests to finish shooting before the Fourth of July rush of tourists. This way, the production company would be spared the expense of the increased rents on the island over the holiday and the island would be spared the extra congestion of a Hollywood movie crew. It was during this time in mid-May 1977 when Director John Hancock joined Joyner on a tour of familiar locations to be used in the sequel.

They planned to shoot at South Beach, the site where part of the Chrissie Watkins pre-attack sequence was shot in *Jaws*. In addition, they also planned to use the Zinn house on East Chop once again as the Brody residence as well as the John Coward House in Edgartown, which

9

was the Amity Police Station exterior in *Jaws*. Of course, Main Street in Edgartown as well as the Chappy Ferry were also to be used once again in the film. Joyner and Hancock left the island and planned to return the following week to officially begin pre-production work.

On May 15, 1977 Shari Rhodes was due to arrive on island to continue work on casting *Jaws 2*. However she was busy casting down in Florida and didn't make it in time. So once again Janice Hull, Rhodes right hand woman, took over the Kelley House on Monday May 16, 1977 and people came from everywhere, even off-island, surely with delusions of grandeur about achieving fame and fortune, hoping to be cast in *Jaws 2*. The Kelley House was the stomping ground for the original *Jaws* crew three years earlier and it was now certain it wouldn't escape the bite of this second set of jaws. Adding to the chaos was the fact that such a motley pallet of specific "characters" were needed. They needed skin divers (both male and female,) a six year-old girl, teenage sailors as well as older people, surfcasters, and even full families were requested. There was no shortage of extras from *Jaws* that wished to return in *Jaws 2*.

The most interesting applicant, above and beyond the usual exclamations heard from many applicants that they "were in the beach scene" or "were in the armada dock scene;" was the young lady, a one-time waitress on the island, who quite literally played Chrissie Watkins' crab infested severed arm in *Jaws*. She recalled for Mrs. Hull how the crew neglected to mention that there would be crabs crawling on her arms and added how she suffered with a case of bronchitis for a month after her arm's famous scene concluded.

So excitement was in the air all over the island as the *Jaws* sequel picked up steam and photos of would be movie stars poured into the *Jaws 2* production office on South Summer Street and the Kelley House. Everyone knew how famous *Jaws* had become so the eagerness to be involved in its sequel was contagious.

There was one more casting session on Saturday May 21, 1977 from 10 a.m.-12 p.m. at the Kelley House where little girls aged six to eight years-old were encouraged to apply.

Come May 27, 1977 the film was already behind schedule and Rhodes had still not arrived from Florida. This was of great concern because the Martha's Vineyard portion of *Jaws 2* production was scheduled

10

to begin in less than a week, on Monday June 6, 1977. Director John Hancock was scheduled to arrive on the island on Sunday May 29, 1977, presumably with Rhodes in tow, to fish through the myriads of extras' photos prepared so diligently by Janice Hull. Jeffrey Kramer, who played Chief Brody's Deputy Hendricks in *Jaws* was briefly reprising his role for *Jaws 2*. However, he quit, citing that the role was far too small and hardly worth his time. He had other fish to fry, no pun intended.

According to the script, the fish that surely were doomed to, quite literally, fry in *Jaws 2* however; specifically 25-foot mechanical ones, still had not appeared on the island and it was believed they wouldn't ever be needed on the island, in spite of the fact that there were shark attack deaths scheduled to be shot in island waters. It would be mere days before the cameras would roll and a headquarters was set up at Coal Wharf in Edgartown.

June 6, 1977 – *Jaws 2* began shooting on Martha's Vineyard. Associate Producer/Production Designer Joe Alves had created shingled walls that hid the crew's trucks like a barricade around the work zone. Main Street in Edgartown was to appear dismal, windows to businesses were boarded up. However dismal Main Street may have looked, down at Coal Wharf things were alive with action. Actors were being cast, people were getting measured, having body make-up applied to seemingly every part of their bodies, hair was getting cut and restyled, and it was very much apparent that the *Jaws 2* production was in full swing.

One islander who was cast with a significant role in *Jaws 2* was Tom Dunlop. Dunlop was selected over 5,000 other applicants to play the role of "Keith." Ironically, Tom completed a moviemaking course at Taft just the year before.

A massive, 3-hinged, 65-foot truck was parked on Dock Street which housed the bathrooms and the dressing rooms for the actors. This along with the other production trucks lined the street, including the return of the lunch truck which was used for the *Jaws* crew three years prior. This time authorized lunch-eaters were given tickets to avoid any freeloaders grabbing a cost free lunch on Universal's dime, which author/photographer Edith Blake stated was a problem on the first *Jaws* set in her book, *On Location – On Martha's Vineyard: The Making of the Movie JAWS*.

Roy Scheider leaves the Amity Police Station

(l-r) Producer David Brown, Production Designer Joe Alves, Producer Richard Zanuck and Director John Hancock

All photos in this section are courtesy of Edith Blake

Behind the Scenes

14

Director John Hancock, with hand on hip, discusses the next set up

At this point things on Martha's Vineyard became very reminiscent of the filming of the original film. Islander Laurence Mercier was hired to tow the shark which was now on island; the position held by Lynn Murphy on the original movie. Murphy was outbid by the Edgartown Selectman for the job on the sequel. The shark, although on island, would only be used for one scene. The scene called for the shark's fin to rise in Edgartown Harbor with the unsuspecting town in the background. Once this scene was shot the giant mechanical shark was sent down to Pensacola, Florida.

Stuntman Teddy Grossman was on island to once again handle some stunts although his actual character met his gruesome demise in the estuary in the original film. Jay Mello, who played Chief Brody's youngest son Sean Brody in the first film, was cast as random teenager for some scenes shot at Coal Wharf which was being rented by Universal for $600 a day. Mello did not reprise his role as Sean Brody because he hadn't aged enough since 1974 so the part was instead offered to then-unknown Ricky Schroder.

Schroder's first big scene involved him being thrown overboard in jest by the older teens. The scene was shot, and reshot, and Schroder took may spills into the water. Tom Dunlop, who was cast as "Keith," was playing the brother of actor Keith Gordon in the film. There were many jokes about "fake" Keith and "real" Keith being passed about the set.

Murray Hamilton was back as Mayor Vaughn and was on island as was Roy Scheider. Islander Paul Trombly, who co-author Lou Pisano, through a strange coincidence, learned was once his aunt's boyfriend, was Roy Scheider's stand-in double.

On Friday June 10, 1977 a big storm hit the island. It was during this storm that actress Lorraine Gary arrived on island. The rain prompted the crew to shoot indoors so they were off to Edgartown Town Hall to shoot in the Selectman's Office. Murray Hamilton was on hand as was Robert J. Carroll, Cyprien P.R. Dube, and John Painter. Painter was originally cast by Shari Rhodes as a non-speaking boater but because she thought he had a great voice, he was "promoted" to being an Amity Selectman in the film.

The following day, better weather conditions led to about 100 extras being sent to the bridge between Oak Bluffs and Edgartown,

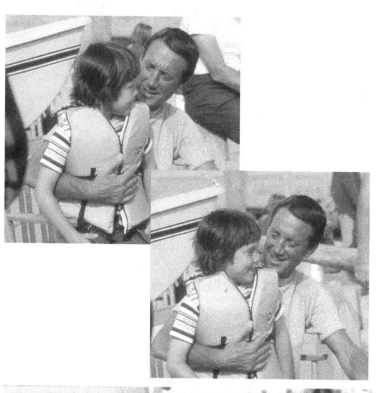

Roy Scheider has some fun with the original Sean Brody, Ricky Schroder.
Photos on this page are courtesy of Edith Blake

affectionately dubbed "The Jaws Bridge" because of its famous scene in the original film. The extras were instructed to act as if they were witnessing a boat burning. Director John Hancock decided at the last minute to shoot a scene involving dozens of extras at the Steamboat Wharf in Edgartown. There was to be an ambulance pulling up to the scene and extras were instructed to act panicked. In the final film this scene was reshot in Florida, thus the clever editing in the final film of Chief Brody's truck speeding through Edgartown toward the Steamboat Wharf only to pull up to an ambulance that was actually in Florida. By Monday June 13th, 1977, with only two weeks left on island before production moved to Florida, the weather had significantly improved and production resumed at Coal Wharf with some of the "Amity Teens."

Fake tans and sunburns were applied by make-up while the On Time II, operated by Richard P. Hewitt, was being shot as well. In spite of the inclement weather and several on-set mishaps, such as the camera dolly truck sinking into the sand, *Jaws 2* was still on schedule and the general consensus among islanders and returning cast from *Jaws* was that the sequel's production was far more organized than that of the first film's production three years earlier.

The arrival of mid-June 1977 saw the hiring of photographer Susan Ford, daughter of former President Gerald Ford. Ford was to be the assistant to Louis Goldman, the *Jaws 2* set's still photographer. Many of the photos taken on set were featured in Ray Lloynd's book, *The Jaws 2 Log*, which was essentially a studio-approved, detailed account of the *Jaws 2* production.

On Saturday June 18, 1977 the pressure was building for the *Jaws 2* crew. Their base at the Coal Wharf was soon to be needed by the Yacht Club for parking. They had to be moved from Coal Wharf the next day. The concern was that, if shooting was not completed over the next 24 hours that Art Director Joe Alves would have to go through the nuisance of having an exact replica of the Coal Wharf built in Florida to finish the needed scenes. However the crew met their deadline, completed shooting on the Coal Wharf, and moved down the street to the Steamship Wharf, affectionately dubbed the "covered dock" by crew.

It was at the Steamship Wharf where scenes involving over 100 extras were to be shot. The scenes involved reactions of concerned citizens to an ambulance for a diver who killed himself trying to escape the shark by giving himself an embolism from rising from the depths too quickly.

Director Hancock became increasingly annoyed while trying to shoot a scene where Lorraine Gary was walking through the crowd towards the ambulance. Extras kept moving in front of the camera, blocking the path previously plotted out by Hancock for Lorraine. Eventually the extras stayed in their proper places and the scene was shot. Other scenes shot involved sailboats coming and going from Edgartown Harbor.

Monday June 20, 1977 was a bright summer day, much to the chagrin of director John Hancock who wanted Amity to appear dismal and depressing. The scene called for the Amity Police truck, following closely behind a speeding ambulance, to cross the intersection of Main Street's "Four Corners" in Edgartown. Of course the intense sunshine was not conducive to effectively portray the dark atmosphere the director wanted so four fog machines were set up. The streets were soaked with water by a fire truck to add to the ambiance of the scene. The plan was to use filters on the cameras and manipulation in the lab in post-production to make one of the nicer days of the summer so far seem like it wasn't so nice out at all.

Bright colors were all but omitted from the film with the color yellow being especially discriminated against by director Hancock. There were even rumors flying that he was going to have the yellow lines in the streets painted black. Blonde haired cast were forced to wear black bathing suits. Sails on boats were made black. There were even extras who were sent home to change clothing because their ensemble was too bright for the director's liking. Ironically, Art Director Joe Alves was to place red roses in between the slats of a picket fence which lined the street; a curious endeavor to be sure considering the dark tone for Amity Island that the director was obsessed with achieving. Supposedly the roses were to add contrast to the scene. Of course red roses were the least of Joe Alves' worries this day.

Originally Alves had planned to once again use the Zinn house on East Chop as the Brody residence as it was in the original film. When Alves learned this was not going to happen, he immediately chartered a plane to fly around the island looking for a suitable replacement for the Brody home. He found six homes but none of the owners were willing to allow Universal to use their homes. So finally Alves settled on using the Cornelius S. Lee House on White Beach because it had the backyard beach he was looking for.

Sunday, June 26, 1977, was quite possibly the most significant day for the *Jaws 2* production. Not only were the cast and crew slowly leaving the island to resume filming in Pensacola, Florida; but a bombshell was dropped this day as well. Director John Hancock abruptly left the film. Obviously following suit was his wife, Dorothy Tristan, who was a co-writer of the script. The couple's departure was a massive setback for the film that not only meant script rewrites would now be required but, it also meant that everything that had been shot so far would have to be reshot.

Plans were announced that Universal would return to Martha's Vineyard in the fall to acquire the now needed reshoots. In the meantime, it was also announced that a significant amount of *Jaws 2* would start shooting near Pensacola, Florida in three weeks for what was planned to be a four month shoot. The three weeks wait was to allow for the special effects crew to test and work on the mechanical sharks which were shipped off to Florida from Martha's Vineyard weeks before.

It wouldn't be until nearly mid-July 1977 that Jeannot Szwarc would be named as John Hancock's replacement as director of *Jaws 2*. Whether or not the film crew would truly return to Martha's Vineyard that fall would be a decision that Szwarc would now make once he reviewed the scenes that were already shot by John Hancock. *Jaws 2* veteran Carl Gottlieb was hired to replace Dorothy Tristan and he rewrote the script. Gottlieb eventually replaced five of the seventeen Amity kids, changed a few of the character's established names, and eliminated two of the Amity Kid characters altogether.

NAVARRE BEACH, FLORIDA

It's CALLED "the Emerald Coast." A beautiful stretch of beach from Destin to Pensacola, Florida. And it was here that Tom Joyner and Joe Alves decided to film the majority of *Jaws 2*.

The production had set up a "boot camp" for the young actors, whose days began with a vigorous round of calisthenics. Prior to heading to Martha's Vineyard to shoot the cast spent countless hours every day learning to sail under the watchful eyes of Ellen Demmy. When the kids weren't needed on set their call sheets always read the same: "Calisthenics and Sailing Practice."

Scheider (on left) relaxes between shots.

All photos in this section are courtesy of Edith Blake

The cast and crew were housed in the Navarre Beach Holiday Inn, the only hotel property in the area. Not only was it a place for everyone to assemble, it became their home away from home.

On Sunday morning, June 26, 1977, a bombshell shook those in Florida as well as on Martha's Vineyard. It was announced that director John Hancock had "left" the film. As the cast and crew were already scheduled to move to Florida to continue shooting, many did, waiting patiently while a decision was made as to whether the production was going to continue or not.

Much to everyone's relief, director Jeannot Szwarc was hired and production was scheduled to resume in late July. Carl Gottlieb was hired and spent most of the month of July in his hotel room, banging out a new script.

On July 28, 1977, Gottlieb turned in his draft, incorporating his new ideas into the existing script. Several scenes were kept, for budgetary reasons, but Gottlieb created a whole new adventure for the Amity Kids to embark on. He would continue to tweak the script until Labor Day.

On Saturday, July 30, the 2nd Unit captured Patrick and Lucy ramming the boat that contained Timmy and Brooke. Highlighted on that day's call sheet were two words: PARTY TONIGHT. In an attempt to loosen up the cast and crew, director Szwarc insisted that each Saturday night would feature a party so that, after a long week of filming, the cast and crew could blow off some steam. This would be even more important in November and December, when Szwarc and company embarked on a 22-day straight shoot so that the film could be finished before Christmas.

Also on that day, after spending two weeks waiting, actor Marc Gilpin and his father met with Szwarc to discuss the role of Sean Brody, which was currently being played by Ricky Schroder. After the meeting Gilpin was in and Schroder was released. With principal photography scheduled to resume on Monday, August 1, the final player in Szwarc's cast had been set. The first shot is described, simply, as "Ed and Tina vs The Fin."

Most of August was spent filming the "Kids" on the water. When the weather wouldn't cooperate, the production moved to a warehouse in

Pensacola, where mock-ups of the Amity City Hall and Police Station offices were built. On August 16th, the scenes where Tina is rescued and where Mike Brody flips his boat were filmed. Later that day, when rain came, the 2nd unit accompanied Roy Scheider to Pensacola and filmed him manufacturing his cyanide-tipped bullets.

If the rain couldn't stop the production, you have to wonder if anyone even realized that Elvis Presley died that day.

The other big news that week was the announcement that Susan Ford, the daughter of former President Gerald R. Ford, would be working on the production as a "special photographer." A photo-journalism student at the University of Kansas, Ford took many photos which later appeared in the studio-assisted book, *The Jaws 2 Log*, written by Ray Lloynd.

As August continued and the kids spent more time at sea, a casting call was put out in the local paper for "Acting Look-Alikes" to spell the kids during long shots and pick-ups. The tallest among the kids was Billy Van Zandt at 5' 11". The shortest was 4' 3" Marc Gilpin.

August 25, 1977 saw the filming of one of the most dramatic scenes in the film, the rescue of Mike Brody.

As Labor Day approached, the cast spent their days frolicking at the Lighthouse. Afterwards, the discovery of the killer whale was filmed.

On September 2, 1977 Carl Gottlieb turned in the final draft of the screenplay.

As the weather got colder the shoot got longer. Shortly after Thanksgiving director Szwarc convinced that the only way to finish the film before Christmas was to shoot seven-days a week. This made the aforementioned Saturday night parties even more important.

On December 22, 1977, Roy Scheider lowered himself down a thick cable and, with the help of the special effects crew, sent the shark to an electrifying death. By the end of the day the Holiday Inn was almost vacant.

You will learn much more about the Florida shoot, through the stories of the cast and crew, later on in the book. To mention certain things here would only spoil your upcoming reading. No one likes to know what happens before they read a book or watch a movie. Read on and we promise, you won't be disappointed.

BACK TO THE VINEYARD

OCTOBER 17, 1977 was a real life sequel of sorts itself, at least it surely must have felt like one for Martha's Vineyard and *Jaws 2* crew. The film-makers returned to Martha's Vineyard to reshoot scenes shot with former director John Hancock months before. The film was no longer to portray a dismal and depressed Amity Island with boarded up windows and dense fog, instead new director Szwarc wanted to portray a bright town that has recovered from its previous shark problem four years earlier.

Bright colors were brought into the film and fog was not used. The idea was that the shark ruining a happy town was far more impactful than a shark ruining an already-depressed town. All of the dock scenes and water scenes that were shot under Hancock had been scheduled to be reshot in Florida however, recreating the uniqueness of Edgartown in Florida was impossible. So it was decided that a small crew of 25 people would reshoot Edgartown scenes. Roy Scheider and Lorraine Gary were brought back to Martha's Vineyard for some reshoots as well.

One scene which never made the final film was that of Scheider exiting the John M. Coward House, the Amity Police Station exterior as seen in the original *Jaws*, and walking a few paces to enter a photography shop. As simple of a shot as this seems, it took Scheider and crew until 9:30 p.m. that evening to finish the scene.

An interesting dilemma presented itself to the *Jaws 2* crew. The scenes that were to be shot, which primarily involved the Amity Police truck racing through the streets of Edgartown towards the ferry dock, were to portray a very hot summer's day with the usual hustle and bustle of tourists on the streets. Well it was now late October in Massachusetts. There were no leaves on the trees and not nearly enough tourists. The weather was cold and a pair of recent nor'easters had effectively blown all the now-colored leaves off all the trees and onto the streets.

Janice Hull hired fifty extras to play the tourists and all of the fallen autumn leaves were swept up off the streets. The crew even went so far as to bring their own blooming, green trees that were meticulously placed in the scenes for atmosphere and then moved to the next filming location, courtesy of islander David Hand and his pickup truck. Eventually, after reviewing dailies, there were several reshoots needed involving the Amity Police truck boarding the "On Time II" Chappy Ferry. They finally got the scene they were looking for and in perfect time as shortly after the scene wrapped, the weather turned foul.

Within a month it would be over. Universal would once again leave Martha's Vineyard and return to Pensacola, Florida for the last month of shooting there. *Jaws 2* had invaded Martha's Vineyard a second time in much the way the shark invaded Amity Island a second time on film. It wouldn't be long before islanders returned to their normal everyday lives no doubt anticipating a return of Hollywood in a few years for the seemingly inevitable *Jaws 3*. For now, *Jaws* was gone and all that remained was for islanders to anxiously await the theatrical release of the sequel to see the results of the invasion that overtook their island once again.

Shooting inside the Holidome of the Navarre Beach Holiday Inn

Roy Scheider (in suit, center) and Lorraine Gary take in the festivities.

Ann Dusenberry is Miss Amity.

The shark attacks the speed boat.

Destin becomes Amity

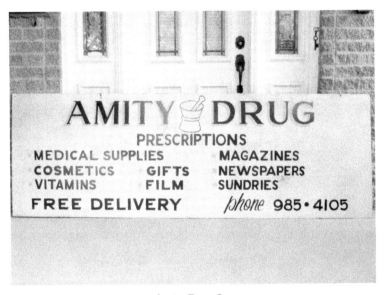

Amity Drug Store

The bandstand and beach cabanas

Snack bar

The light house, built by Joe Alves and his crew.

Have dinner at the Amity Whaler

Grace Witherspoon's house.

A shark tower....or just an observation platform.

Cable Junction

Sculptor Chris Mueller, Jr (seated) with model makers Gunnar Ferdinandsen and Werner Benczek. Dated April 2, 1977. The finished Orca sculpture would measure 20' 9" long.

SCREENPLAY BY...

BEFORE 1975, if you knew the name Howard Sackler it was because he was the author behind the 1969 Broadway play *The Great White Hope*, which won Sackler the Tony and New York Drama Critics Circle award as the year's Best Play as well as the Pulitzer Prize for Drama. A friend of film producer David Brown, Sackler accepted the offer to do a re-write on *Jaws* author Peter Benchley's script for the film version of his novel. Sackler's main contribution to the story was the back story that the shark fisherman, Quint, derived his hatred for sharks from having survived the sinking of the U.S.S. Indianapolis in July of 1945 (in the film, Quint errantly states the date as "June the 29th, 1945").

When Brown and his producing partner, Richard Zanuck, approached Sackler about writing *Jaws 2*, Sackler's first idea was to write about the Indianapolis incident. However, after being told that the studio wanted to stick to the familiar landscape of Amity Island, he created a dark world where Amity was almost a ghost town and Police Chief Martin Brody is beyond paranoid and haunted by nightmares from his experience.

The character of Len Petersen is introduced as a real estate tycoon who promises the town fathers that he can bring Amity back to the destination showcase it once was. Mayor Larry Vaughn must deal with a town in the depths of its own depression as well as a Police Chief who is trying to get the funds from the city treasury to pay for fencing to be put in the water at the city's main swimming beach. Another new character is a gentleman named Boyle. Boyle has tracked down a relative of Quint's and has purchased the fisherman's shack and belongings, planning to turn the building into a tourist establishment called the "Shark O' Rama Shark Den."

While there are quite a few youngsters in the finished film, Sackler only concentrated on four: Mike Brody, his little brother, Sean, and two friends of Mike's; Andy and Doug. Tina and Ed briefly show up just in time for Ed to get eaten. Brody is now beyond paranoid, dealing with sharks in his ever darkening dreams. One nightmare has him seeing sharks in every body of water he looks in, be it the ocean or the town swimming pool. It ends with his body washing ashore at Ellen Brody's feet, dead from a shark attack. After a dead killer whale washes up on the beach, the victim, in Brody's eyes, of sharks, the Chief takes the police boat out and ends up destroying it, losing his job in the aftermath.

Eventually the shark makes his presence known to others and Brody, Boyle and Petersen head to sea on Petersen's twin engine boat. They search for the shark, who finds them and begins ramming the boat. Boyle is knocked overboard. With Petersen at the helm, it is up to Brody to rescue him. As the boat pulls alongside Boyle, Brody reaches down and pulls the man up. But he is too late as he only pulls the top half of Boyle out of the water, the man having been bitten in half below the waist. The shark continues to attack. Brody has Petersen raise the boat's twin engines out of the water and then centers himself between them on the back of the boat. He begins kicking his legs, hoping to attract the shark. As the shark heads towards him, Brody at the last minute pulls himself up into the boat while Petersen drops both engines into the water, their whirling propeller blades chewing up the shark in a red blaze of glory!

This was the script that director John Hancock was handed. Hancock showed the script to his wife, actress/writer Dorothy Tristan. Tristan read it and suggested some ideas that Hancock liked. He asked her to do a rewrite and, when she was finished, he showed it to producers Richard Zanuck and David Brown who liked it enough that Tristan was hired on as co-screenwriter. Tristan made several changes to the story, adding a major action scene (the shark attacking the water skier), dropping the Boyle character, fleshing out the character of Ellen Brody, adding more teenagers and now having the shark meet his end via electrocution. Instead of the four major teenage characters (or six, if you include the brief appearance of Ed and Tina) in Sackler's script, Tristan had seventeen, including a young man known as "Sideburns" who would be revealed to be Quint's son. This was the script in place until director Hancock was removed from the project. Enter Carl Gottlieb.

A friend of Steven Spielberg, Gottlieb had been brought in by the director to punch up Peter Benchley's script, giving the first film a well needed dose of humor. Gottlieb had been approached in the early discussions to write the script for *Jaws 2*, but turned the offer down because of the money being offered. Now, with Universal in a bind, Gottlieb received a healthy raise in agreeing to return. As he had on the first film, Gottlieb streamlined the story. Gone was Quint's son, "Sideburns." Instead the character became Bob Burnsides. Gottlieb named him Bob because originally the character was to meet the same fate as Boyle in Sackler's script. Bitten in half, the upper part of his body would "bob" on top of the water!

Gottlieb also solved the problem of trying to get all of the teenage characters out on the water at once. Thinking back to an earlier time in history when young boys would cruise up and down Main Street in their cars trying to impress the girls, he resolved that in a community like Amity, where boats outnumbered cars, the teen culture would be to "cruise" with their friends in their personal boats.

Like the first film, Gottlieb was writing a step ahead of the production, often finishing scenes mere days before they were scheduled to be filmed. Because it was 1977, and personal computers were just being introduced, Gottlieb spent his days in his room at the Navarre Beach Holiday Inn banging out the story on his reliable typewriter. Occasionally the changes were immediate and a note would accompany the Xeroxed pages. Here is an example from September 1, 1977:

"Scenes 63 through 73, the Lighthouse/Whale sequence, have been edited prior to their inclusion in the final script. Since the final script will not be back from Mimeo until next week, we will shoot these pages today. I figured you would like to have them today.
Thank you for your attention.
Carl"

When the final film was released the script was credited to Howard Sackler and Carl Gottlieb, based on characters created by Peter Benchley. This credit was appealed by Dorothy Tristan to the Writers Guild of America, who upheld the credit.

The death of Marge

Tom Andrews in trouble.

The shark attacks the kids Armada.

Keith Gordon, Donna Wilkes, Billy VanZandt and Gigi Vorgan.

David Elliot and Billy VanZandt

Donna Wilkes and Keith Gordon

Readying the shark for his electrifying finale'.

Roy Scheider prepares to get into position

Scheider works his way down the cable.

The shark's first attack on Brody.

"Open wide!"

"Say ahh!"

Sparks fly

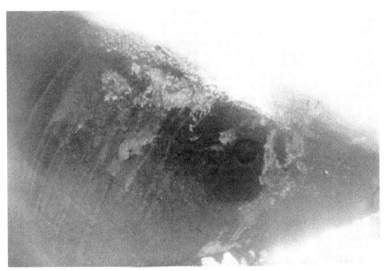

The shark gets his close up.

The shark platform

The shark being unloaded

Out above the water.

Charles Chasarik, one of our featured photographers

Moving into position.

81

On the surface

The shark relaxes on dry land.

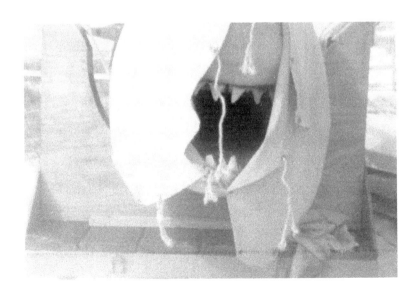

AUTOGRAPHS FROM THE SET

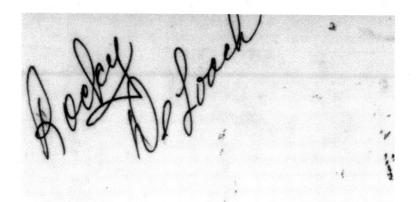

Crew member Rocky DeLoach

Ken –

Thank you for finally [...] this to me to sign. [...] wishes on getting this [...] done & in the theaters. [...] we buck-up and [...] each other's company.

Always,
Ann Dusenberry

Ann Dusenberry

Camera Operator John Fleckenstein, Director of Photography Michael Butler

Crew member Bob Forrest

Lorraine Gary

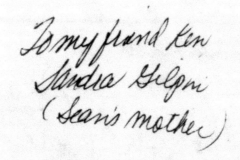

To my friend Ken
Sandra Gilpin
(Sean's mother)

Sandra Gilpin, Marc "Sean Brody" Gilpin's mother

If it wasn't for you I would have died of thirst a long time ago! Best Wishs, and enjoy life to the fullest.

Your friend,
Mark Gruner

Mark Gruner

Best Wishes

Murray Hamilton

Murray Hamilton

For You thank you for all your kindness. Best, Jeffrey Kramer

Jeffrey Kramer

Phil Leto – Hair Stylist

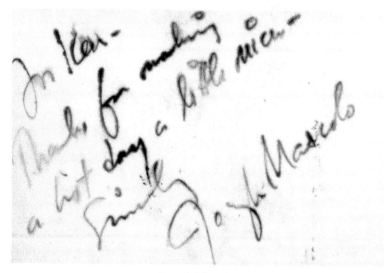

Joseph Mascolo

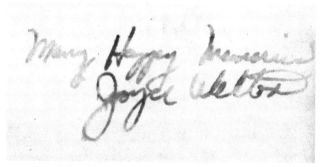

Casting assistant Joyce Welton

First Assistant Director Don Zepfel

To Ken,

affectionately,

Jeannot
Szwarc

Jeannot Szwarc

DELETED SCENE
The death of Bob

Sorry for the inconvenience! (from the collection of Jim Beller)

Waiting for Dick or David.

Joseph Mascolo rehearses for the beach panic scene.

Amity PD vehicle.

Amity Police Boat

Amity Police Boat

Filming Roy Scheider on the way towards Cable Junction

ON AND OFF SET

A cake for the crew.

November 21, 1977 – director Jeannot Szwarc turns 38

DIRECTED BY...

By now, you know that John Hancock had been hired to make the film and that he had been replaced by Jeannot Szwarc. But what about the man in the middle – Steven Spielberg.

You will read in later chapters various stories about Spielberg's interest in making *Jaws 2*. In our research we found some stories from the horse's mouth.

In October 1975 he told a film festival audience that "making a sequel to anything is just a cheap carny trick. Universal offered me the opportunity to direct the sequel, but I didn't even answer them. I didn't call or write or anything." (4)

After John Hancock was fired, Spielberg was contacted by his mentor, Universal Studio head man, Sid Sheinberg. This time he gave them an answer. "I said I'd spend the July Fourth weekend trying to find the solution to a sequel and that if I could write it and Zanuck and Brown would push the production to the spring of '78, I'd do it. I spent three days at the typewriter and wrote seven or eight schematic breakdowns. I kept the Dreyfuss and Scheider characters in it. Then I finally said to myself, 'I can't, I can't.' I called Sid back and said I couldn't do it… I decided a sequel would not be an exercise in expanding my own horizons. It would be corporate business." (5)

In June 2011, Spielberg chatted with author Brian Vespe, better known to his readers as "Quint," for a piece on the *Ain't It Cool News* web site. Asked if he was offered *Jaws 2* he replied, "Yeah, of course. And *Jaws 3*. I was done, I was done with the ocean. I would have done the sequel if I hadn't had such a horrible time at sea on the first film. I would have absolutely jumped at the chance to own the sequel because I knew that when I was walking away from the sequel I was walking away from a huge piece of my life that I had helped to create, but it wasn't a hard decision to walk away from it. I just could not imagine going back out to the ocean and sitting in a boat for 9 months. I just couldn't imagine it.

So, I was happy and relieved not to have made the movie, but also I wasn't happy with the sequel and I realized I had let a franchise go that I could have made a good contribution to."

When asked if he had any idea what he would have done with a sequel, Spielberg replies, "No. No idea at all. But I have a very, very good scene which I thought would have been good for a sequel someday."

He didn't share his idea.

THE AMITY KIDS
(PART ONE)

IF YOU'RE A FAN of the film *Jaws 2* then you may know there were seventeen young cast members who made up the teenage clique' in the movie. Many were cast by, and also released by John Hancock but, after he was replaced, new director Jeannot Szwarc made some changes as well. The actors who started out with John Hancock and finished the film with Jeannot Szwarc are: John Dukakis, Tom Dunlop, Ann Dusenberry, David Elliot, Keith Gordon, Cindy Grover, Susan McMillan, David Owsley, Gary Springer, Martha Swatek and Billy Van Zandt. They will all be covered in the next chapter. This one is devoted to the ones that got away.

Karen Corboy (Lucy)

Karen Corboy was a student at Chicago's William Howard Taft High School, an institution that boasts guitarist Terry Kath from the band *Chicago* and Jim Jacobs, the co-writer of the Broadway musical *Grease* among its alumni. She modeled locally and, thanks to her theater work, gained an occasional mention in Irv Kupcinet's popular *Kup's Column* in the Chicago *Sun Times*. She recalls an open audition at her modeling agency as her way onto the film. "I had just wrapped up a production of *Guys & Dolls* with the Chicagoland Theatrical Troupe where I played Adelaide. I met with casting director Shari Rhodes at the Shirley Hamilton Agency in Chicago. There must have been 400 girls auditioning but I was one of the ones flown to New York City twice to test with Dorothy Tristan. I got a call the first week of May 1977 and was told that I had been cast as a small character by the name of Lucy and that I would be gone five weeks. A week into filming Sarah Holcomb was let go and they asked me to take over her character, which was originally named Angela but which was later changed to Jackie."

Karen Corboy

On the dismissal of Hancock and Tristan, she recalls "I was released after the cast and crew went on hiatus...when John and Dorothy were at odds with the producers about the film. I was TOLD that the new director, Jeannot Szwarc, had different ideas on the way the film should look and changed seven of the characters...one of them being mine."

When asked if she recalls any particular scenes from filming she mentions two. "We were filming and a catamaran that I was sailing on with David Elliot, Billy Van Zandt and Nancy Sawyer flipped over. The waters were really rough and it took a Boston whaler to turn it back over. We were in the water at Navarre Beach. . . we were hiking out and the wind came about really quickly and we just turned over. I remember we lost a $1500 radio. Scott Maitland, the assistant director, wasn't too happy about it I recall. Another time we were filming with Ricky Schroder, who was just a little kid about seven years old I think, and he was supposed to hit a certain mark and say a line and then jump onto the boat. We did, like, twenty-four takes and it took most of the afternoon and I still don't think they were happy with the results. Coming from a background in theater this was very foreign and a little frustrating to me since I wasn't used to getting any more than one take."

Asked about any on-set romances, she will only say, "a lady doesn't kiss and tell but David Elliot did take me to my senior prom." As for memories, she shares a couple. "I remember getting second-degree sunburn on the back of my legs and having to either stand or keep my legs elevated for two days so I wouldn't blister and peel. I had to have towels soaked in Sea Breeze antiseptic applied every hour. I had been laying on the dock early in the morning, about 9:30 a.m., doing whatever homework I was working on at the time. I didn't feel it, but the sun bouncing off the water just flash fried my skin. Coming from Chicago, I wasn't used to that intense weather. I also remember that we were first being taught to sail in Florida. We started off with Sunfish, which is/was a small sailboat only big enough for one person. We had to sail out to a certain point and back to practice. The wind was fine on my way out but suddenly died down and I remember having to try to tack back and forth and back and forth to try to get back to shore. It was an exhausting and nerve-racking time, since I was so unfamiliar with sailing to begin with.

My summers were spent on boats in Lake Geneva, Wisconsin, but I was usually just skiing or tubing."

David Elliot and Karen Corboy

Sarah Holcomb (Angela)

Sarah Holcomb was 16 years old when she was cast in the role of Angela. She was let go while still rehearsing in Florida. More on Sarah can be found in the *Catching Up* chapter.

Lily Knight (Kathy)

Lily Knight was already acting and in college when she got wind of *Jaws 2*.

"I was in acting school at the time at NYU and the audition was such a huge thing. I found out about the audition from a good friend who was also good friends with Dorothy Tristan. I had understudied a role in a play that Dorothy had done at Centerstage and my friend suggested to her that she read me for the film. So, after reading and about five more callbacks, I got a part in the film.

Of course I was crushed when I got fired. It took me a long time to get over it. After John was fired we were all sent home so they could regroup and I got a call a couple weeks after I was home that said I was not going to go back with the others. I mean, a lot of us were let go, I think maybe ten of us, so I don't think it had anything to do with me but I had never been fired.

But I'm still good friends with most of them today. I see Lenora May often at commercial auditions and I see a lot of Billy Van Zandt."

Like the rest of the teen cast, Lily headed down to Florida to learn how to sail. "We had to go to sailing camp and that was extremely challenging to me. I was bad at it and had to have special coaching. I do remember one day we were shooting on Martha's Vineyard in the bay and I did this thing that was so much fun, a slice through two other boats. I caught the wind at just the right angle. It was amazing! You really get an adrenaline rush when you do something that is so far out of your wheelhouse, so far out of your comfort zone. That's a happy memory for me. That and spending a lot of time with Lenora out on the catamaran.

I also remember being out a lot with Keith Gordon and Billy Van Zandt and just really enjoying the people. It was such an unusual experience for me. I mean, I've done a couple big pictures since then and I sort of recognize the politics of what goes on. They couldn't afford to take chances when it was that much money involved and the fact that they had this husband-and-wife team directing and writing was kind of a big chance.

So now I look back and kind of understand why they did what they did. John was a little too far outside of the Hollywood formula, you know what I mean? I think they could've probably worked with one of those personalities but both of them at once took them too far outside their usual domain.

Here I was with a career I thought was heading towards Broadway and I found myself catapulted onto a movie set on location, which was a completely different world. I had more money than I'd ever had before. It was only scale but to me it was a huge amount of money. Staying in hotels and eating out all the time, it was just like a fairytale. And then it ended."

Lenora May (Laura)

Lenora May was a graduate from the University of Miami's Theatre Department and hung out with some well-known fellow students.

"I had gone to the University of Miami and got a Bachelor of Fine Arts in theater. Some of my classmates are pretty well known. Ray Liotta, Steven Bauer. Ernie Sabella was a grad student when I was there. It was a great department and after I graduated I moved back to New York to start my career. I signed with a manager who got me many, many agents. Back then you had to have several agents, you couldn't have just one.

Even though I was 20 years old I looked like I was 16 because I had long hair and freckles and was really skinny. I started going out for commercials and I got the first one after about a month, and after that I got my SAG card and started working.

For two years I was doing equity theater and other shows and commercials. One day I got an invitation to meet the casting director of *Jaws 2*. I read for her and she said, 'Yes, ok.' The whole process took months. I think I had to go in and read five different times for different groups of people. They were sorting out all of these teenagers that they'd seen all across the country. People in New York, people in Boston, people in Chicago. I finally came in to read for Dorothy and John and they gave me a monologue to do from *The Glass Menagerie*, the Tennessee Williams play. I was like, 'Thank you, this is right up my alley.' I'm a very sensitive actress. In school I was like the star of all the dramas. Not the musicals, the dramas. They gave me this piece and I loved it. Dorothy told me that I reminded her of a friend of hers. They had us line up in front of a group of Universal executives. We were all standing there freezing in our little bikinis because it was the middle of winter.

They sent me home and I didn't hear from them for a while. Then they called me back and told me to come in with makeup on. Back in those days I didn't wear very much makeup because I was trying to look as young as possible. I remember getting into the elevator at Universal and riding up with Joe Alves. He looked at me and said, 'I liked you better without the makeup.' (laughs) I was so young that I looked silly with all the makeup on.

Anyway, that day we came in to read and they mixed and matched us. They put different people in different groups and had us read different scenes. I thought my work went very well. . . that I'd done a good job. I put forth a lot of emotion and tried to make it very real. I'm not sure when I got the word, but I got the word that I'd gotten the film. Of course it was huge for me.

So we went off to Florida. To Pensacola, the panhandle. We were in Navarre Beach and we were learning how to sail the sailboats. We had to learn how to sail so that when we got to the Vineyard we could really sail and make it look real. It was great for me because here I am on location with all these people in Florida. I had relatives in Jacksonville and they came to visit me. But there was also a lot of confusion. It wasn't really organized and we were never sure what were supposed to be doing. I think we were there for two or three weeks and then we finally flew up to the Vineyard. That water was a lot colder as you can imagine."

Lenora also had an association with *Jaws* while on the Vineyard. While there she dated Jonathan Filley, who had played Cassidy, the young man who misses out on Chrissie Watkins midnight swim in the first film.

"There was a three-week period of rehearsing. We would be out on the water and we'd have to pretend our boats were messed up. We'd have to pull the boats together and make a raft out of them. And then the shark is supposed to come around and we'd all have to have these different reactions.

I did one scene on land on the dock and then John Hancock got fired. He actually fired two people before that. He fired this beautiful girl who was one of the leads named Sarah Holcomb. He also fired Bryan Utman. Sarah and I had become friends but there was something about her that was mysterious. She was sort of an odd girl. There seemed to be something in her that was very disturbing, she had a lot of issues. I never found out why she was like that. I liked her so much, I really did. She was so nice. There was always something a little off with her. When she did *Animal House* (1978) she became good friends with Tommy Hulce. I stayed friends with her as long as I could. Until I moved to Los Angeles she and I stayed in touch. It was kind of heartbreaking. It WAS heartbreaking.

115

We spent about eight weeks together and then everything was shut down. We were told that in two weeks' time they would let us know what would happen."

Even this newcomer to film could sense something was awry on the set. "John was vacillating so much, he was never sure of his shots. He would set up something and say, 'No we don't need a crane' and then an hour later he would ask for the crane. Things like that. I heard he was costing them a lot of money. He just wasn't efficient. He was extremely vacillating, he kept going back and forth. I just think the studio didn't trust him.

They sent us back to our original places—mine was New York—and in two weeks I got a call that said 'You're not in it anymore, they replaced you,' and that a guy named Jeannot Szwarc was going to direct. As you can imagine I was heartbroken.

What was interesting is that they replaced some of the kids and not all of them, and I never understood that. Why only some and not all? Of course, some of us had bigger parts and I think the director wanted to put his input into the film. He wanted to find his own people. And I think the majority of the people that remained ended up with lesser roles. It would have been harder to replace twelve people than just four. So he recasts those four main people and makes the film as he wants it. That's just a guess, but every director wants to put their own stamp on their project and they don't want to inherit somebody else's taste.

I may not have been his idea of what Mike's girlfriend would look like. Teagan West was Mike and apparently he didn't fit Jeannot's idea of Mike. I think we were targeted because we had much more important roles in the film. Again, with a lot of the kids in the film, their roles are really nothing more than glorified extras. You can work on a film for weeks and weeks and weeks but really in the end you only have just a few principals that have the bulk of the storyline. There are only a certain number of roles that are key roles. The rest are just minor roles and I imagine that some of the kids were good enough to play the minor roles so they didn't have to switch them. I think they were more concerned with whoever was going to play Roy Scheider's son and myself and others.

I had a great scene, and Lily Knight played my best friend. It was a scene where I was very sad because Mike Brody had gone out with another girl and in the scene I was crying about him. THAT's a real scene, that's not some rinky-dink bit. That's a part of the storyline. Now, whether or not that scene was ever going to make it into the film who knows? But I know that was in the script. I know when I saw the film after it came out I was disappointed because it seemed more "jokey," it was more by the numbers.

I was also still very bitter about what had happened so I probably wasn't watching the film with an open heart. I really went just to see some of my friends in the film. In the original script we were a major part of the storyline. I was his girlfriend and he was going out with another girl. They go out in a boat and there's a storm. It was just a lot of stuff going on, I don't even remember how I got out there with them.

It looked like they just cut out a lot of stuff to make the film simplified. Of course, once they fired Dorothy I guess they had to get another writer to change the stuff they didn't like. This film was the motivation that made me move from New York to LA. I had shot a lot of footage and I wanted to see it. I had a really emotional scene and I remember the day after we shot it the cinematographer and a bunch of the crew people came over to me and started kissing my hand. They were saying, 'Oh my God, you were so great!' And the next thing I know I'm out of a job.

Anyway, I came out to Los Angeles and I demanded to see my footage because I knew that scene had gone so well. I mean, I didn't know what had happened. Everyone said how great I was so why was I fired? I couldn't wrap my mind around it so I came out here. They set up a private screening for me in one of the screening rooms at Universal and I went and saw it one day and it was good. I wish I had my hands on it. And that was the end of it. But I decided to stay in Los Angeles because there was a lot of work here and I was too depressed to go back to New York because I was still sad about the whole thing. So, staying in Los Angeles was the right thing to do for me.

The first job I got out here was a guest role on *Little House on the Prairie.* The whole experience had fired me up. So I got my first job and the first person I read for was Michael Landon. I knew I had made the right decision right away. In fact, the show I did was all about my character. Poor girl lives out in the woods with a crazy father. I secretly have a baby and send it down the river for someone to find. Of course,

Laura Ingalls finds the baby. They actually turned it into a 90 minute special.

Michael Landon kept writing more stuff for me to do and, of course, it made me feel much better because I was in a show that was all about me. And then he made it even bigger. That was Michael. He was the nicest guy you'd ever, ever, ever, ever want to work with. He was a sweet, sweet man. A gorgeous man. With a great sense of humor and a big, big heart."

(l-r) Lenora May, John Dukakis and Lily Knight

Lenora May and Ricky Schroder

Lily Knight and Lenora May

Lenora May

Nancy Sawyer (Brooke)

Nancy Sawyer was still in high school when she was cast in *Jaws 2*.

"I'll never forget the day that Shirley Rich came to Staples High School in Westport, Connecticut. Little did anyone realize that my dream was to be an actress and I was hoping to move to New York City on my own as soon as I could. Until that day. When I heard they were coming to my school to find new talent. . . it's hard to explain. . . but I knew in my gut the part was mine. When Shirley Rich cast me and said, 'You're the most talented person I've ever seen at your age,' I remember feeling like I'd found my home.

At the time I was seventeen years old and still in high school. I was very involved in the drama department. I knew I wanted to be an actress, though I had never worked on films or anything. I planned to graduate, go to New York and study with Lee Strasberg. What happened was one of the casting directors came up to my high school, which had a very well-known theater department. They auditioned pretty much all the kids in the drama department. They called me back so I went back in and I got the part, which was very exciting. And the role kept getting bigger and bigger the more they wrote it, which was very exciting at the time.

Rick Schroder was an adorable little towheaded boy. Sarah Holcomb was from the town next to mine. In fact, we used to use the same YMCA. After the whole *Jaws 2* fiasco I would run into her. Her boyfriend at the time was a tenant of my dad's. It was a shame because we were like a team. She was Angela and I was Brooke—we were cousins. I don't know that we **were** cousins, I think we just made that up. But we were friends. You really get that close comradery when you're working together on a film for a while, especially when you're young. I heard about some of her circumstances and my heart went out to her."

Nancy is very frank when she talks about her dismissal from the film. "I was pretty young at the time; I really didn't understand the politics involved. That's showbiz, isn't it? We went to Florida for rehearsals because they wanted us tan. Then we went up to the Vineyard. Every night we would go to our mail cubbies at the hotel to see what was planned for the next day on set but, because the shark was not working, we would get notes that would say 'on hold.' We were on hold several days in a row. Nobody could figure out what was going on and people

120

were getting frustrated. I'm sure if you go through the archives at the Martha's Vineyard *Gazette* you'll see a quote from a certain star who didn't want to play second fiddle to a bunch of teenagers. (laughs) I'm not going to say who that star is.

I was very good friends with Keith Gordon. I really enjoyed working with Dorothy and John, they were very complementary towards me and my work. I was so young and they gave me a lot of support, a lot of encouragement, and a lot of praise. Looking back, it really meant a lot to me. There's a whole other side to this story that a lot of people don't realize. It got me into the Screen Actors Guild. I still act occasionally. I'm still trying to reignite my first love, which was acting, now that my kids are older."

Ricky Schroder (Sean Brody)

By the time six-year old Ricky Schroder was cast in *Jaws 2* he was a veteran, modeling for catalogs and appearing in commercials. If you bought film in the mid-1970s you may remember him as the "Kodak Kid."

"I lived in New York and I went in and auditioned. I had done commercials before but this was my first film. I was seven when we went to Martha's Vineyard. I love to fish so whenever I wasn't needed I always had a rod or a crab pot in the water."

Rick remained part of the production until July 30, 1977 the day before production resumed with Jeannot Szwarc at the helm. Being a young boy at the time, he is unsure why he was let go. He knows his parents were upset, but that anger could have been two-fold.

His hair had been dyed brown to better make him look like Roy Scheider's son and his contract stipulated that, when he was done filming, that it would be restored to its original blonde color. Sadly Ricky flew home with green hair!

Skip Singleton (Patrick)

Skip Singleton was a senior in high school when he heard about a local casting call. "I'd come home from tennis practice one day and someone said that they heard they were looking to hire people for *Jaws 2*. They said, 'You should go out there and interview,' so I did. They were looking for someone who could sail and who didn't have a southern accent. Because of my father's military background we had lived all over so even though I was from the South I didn't have a southern accent like so many others in northwest Florida do.

So I went and I interviewed and literally I was hired that day. I knew how to sail a little bit, not a lot, but I was just hired on the spot and started the next day. I was a senior in high school, but I had finished all my credits. I informed them I wouldn't be finishing the year and, literally, started the next day. We spent our time reading the script and practicing sailing. We also practiced how we would end up in the water, with all the boats banded together. I remember Zanuck and Brown coming out and watching this. We practiced who was going to be here and who was going to be there.

It was during rehearsals that Skip asked for the weekend off to attend a family event. "I got axed because I went to my sister's wedding. My sister was getting married in Williamsburg and I asked to leave to go to her wedding. They were not pleased that I wanted to leave to go to a wedding. I have one sister... I have one sibling and I told them I needed to go. My parents told me, 'You're going,' and so I went to the wedding. And they fired me.

I ended up teaching tennis for the summer in San Destin, then I went to Ole Miss on a tennis scholarship, liked I planned to do."

Alan Stock (Eddie)

Alan Stock was an economics major at Harvard with an interest in politics when he was selected for *Jaws 2*.

Jaws 2 was my first professional acting gig. I'd only been in school plays before. I was actually going to Harvard at the time and I'd spent the previous two summers in Washington D.C. working for then-Congressman Ed Koch. If I remember correctly they held local auditions in either Cambridge or Boston."

Alan had no idea John Hancock was in trouble. "I was not aware that the studio was unhappy with how things were going. I was a self-obsessed teenager. I didn't even know there were any problems. I was just happy to be getting a lot of money and having the chance to go

(l-r) Tegan West, Sarah Holcomb, Martha Swatek and Gary Springer.

(l-r) Karen Corboy, Tegan West, Gary Springer and Nancy Sawyer

Nancy Sawyer

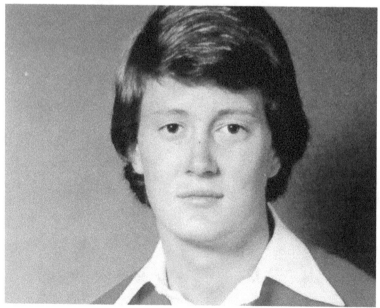

Skip Singleton

Alan Stock

sailing with pretty girls. I don't think I filmed anything major. . . maybe one scene where I was in the background. I was replaced during the hiatus when they switched directors.

Everyone was very nice. I was busy during much of the time writing papers and studying for my final exams for Harvard. They had a tutor come to the location to give me the exams. The person I remember best was Sarah Holcomb. She was incredibly beautiful, with the most amazing personality."

Jaws 2 wasn't all bad for Alan. "My experience on *Jaws 2* did lead me to being an actor for a while. After I was fired I had enough money from the shoot to come out to Los Angeles and try my luck and, after a couple of months, I was cast in a series and put under contract by Universal. Universal was the last studio to still have contract players. I think they eliminated the contract program in 1981 or 1982. Ann Dusenberry, who was very nice to me, was also a contract player.

After that I worked fairly steadily in the industry for the next dozen years or so. Donna Wilkes and I both guest starred in an episode of *T.J. Hooker* in 1982.

The credit I'm most proud of is acting opposite Gena Rowlands in John Cassavetes last work before he died, a play called *A Woman of Mystery*. He was an exceptional human being as well as an incredible talent."

Bryan Utman (Doug)

Bryan Utman had to work to get chosen for the young cast.

"I had eleven auditions at Universal Studios' offices in New York. Eleven! (laughs) At that point I guess the director was sure he wanted me in the film. **After eleven auditions!** Rick Schroder was also there auditioning for his role. Of course, he too was asked to leave.

The way they did it to me was really low—very low. In fact I think it was illegal. I was out rehearsing on a beach somewhere, maybe during the third or fourth week in Pensacola, Florida. What happened is that one of the transportation guys tapped me on the shoulder and said, 'Bryan, could you get into the van?' They had gone into my hotel room and had packed all my bags for me. They brought me to the production office. The guy who had tapped me on the shoulder told me I had been paid three more days per diem for that week and took that money back from me. Then they sent me off on a plane to New York. I didn't even know they had a ticket for me. They were obviously planning this. I was a kid.

I was in first class because I was a Screen Actors Guild member. I'm sitting towards the back of first class when who should come over because he heard me crying and whimpering but Roy Scheider. He sat down next to me. He kept saying, 'Don't worry.' He was consoling me. He was a very nice man.

He said John Hancock was the one who fired me and that he was a royal pain in the you know what! But he said, 'Don't worry.' He extended a hand of friendship for the future. He lived in New York, as did I. He was very friendly to me and he told me to call him whenever I could. He gave me his personal phone number. He said the director was extremely disorganized and insecure and, in his opinion, he wouldn't last.

Years later, when I was working as a publicist at an event in Manhattan, I saw David Brown and his wife standing outside. I walked up and said, 'Hello Mr. Brown. You don't know me but I was in the original cast of *Jaws 2*. We had a good laugh and he told me that John Hancock had been a pain in his ass. (laughs)

I do remember the actor that ended up playing the part of Doug, Keith Gordon, told Hancock that I was his friend and he didn't want to play the part. I guess they told him 'Well, then you can go home with him.' I mean, he really had no choice. The director had created such a tenseness on the set, because no one knew who was going to get the ax next. It's not the way to run a production.

He just made me so angry. He hired his wife to work on the script and she was such a busybody. She was always spreading gossip around the set. The whole thing was just so unprofessional. And it wasn't David Brown's fault, God rest his soul. He was such a sweet, wonderful man. I met him many times afterwards at Hollywood parties and he was such a good person. Kind and fair. He was always a very nice man.

After I was cast, a major book publisher came to me with the deal of being the eyes and ears on the set. They gave me a $10,000 advance to write a book. I met with a ghostwriter at my manager's place on Central Park West and signed a contract. That $10,000 was a heck of a lot more than I was going to make on *Jaws 2* and, of course, I had to give it back.

I went on to work with Dean Jones on television in *Herbie the Love Bug* and I went on to do *Seven Brides for Seven Brothers* with Richard D. Anderson and River Phoenix. I had a good career that lasted into the

90s, but I think my career would've been so much better had I gotten that start in a major motion picture like *Jaws 2*.

Years later I ran into the production manager whose responsibility had been to have me packed up and sent home. He was working on a film that Bill Badalato and his son were producing. He felt really bad about how they treated me and he hired me on the spot."

Did Bryan ever see Roy Scheider again? "I never called Roy after that. I never asked him for anything. But the fact that he did what he did meant so much to me. I know in my heart that he was so sincere and so good. He was an actor's actor. He didn't think he was any more important than the next guy. He was just that way. He was a really good person and I miss him. I really miss him."

Bryan Utman

Tegan West (Mike Brody)

Tegan West had only done a few high school plays when he was cast as Mike Brody. "In retrospect what I find particularly astonishing was the fact that I was cast at all. I'd had zero professional experience. Zero.

A manager named Bob Thompson was calling around to Los Angeles high school drama departments and asking about young men who might bear a resemblance to Roy Scheider. My teacher recommended a guy who had Roy's swarthy complexion, but suggested the manager meet me as well. We met over lunch and he mentioned that the *Jaws 2* casting people were scrambling to fill several roles; that they'd burned through the rosters in L.A .and New York and come up short.

Bob decided to arrange for me to read for the casting director. He also gave me a tip, 'If they ask you how tall you are, say 5'10.' I am 5'11". He was concerned I was taller than Roy Scheider. I went up into the "Black Tower" at Universal Studios and met a gentleman whose name, unfortunately, escapes me.

I wasn't particularly nervous. To me, this was a lark. I read for him. He took a long beat and thanked me for coming in. I got up to leave and he said, 'Wait. Come upstairs with me. I want you to meet someone.' While standing at the elevators, he gave me a once over and asked, 'How tall are you?' "5'10." 'No you're not. You're 5'11".' I froze, but he didn't press the point. I read for another man upstairs, chatted for a bit, and said my goodbyes.

The following weeks were a blur, punctuated by a few very clear memories, one being Bob Thompson calling me to say, 'Pack your bags, you're going to Florida.' I was to be paid something like $650 a week. I had to join SAG. I had to graduate early from Harvard High School. We were going to Florida to be trained by "Olympic-class sailors," including the Whitehurst brothers.

The first time I met the producers was in Florida. I remember David Brown as pleasant and friendly, while Richard Zanuck was a cooler character—all business.

Several actors were fired in the early days at Navarre Beach before actual filming began. I'd become friends with an actor named Skip Singleton, however he was fired within two weeks. I described him as a scapegoat in my diary, a message to the cast to knuckle down and get to work. He was replaced by Ben Marley, the son of John Marley. A week later two more actors were fired, Bryan Utman and Sarah Holcomb."

Tegan was unaware of any problems the producers may have been having with director John Hancock. "When our director was fired, the only scuttlebutt I picked up on was the studio didn't like the grey, gloomy look he was creating. So, the film was shut down for a few weeks. Within a day or two of the news, we were sent back to our respective cities. Not long after, I invited the actors who were in LA over to my parent's home for a barbecue. A few days later I was told by my now manager Robert Thompson that I had an appointment over at Universal to meet the new director, Jeannot Szwarc, and that I had to read for him. Unusual, I thought. I mean, there was plenty of footage, wasn't there? I was too green and naïve to see what was coming.

I happily went for what I thought was a meet and greet. In the waiting room were several of my fellow cast mates from the movie. In retrospect, I should have picked up on their frozen smiles, but it was Hancock who'd been fired, not me. I entered the office to meet Verna Fields and a grim faced Jeannot, who shook my hands and said, "Thank you for coming in. I hope you know how difficult this is." I was completely agreeable and utterly oblivious. I read for them, said my goodbyes and left, cheerfully passing my cast mates.

I don't recall how many days passed but the call came from my manager that the director had sacked several of the kids, including me. I recall he was quite incredulous. I called several of the cast members to talk about what had happened and it was then they revealed they knew my head was on the chopping block at the barbecue at my parent's house. Awkward for them, to say the least, but none of them said a word.

I can appreciate their quandary, as I can appreciate Jeannot's. Who wouldn't want to pick their own cast? I never carried a bit of ill will toward any of them. It was a great adventure for me—learning to sail catamarans and, of course, the first time I'd ever been in front of a camera. I do wonder what those dailies looked like. We weren't allowed to see them.

I graduated early from high school, worked on *Jaws 2* for a couple of months and headed off to the start of the fall quarter at USC, all without missing a beat. It was an amazing summer."

For Tegan, *Jaws 2* was the gift that keeps on giving. "I still get residuals! For a couple of years I chalked this up to some accounting error and kept this secret to myself. Several years after the movie came out, I ran into another actor from the film and delicately broached the subject. 'Do you ever get. . .' 'Residuals? Yeah.' As to why this is, my best guess is I'm in the movie. The final film contained what looked like several familiar master shots of us sailing in the harbor. Perhaps someone in legal decided it was simpler all around. Again, that's just a guess.

Tegan kept a diary during his time on the film and he shared a couple entries:

* Diary - May 9, 1977 *"What a day! There's so much involved, it's really exciting. I've met just about everybody in the cast (except Scheider and the big stars). Hey! John Hancock went around telling us what part he wanted us to portray and he said I was MIKE!"*

"Upon reading that, I recall more clearly that there was some mixing and matching after everyone arrived in Florida. And a later entry talks about how they tried another actor in the role of Mike for a day, much to my confusion and chagrin. But that was just for a day. By the time we settled into Martha's Vineyard, my hair was to be dyed a dark chestnut to closer resemble Scheider's hair. Another entry, June 12, 1977 in Martha's Vineyard, talks about 27 takes – all day - for one shot – **"preparing to leave the harbor."**

As much fun as he had on set, Tegan also enjoyed a trip off the Vineyard.

"A highlight involved traveling with John Dukakis and a few other actors to Boston. We stayed in the governor's mansion and that night it was arranged for us to see John's grandfather, Harry Dickson, conduct the Boston Pops. As an encore, he did the theme to *Jaws*. I'm not sure how the Pops felt about it, but everyone in our group was tickled.

I spent the night at the Dukakis home and the governor made us pancakes in the morning before we toured Harvard and Boston. I was very impressed that there was an unmarked car and a security detail outside their home. The Dukakis' later visited John on the island and

I joined them for dinner that night. They were charming people. The governor, in particular, was genial and friendly and relaxed around everyone."

Tegan also remembered the little blonde haired boy who for a brief time was his little brother. "Being a southern California boy, I'd never heard a Brooklyn accent quite as thick as little Ricky Schroder's. I was endlessly amazed by his ability to turn his sister's name, "Dawn," into a two syllable word. I liked Ricky. He had the ability to cry right on cue, which he displayed in *The Champ* (1979) shortly after *Jaws 2*. I'm afraid the cast of teenage actors kept Ricky at arm's length, as teenagers are want to do."

Tegan West

THE AMITY KIDS (PART TWO)

THE AMITY KIDS. If you were a teenager in the late 1970s (and a *Jaws* fan) you wanted to be one. Boats. The Ocean. And an apparent unlimited supply of beer for the under-aged. Here now is the story of the young actors who may not have all survived the shark but made it through the production of *Jaws 2* alive!

Gary Dubin (Eddie Marchand)

Gary Dubin played Eddie Marchand, the doomed boyfriend of Tina. Gary remembers the Holidome of the Navarre Beach Holiday Inn with the word "getaways." Gary added, "I was able to rent a car and sometimes get permission to leave if I wasn't on the call-sheet. I drove to New

Top row (l-r) David Elliot, Ben Marley, Gary Springer, Martha Swatek, Ann Dusenberry, Suzie Swatek, John Dukakis, Marc Gilpin sitting on David Owsley's shoulders.
Middle row (l-r) Susan McMillan Owsley, Cindy Grover, Tom Dunlop, Billy Van Zandt, Donna Wilkes, Keith Gordon, Gary Dubin.
Bottom row - Mark Gruner and Gigi Vorgan

Orleans on Labor Day. . . good times. . . but there were tons of hours/days/weeks just waiting for the shark!"

Gary Dubin's scariest experience on *Jaws 2* was, as expected, during his death scene. "I had a real scare in my death scene, the shark is chasing me and when I was swimming towards Tina, I looked over my shoulder and swear I saw a real shark fin!!"

The authors contacted Mr. Dubin's representative but were never able to schedule a time to speak with him. The above comments were taken from a conversation Gary had with Lou Pisano for an article that ran as a three-part series in *SCREAM* magazine beginning in July 2012.

John Dukakis (Paul "Polo" Loman)

The son of the then-Governor of Massachusetts (and 1988 Democratic President nominee) Michael Dukakis, John Dukakis was in college when he heard about *Jaws 2*.

134

"I was at Brown. I intended to be a theater major there. I was very active in high school and I had done some theater in Boston as well. My dad was in his first term and I got a call from somebody in his office saying they would be holding open auditions at the Harvard campus and, while he couldn't do any favors for me if I took the bus up from Providence they'd make sure that Shari Rhodes would see me.

So I went up and met with her and I read for, I think, the Mike Brody part with her and then I kind of forgot about it because I didn't hear back for a while. Then one day got a call and I was brought to New York. There were a bunch of us there. As I remember it I was told to do some improv and make fun of Shari's clothing, which I must've done with great gusto.

It was probably in March 1977 that I went back again. I met with Zanuck and Brown and they kept pairing us up with different people. Obviously I knew it was about a bunch of teenagers and they kept pairing us together to see how we looked and interacted with each other.

I didn't hear anything for a little while and then out of the blue I got a call that says 'you're in, it starts May 8 and were going to need you to get on a plane to Florida.' I believe I was given a four-week guarantee contract for scale so I kind of looked at this as my summer job.

I had to leave school a little early before finals my freshman year. There was another kid in the cast from Harvard named Alan Stock, and we both ended up taking our finals on a picnic bench in front of the Holiday Inn, which is not exactly how we would've taken them back at school.

I had to go back and make fun of Shari's clothes once again for the final audition and the next time I saw anybody was when I flew in from Providence. I flew to New York and then, when I got on the Eastern Airlines flight to Pensacola, or it may have been to Atlanta, I'm not sure. . . actors had to fly first-class and I remember we took up the entire cabin.

There was Lily and Billy and David and Lenora May. I know Tegan flew in from the West Coast with Gary and Ann so we pretty much had the run of the place before they got there. We met up with Sarah Holcomb and Nancy Sawyer. I know we all went out and swam, and that was the only time I ever went out and swam voluntarily after we got there."

Like many of the young cast, John didn't sense a lot wrong during the Hancock era. "I know there were a fair number of rewrites that Dorothy was doing. You have to remember that most of us, particularly me, had never been close to anything like this so I had nothing to compare it to. But it didn't seem to be very organized.

Dorothy and John would bring us in for rehearsals and we would improv things, but it didn't seem very cohesive. Also, they were beginning to replace members of the cast even before John and Dorothy left. We would sail in the Intercoastal Waterway near Navarre and then suddenly you would see a zodiac coming from the shore. Whenever I saw it I would start doing the *Wizard of Oz* (1939) music – 'dun da dun da da da.' And invariably they would be coming to get somebody to take them away and we would never see them again. That happened several times. I was sailing with Sarah when they came to get her and it was painfully sad. I put Skip into that category as well, although he was local.

Sometime after that we were all brought into a room and were told we were shutting down for now. 'Don't know what's happening, here's your plane ticket. Someone will call you when we find out what's going on.' And I ended up going to LA with Gary and Ann. Ben Marley was also there with us and so we just waited.

Because Ann was a contract player at Universal she had access to a little more information and I remember her getting on the phone at one point with a bunch of us sitting around her apartment. She started writing down cast member's names and then, when she finished, she would either leave the name as it was or draw a line through it and that's how we knew what was happening.

I remember she got to the end of the list and I wasn't on it one way or the other. She asked the person on the other end, 'What about John,' and they told her that they'd been looking for me. Of course this was way before cell phones. I had left my dorm room phone number with them but I found out I was still a part of it. They told us about Jeannot and they told us that they were bringing Carl Gottlieb back in. I think we waited a couple more weeks and then we all went back to Navarre."

One of the more exciting scenes in the film was also exciting to film.

"Saving Mark Gruner was incredibly terrifying. We had done it already, God only knows how many times, and it was taxing because we had to keep one eye on where the shark was, because we had to time it. We would keep on dropping him and then get a good hold of him and pull.

We did a couple great shots, including a few with John Fleckenstein in the saddle on top of the shark. This was the shark that had to be dragged and it had a number of hoses underneath it and I remember we did a couple of takes where Mark's feet would get tangled in the hoses so we were afraid of that. I know there were scuba divers in the water but still. . . . You have to remember that he was acting like he was unconscious. He was completely reliant on us to make sure he stayed safe. But on that one particular take both Tom and I could see that the shark was coming really, really close and really, really fast—much too close for comfort.

And when the moment came, you can see it on our faces, I was really terrified. The shark caught a wire on the boat and it made a horrendous noise but it still kept on coming. I thought it was going to knock the boat over, which was really, really scary.

I remember after the scene just sitting there in the boat stunned that we just gone through that. It was amazing, and of course it's all on film. If you look close enough you can see it's obvious the mouth is just a little too wide open. We had done it so many different times but the last time was the best."

G. Thomas Dunlop (Timmy Weldon)

For those of you who enjoy trivia (and who doesn't?), can you name the Amity Kid that appears in both *Jaws* AND *Jaws 2?* Time's up! The answer is Tom Dunlop, who is clearly visible on the beach early in the first film. Tom talks about how he was cast.

"I have a woman by the name of Janice Hull to thank for that. She was Shari Rhodes' assistant and she was a friend of my mother's and my stepfather also. This was in very early June 1977. I was in boarding school and just getting ready to come home for the summer.

Mrs. Hull knew that they were interested in finding a kid who could sail an old-fashioned kind of sailboat, a Heffeshoff 12 ½. 12 ½ means it is the length of the boat at the waterline. My stepfather owned a replica of this boat. In fact, it was the first replica to ever come to Edgartown

137

Harbor. Janice got in touch with my mother to see if I wanted to come in and audition because my stepfather owned one and presumably I had sailed one.

This was towards the end of the John Hancock/Dorothy Tristan era. The rest of the kids had already been hired and had been sailing together for about a month. I didn't know any of them and I came in and I initially auditioned for Shari. I remember I read a couple of lines from the scene that had a couple of the prep school kids giving a couple of the local kids a hard time. I read my lines. Shari knew my stepfather had one of these boats but the part I read for was given to somebody else.

A couple of days later I was called back in by Shari who wanted to know more about my particular knowledge of this boat. I won't bore you with the subject but if you take the boat my stepfather had and compared it to the sailboats of today it would be like comparing a biplane to a Piper Cub.

I walked into the next audition knowing they really needed someone that knew how to sail this boat and I laid on the thickest line of malarkey that I had ever laid on in my life. They asked me if I knew about this boat. I told him that I did; that my stepfather had bought the first one ever to the harbor and that I'd been sailing it with him now for a couple of years. Oh, and they're really complicated. I then started dropping technical terms and started drawing pictures on napkins about how it worked. Why the boat was more old-fashioned than modern.

And I dazzled them. I could feel it. I just had Shari completely awed with my knowledge of the boat. I told her, 'I'm going to be perfectly honest with you, you're not going to find another kid my age in this town that knows how to handle one of these boats because it's so complicated.' That was utter garbage, there were plenty of kids in that town that could sail it, and could sail it better than me. You could've thrown a fistful of gravel and hit six of them all at once. But here I was, insisting that there were none. And this beautiful woman, Shari Rhodes, took it hook, line and sinker, God rest her soul.

The next meeting I had was with Dorothy Tristan and I laid some of the same preposterous mess on her and she had me read a larger scene. I don't remember what it was exactly but it was some legitimate part in the film. She actually had me do some really interesting stuff. She would tell me to read the scene again but this time as if I had a speech impediment, that I didn't have the language to explain what I'd just seen. We did this for almost an hour, all kinds of different ways, and I walked out of there feeling as high as I possibly could.

I had done maybe two plays in my life. I had no professional experience. I had done two plays in high school and this was the most galvanizing hour I had spent over the past two days. It was about a fifteen minute walk from the production office and by the time I got home the production called and said I was in.

I think initially what they really had in mind was that I would be not only sailing the boat they wanted but that I would also have a walkie-talkie on me to talk to the people on the camera boat to see if my boat and the other boats could go in a certain direction. Can we shoot port to camera from this angle, or do we have to move? And that's how I got hired.

The part expanded as they started working on the script more and they were constantly asking us about our lives. We would tell them our own stories about who we were, what we were doing and what we wanted. So my part grew from a guy was supposed to make a boat move efficiently to an actual speaking part. I was a sixteen-year-old kid when I was hired. It's one of the things I look back on that's truly amazing because that would never happen today.

When we reassembled down in Florida in early July for part two with Jeannot I was down there as a sixteen-year-old kid completely alone, absolutely unsupervised. No parents. No official guardian. Just me, on my own. And this movie company, Universal, expected a completely untried and untested kid to completely behave. To act and follow through and be responsible just like an adult. This went on for almost six months, until we left in late December, and I'm amazed. I mean, if I was a shareholder in Universal Studios I would've sold. If I'd known that the studio was relying on a scrawny little dweeb like me, completely unsupervised, to keep it together and to do my job I would have sold my stock.

But I am eternally grateful to each and every one of them. Not just the people that hired me and trusted me, because that was an amazing leap of faith for them to take, but also to the other "Amity Kids." They were are all older than me except, for Mark Gilpin, and they protected me. They included me. I didn't even have a driver's license. And I know there were times when they would go off and have grown up time. They didn't have a sixteen-year-old kid with them all the time, but they never forgot me. They would listen to me when I was confused or upset or bored or whatnot, and they became my family. It was a great turning point in my life.

Billy Van Zandt put it brilliantly at one point when he was asked, 'what did it mean to you?' and he said, 'it changed my life.' And that's exactly what it did for me. My gratitude begins with the fact that they trusted me to carry off my part of it, and the friends that I made then are my friends to this day."

Did Tom fess up to being in the first film? "I may have told Shari Rhodes the story about the day I snuck onto the set. I was very sure that they would find that story funny, that I was so determined that I wormed my way into some shots and that they were forced to bring me back and pay me for two more days. Today you would never get anywhere near the set on a movie like that. She may have found that story charming in and of itself." When asked if he had filmed anything with John Hancock at the helm he notes, "I did one scene with Keith Gordon. At that time, Keith's character and mine were supposed to be brothers—they kind of invented that on-the-fly when they saw that there were two of us that looked a little bit alike. We were close to the same age. And in the scene we shot we were supposed to go down to the dock, get in our boat and sail away.

A lot of the time they just took the kids and had them practice sailing all day. There were a couple sequences that they filmed in Edgartown where the camera barge was really far away. They were establishing shots. I was never formally introduced to John Hancock and never auditioned for the guy. I remember him seeing me and Keith together and turning to an AD and saying, "how about these two guys being brothers?" That was sort of established and then it went away. Remember, this was probably the seventh or eighth of June, about twenty days before he and Dorothy were let go and we went on hiatus, where we all went down the Florida."

How did he hear the news that Hancock had been let go? "We got a phone call at my house from Shari and we were told that the production was being suspended - going on hiatus was the term they used. They were going back to Los Angeles and we were not going down to Florida the next day or two days later. They were going to be reconstituting the whole thing.

I remember I was called to the set when all of this happened. All of this happened at night, and I remember everyone seemed very unsettled that day. Rumors must've been circulating and nobody was going to talk about them that night or the next morning. Shari called. She spoke to my mother, not to me. I think she tried to assure my mother that my job was probably safe and that they would be back in touch when they figured out who was going to take over.

In the interim, after they had gone back to Los Angeles and hired Jeannot, I must've spoken to somebody. I can't remember who but I was told that my job was safe and that I was going to be called out to Los Angeles to meet whoever the new director was. That happened a few days before we all moved to Florida. I'd never been to the west coast in my life. I got a call and was told I needed to be on a plane with my mother, because I was underage. We flew out to Los Angeles from Boston I had never been there. We were met at the airport by a limousine. I got in the back seat and my mom got in with the driver. The backseat was about 6 feet behind the door. We spent the night at the Universal Hilton.

The next morning I was summoned to meet the new director, Jeannot Szwarc. David Brown was there; I think Carl Gottlieb was there and Shari was certainly there. I was wearing a jacket and tie. I had this little plaid jacket at the time. I'm sure I looked adorable…so earnest…

Jeannot asked me to tell him about my work. I was very professional and I told him about the two high school plays I had done. I then told him that I had also done a monologue from *Missiles of October*, playing Robert Kennedy, and then suddenly I realized that they're going to ask me to do it. (laughs) I'm thinking I need to work up a Bobby Kennedy accent but as for the speech, I didn't have any idea what Bobby Kennedy said during the *Missiles of October*. Everyone looked at me but then Jeannot shook his head and said, (mimicking a French accent) 'Thank you very much for coming in, we will be in touch with you very soon.' I think I flew home still not knowing whether really and surely I had been hired for the next go around. We flew back to Boston, then to the Vineyard and 24 hours later we were summoned down to Florida.

My mom came with me again to sign all the documents. We were down there around the Fourth of July and then my mom went home. I didn't see anyone again until after we were done shooting, except for a quick lightning trip home at the end of November. But it was the longest period of time I'd ever been away from home without a break. Once again, I was entirely on my own. Unbelievable.

I recently saw a boy that was obviously heading off for a long trip and it took me back. I was a boy. I was shaving once a week. I wanted to go up and ask his parents, 'How do you feel about your son leaving home for the next six months and having to look after himself? And you guys won't see him because you're taking care of your other kids and have to go to work. This is the start of summer and you're not going to see him again until the time you get around the carving the turkey.' I'm sure they would've said, 'Are you out of your mind?'"

A burgeoning author, Tom kept a diary during the production and he shares his memories of shooting one of the film's most dramatic sequences.

"August 25, 1977. I have to tell you, I saw it on film opening night when I saw the movie. And I'm sure on the six or seven occasions where I may have seen the film again that I've actually had to force myself to watch it. It was terrifying – I remember that scene microsecond by microsecond. There is a lot of misinformation about what happened to the boat as well as to the actual jeopardy that Mark Gruner was in. I tip my hat to the crew, to the designers of the shark. . . everybody. It was a tremendously complicated piece of machinery out in the wilds of the Gulf of Mexico. It was 25 feet long and I don't know how many thousands of pounds. It was as if you were being slammed into your boat at 70 miles an hour. I mean, that's like being hit by a truck. Everyone was really impressed at how they could move and maneuver this thing around the sailboats. Of course, most of the time the sailboats were anchored so they were just targets.

First off, it's really easy to haul somebody out of the water into a boat and one of the things I'm really proud of is that John and Mark and the cameraman and Jeannot and I all worked really hard to make it look as difficult as it was. We came up with the idea to try to pull him up, drop him and then pull him up again. In the scene we shot that's in the film, while we were pulling Mark up, I looked over and I saw an awful lot more of the shark snout and an awful lot more of the head then I had ever seen before.

I also noticed that it was coming at us a lot faster. More "at us" to the point that I thought it was actually going to hit us. So here we are in a boat anchored to the bottom with the camera boat right behind us and I knew our boat wasn't going to move at all. And I remember suddenly going cold. It was loosely like how you feel when you know you're going to have a car accident. Suddenly the shark was in my face, it was blocking out the sun.

And here's the part that in the end I thought was really scary. The shark actually snapped a wire that held a part of the sailboat in place. That's why you see its nose crushed in and you hear that tremendous bang. That came from the wire and the turnbuckle attached to the mast ripping out.

I heard that thing go whistling over our head at about one million miles an hour. A flying projectile made of metal and whipping around with the wire whipping overhead and I realized if Mark's legs were still sticking out towards the water that this thing would come crashing down and snap his legs backwards. That is the sickening and overwhelming thought that I have whenever I see that scene because I was sure that thing was going to shatter his legs. Of course that all goes by in a half a second, the shark is gone, we got up in the boat, the shot is over and there is total silence on the camera barge. Jeannot yells 'Cut!' and eighty people erupt into cheers.

And John and Mark and I—Mark hadn't really seen it because he was supposed to be unconscious, his eyes were closed. We just sat there for a few seconds and waited for someone to ask if we were okay. They didn't. I think it was Jeannot that said, 'Good job, guys, terrific, super.' They were just thrilled. They had no idea how really dangerous this thing had turned out to be.

When they saw the dailies a couple days later it just sent shock waves through everyone that saw them. There were cheers and screaming and yelling about how good the scene looked. It looked great, dramatically, and I kind of forgot but when I saw it again in the movie I remembered. The reactions on our faces are genuine looks of fear and shock. Now

143

that I know what was really happening—what was really breaking—the danger involved; what was letting go and what was breaking, it's still really hard for me to watch it."

Asked if he has a fun memory to share, Tom replies, "I like the parts were we got to be real teenagers. I liked going to the Holidome. We got to talk and work on scenes and block scenes together. We got to be real kids."

Ann Dusenberry (Tina Wilcox)

Ann Dusenberry began acting as a young girl and was under contract to Universal Studios when *Jaws 2* was his being cast.

"I started my contract in 1976 and, of course, *Jaws 2* started filming in 1977. They called me and said, 'were sending you out on it." I hadn't even seen *Jaws.* I was afraid to see *Jaws* but I went to see *Jaws.* I really didn't want to do *Jaw 2* because sequels weren't really popular at the time. There were only a couple that had been well received and I didn't think it would do my career any good. I was thinking I'd rather stay in Los Angeles and do other things, because I knew it was going to be a long shoot. But the studio said, 'No, you're under contract to us and you'll go where we tell you to go.' So I said 'Okay' and they sent me down to Florida and that's how it started. I don't even recall having to read for it.

We went down to Florida to learn how to sail and Roy Scheider was there and John Hancock. I know we rehearsed some scenes but at the time that was pretty much all that was going on down there as far as the crew goes. We were just in rehearsals and learning to sail and then we went up to Martha's Vineyard. And of course, from there, everybody got fired and then we came back with an all-new story. What was interesting is that originally I just had a tiny part as one of the kids but I guess, based on the footage that had been sent back to Universal, they decided to write my role a little bigger. They said they liked what they saw and they wanted to make the role bigger. They wanted to make Tina a co-star.

With more experience than some of the other young actors, did she ever sense a problem under John Hancock? "I wasn't sure what was going on but it felt a little discombobulated to me. We were shooting on Martha's Vineyard and everything started to feel a little less focused, for lack of a better word. I just didn't feel there was a very strong focus. We,

144

the kids, stayed focused on sailing because they kept us out on the water a lot. We learned how to get from one town to the next. It was a bit scary.

I remember one time we left Edgartown Harbor. I was with one other person and one of the pontoons had a hole in it. I remember saying something about it to the woman in charge... she was a tough lady. She said they had looked at it and patched it up so there was nothing to worry about. So, of course, we get out to the middle of the ocean and it capsizes. We couldn't ride it because the water had gotten in. We couldn't bring it up because the water had gotten inside it and was just sloshing from one pontoon to the other. There was no way to bring it up on the water so one of the speedboats had to come by and tow us in. All I remember is that it was really cold and we were still learning how to sail. We were in the water a lot so, no, I don't feel there any rumblings per se. But there was a kind of lack of focus, that's how it felt to me."

With a featured role, were there any scenes she had shot that didn't make it into the final film? "There was a shot they did of me in the boat by myself. I'm in the middle of nowhere after everybody had gone and after Eddie had been killed. They shot that one day out in the Gulf of Mexico. There were waterspouts behind me, and I was freaking out because the people on the camera barge didn't know what I learned from training. What I learned was that waterspouts are really, **really** dangerous. But of course, in typical Hollywood fashion, the shot was more important.

I got on the walkie-talkie and said, 'Hey you guys, there's waterspouts out here' and they would say, 'Yeah, yeah... those are cool.' I told them that I thought it would be a good idea that I get out of here and they'd say, 'Just a minute, we've almost got the shot, just hang tight.' I was anchored out there and there wasn't anything I could do. I guess I could've pulled up my sail and just said forget this and gone in. So that was funny. Now. But at the time it wasn't funny at all. They sent me out some alcohol, some brandy or something. They were like, 'Just drink some of this, you won't mind. It'll be okay, just sit tight.'

And you must take note that I was over twenty-one, it's not like they were contributing to the delinquency of a minor. It's just that I was scared and they thought of I had a drink I would calm down."

Not to worry, Ann. In 1977 the legal drinking age in Florida was nineteen.

Ann Dusenberry

Ann Dusenberry

Cindy Grover

Mark Gruner grabbing a drink

Marc Gilpin and Mark Gruner between shots.

Ben Marley and Gigi Vorgan

David Elliot (Reeves Vaughn/Larry Vaughn, Jr.)

David Elliot was already an accomplished actor when he was cast in the film. "I started acting professionally at the age of 9. I sang and danced with Rod McKuen on *The Ed Sullivan Show*. I played Shirley Maclaine's son in *The Possession of Joel Delaney* (1972) when I was 11. I also played Billy Allison on the television soap opera *The Doctors* for four years."

David almost missed out on the film. "By a twist of fate, I was somewhat disillusioned with life as an actor and went down to the Marine Recruiter's office to sign up. However the office, which was supposed to be open until 5:30 p.m., was closed at 4:30 when I got there. When I got back to my apartment there was a message on my machine that I had an audition for *Jaws 2* the next day. After about six callbacks I was offered the job. Needless to say, I didn't return to the military."

Despite his experience David did not sense anything "wrong" on the shoot under John Hancock. "I had no clue. The "shut down" took us all by surprise. We were just told that they were delaying the rest of shooting, to

149

go home and that we'd be called about when to return. I don't know what the studio didn't like specifically. John and Dorothy's script was much darker and I had a much better part in their rendition. The character was way more evil in the beginning but ultimately heroic. The version that got studio approval had fewer sharp edges."

We're there any scenes from the Hancock period that he wished had made the final film? "There was a fun scene where I threw Ricky Schroder into the water off a dock in Martha's Vineyard. The shark is supposedly in the water and I'm saying to Tegan West, who at the time was playing Roy Scheider's elder son, 'What do you think of your little brother as Shaaark Bait?' with a thick New England accent.

There was also a great scene where Roy Scheider gives my character a ticket for riding my bike on the pier and I get all, 'I'm the mayor's son, piss off' with him. It was a lot of fun to play."

Speaking of "fun," does he have any funny stories to share? "Wow, funny stories? Plenty. Ones that I can share? Not many. I'm sure you've heard about the shark biting into Keith Gordon's rubber boat and all its teeth falling out? Thanksgiving dinner served to us in the Holidome by the pool, which made everything taste like chlorine? The umpteen radios I ruined flipping the "Sizzler," Billy and my steel hulled catamaran, which had the handling delicacy of an air craft carrier, but that they wanted us to "fly the hull" in? The Halloween party we had where my costume was a speedo and a mattress from the hotel tied to my back?

Perhaps my favorite, which I can tell without embarrassing anyone, is about how when the crew all got to Martha's Vineyard the producers held a big meeting in the restaurant of the hotel where they admonished us to be on our best behavior. Because the locals still had a bad taste in their mouth from being invaded by the crew from the first movie. They expressed how important it was to the film that we all comport ourselves respectfully. Only this was the late '70s in the film business when cocaine was a breakfast cereal and the next morning, around six a.m., I'm walking to the set and a crew member who has been out all night on a pub crawl and after parties is standing on top of one of our semi-trailers in nothing but a pair of red-heart-polka-dotted boxer shorts, singing at the top of his lungs, 'Suck my dick, I'm a stranger in Paradise.'

Mostly I have fond memories of being a seventeen-year-old kid, pretending to be an eighteen-year-old kid, so the studio didn't have to pay for me to go to school or be accompanied by a chaperone, having the time of his life with a bunch of other crazy kids, at a nine month sailing camp with an open bar.

Of course there's also the fact that I ran into one of the grips about ten years later, and he said to me, 'Man did you have any idea that they were paying us $100 a day cash not to tell you kids when there were real sharks in the water?'

Down in Florida we actually shot a "Billy Van Zandt being killed" scene and my reactions but they didn't use it."

As for his famous comment when he first lays eyes on Donna Wilkes' character, Jackie – "She has tits like a sparrow" – David says, "Much to my chagrin I have to admit that the "tits" line was an improvisation, which Donna has graciously forgiven me for. But I wish those words never left my mouth."

Marc Gilpin (Sean Brody)

Ricky Schroder may have had dozens of commercials under his belt at age 6 but that achievement pales when compared with Marc Gilpin. "I had been acting since I was four years old. Up to that point, I'd done over three-hundred commercials. I was the original "DQ Kid" for Dairy Queen and, for a short time, I was featured in the ad campaigns for Burger King. The year before working on *Jaws 2,* I had starred in a film called *Where's Willie?* (1978) where I played a computer whiz kid.

It's funny, I can't recall how many times I had a birthday on a set. I shared my birthday party with Cindy Grover during *Jaws 2.* Our birthdays are close to each other's."

Of course, Marc wasn't the only one up for the role of Sean Brody.

"Shari Rhodes cast me in *Willie.* We were good friends and when *Jaws 2* came up, she wanted me immediately. As it turned out, I lost to Ricky Schroder. But when they recast the film it was Verna Fields who stepped up and argued for me being cast. I was her first choice and she went to bat for me from the beginning. She convinced Jeannot to meet with me in Florida.

So, my dad and I hung out on the beach for almost two weeks before he had time to meet with me. We talked for about ten minutes and he said, 'You've got it, see you tomorrow.' So, first day, first shot. And, if you think about it, how serendipitous is it that Jay Mello (Sean Brody in the first film) and I looked so much alike back then."

As the new kid on the block did the other young actors fill him in on what had occurred with John Hancock? Or, because of the age difference, did they really hang around with him? "I had heard that the original director wasted a lot of film and about $4 million. That's what I remember hearing, but I was ten years old so take it with a grain.

I actually did hang out with all of the teenagers. Most of them actually. My mom was very popular on the set and would throw parties at our house for everyone. We made some lifelong friends during that project. Mostly crew. I've always been more comfortable hanging out with the people behind the camera.

I was totally head over heels in love with Cindy Grover. She was so great to me. She knew I loved her and we had a great relationship. She's a very kind, warm person that is so beautiful, inside and out. She put up with me hanging around all the time. I was ten and she was nineteen. It wasn't meant to be. If I had been old enough, I would have asked her to marry me. The first great love of my life. When shooting was over I literally cried for two weeks because I missed her so much."

One of the great *Jaws 2* rumors is that, if you watched the film on Irish television, you saw an extended scene of Marge's death, showing her in the shark's jaws. True or false?

"Well, that's the magic of film right? When I did that first close-up shot, I was staring at the water just below camera. No shark. No Martha. Just the crew and pure fantasy. I had to pretend that Martha was being consumed by the shark while I'm holding on to the keel of the overturned boat. I did one take and the entire barge applauded me. I guess they were so relieved—and behind schedule, that they didn't have time to mess around. So, if I couldn't do that scene, they couldn't use me. The rest of the shoot was a cakewalk.

For the long shot, the shark was actually about 20 feet or so behind Martha. The angle of the camera just made it look like it was right on top of her. There were scuba divers under her that pulled her down at the right time. I don't see how they could've pulled that off anyway. The jaws were hydraulically controlled and it would have been too dangerous to put a person in its mouth."

Keith Gordon (Keith/Doug Fetterman)

The son of actors Mark and Barbara Gordon, Keith was already in the family business when *Jaws 2* came around. "I was doing a play at the National Playwrights Conference at the Eugene O'Neill Theatre in Connecticut. "I believe somebody saw me in the play and recommended me for the role. Of course, it's also possible that my agent submitted me like every other young actor in New York and Los Angeles" (laughs)

Reference John Hancock, Keith says, "This was my first film job, there may have been things I might have been more aware of now or I might have picked up a vibe that things were not going well but I was really taken aback. I don't think I had any clue or felt anything in the air, but I also wouldn't know what to have been looking for. I had only done one episode of a television show, *Medical Center*, so I hadn't been around a movie set long enough to sense if something weird was going on. I didn't know what was weird and what was normal. I was like 'What, they fired him and they're shutting down the movie?' I, of course, was worried that the film wouldn't get started again. This was my first movie and it wouldn't get made. It was very upsetting on a number of levels.

It was also upsetting when we started back up because a lot of people that I become friendly with had been fired for no particularly good reason that I can figure out one way or the other. The weirdness of who stayed and who left, given how little had been shot. . . the little that anyone really had a chance to do anything with, I never understood the selection process. I always figured I didn't get fired because my part was so small and nobody noticed me enough to fire me. (laughs) It was a very weird and strainful time because people I grown very fond of were no longer part of the film.

There was a long time I remember having the vibe that this might not even happen. They were searching for directors. They were rewriting the script. It was a pretty major shutdown and though it was my first movie I was pretty sure that most major movies didn't stop in the middle after they started shooting.

We shut down for almost a month and there was always the feeling, 'Is this movie even going to happen and if so, in what form? Who's going to get fired next?' It was just a really stressful time as to what was going to happen with the movie.

And what was weird is that they kept us down on the location the entire time, which was very odd. I don't know if they thought we were going to start up right away or what. So here we are, sitting in a hotel in Navarre Beach, Florida not knowing if the movie was ever going to happen. If you are going to be fired or written out. It was a very odd situation, certainly nothing that I've ever encountered since. I don't think it's a very common one in Hollywood movies, big or small. That kind of breaking continuity and then to pick back up with a whole new team and a whole new script. With the entire crew waiting and standing by, it was a very odd thing. It was very disquieting because I had no idea what was going to happen."

Keith was originally cast as a young man named. . . Keith. Only later did he get the role of Doug. "Yes, I remember, I was there on my own name and I had one line. When they rewrote the script they kept the name "Doug" and I think they changed the nature of the character. It was an instance where they kept the character name and the nature of the character changed. I remember Bryan Utman being a very sweet guy and I don't think he did anything wrong. It seemed very arbitrary. Like suddenly a half or two- thirds of the cast were gone and I couldn't understand why. It was very strange."

Bryan Utman relayed a story about how the actor that took his place offered to quit. True? "I don't remember doing that. I wish I could say I made that grand a gesture but I really don't remember. I didn't find out I was going to be Doug until Carl Gottlieb rewrote the script. I don't remember that I was ever told I was going to be replacing him so I don't remember making such a noble and gallant gesture. I wish I could take credit for it because that's a really cool thing to do but I don't think I was ever aware that I was replacing anybody. I just felt that I was a survivor of the tsunami that had swept through."

Even back then Keith was a writer, and in his spare time he turned out a script of his own entitled *Jaws 2.5*.

"Billy Van Zandt and I hung out a lot during the filming and we were writing the most absurdist comedies. We wrote one called *Murder in the Sanitarium*. And I wrote a parody of the first five or tem pages of the *Jaws 2* script and it got circulated. I don't remember many of the specifics but it was just full of all the absurd things that were going on, like the shark sinking and the wild lives that the kids were leading. I can't remember any of the particular jokes but it made the rounds. I gave it to one person and before I knew it everybody had read it. Luckily, I don't think there was anything too mean in it so I don't think I hurt anybody's feelings or I'm sure I would've gotten myself fired.

I remember when I heard that David Brown had read it and I thought to myself, 'Oh gosh, I'm dead,' because I didn't know if these people had a sense of humor, especially after everything the film had been through. The people actually seemed to be able to laugh about it so I was very relieved. I had written it for one or two friends and before I knew it everyone had seemed to have read it. I mean, it wasn't a major document. It was only like five pages but it was sort of my imaginary making of the movie. It was just so bizarre, people were being fired left and right than the shark would work. I wish I still had a copy. I still have a pair of glasses and a few souvenirs or two but when you start to keep everything you require on a movie set you end up looking like somebody on *Horders*.

I was one of the youngest kids on the set. I was more like the younger brother so when everybody else was out partying or coupling up I was never a part of it. I was always like the little brother that gets left behind. I remember that I was jealous of everyone. I remember trying to flirt with all the girls and politely being turned away which, looking back, to me makes perfect sense. There was definitely a party atmosphere in this hotel in the middle of nowhere with a bunch of libidinous young people and a lot of times where no shooting was happening.

A lot of times the shark wouldn't work and we'd spend the entire day just sailing back and forth in front of the hotel for eight or ten hours, which was such a weird, weird experience.

Again, my closest friend on the set was Billy Van Zandt and we would spend our time writing comedy scripts and having a great time doing it. Billy and Tom Dunlop. Tom was great – very, very funny. He would always leave me letters. We basically had the run of the hotel since there was no one else there most of the time. Each of us had their own mailbox and Tom would leave me letters in them saying everything from 'Your fired, signed Tom Joyner' to that New York had called and they wanted me to come host *Saturday Night Live* and then another letter from Ringo Starr saying he would only do the show if I did the show. He was very witty and very funny. I wish I still had those letters. I remember looking forward to them because it made me happy. I remember once a week I would get a letter from somebody important in the world. I remember one week I got a letter from Jimmy Carter saying that he wanted to meet me and hear my plans for world peace. I also remember spending **way** too much time in the Pinball Room."

Like Ron Howard before him, Keith acquired a love for filmmaking at a young age. "Even before I became an actor I was one of those nerdy kids that was always carrying a camera around back in the day. I mean, I kind of fell into acting and it was great, but *Jaws 2* was really the first film I really tried to use as a film school. And I was very lucky because people were very nice about letting me hang around on the set even on days I wasn't scheduled to shoot. I would spend a decent amount of time in the editing room with Neil Travis, which was really cool because I had a great chance to learn about editing and how that worked. To see how a film went from raw footage to a cut scene. I would go to the dailies, and not just to see shots that I was in. I would sit there and watch hours and hours of film and then go hang out in the editing room at the hotel to see how they took that footage and transformed it into scenes. It was a great film school at that level—everybody from Jeannot to Michael Butler to Joe Alves, they were all very indulgent of this nonstop chatter box full of questions. 'How do you do that? Why do you do that? How does this work?' And they were all extremely generous and kind with their time in terms of indulging me in how to make a real movie. Those are probably my favorite movies because I've loved movies ever since I was eight years old and my dad took me to see *2001* (1968) on its opening weekend.

I just remember being blown away. I didn't understand it, of course, because I was too young, but I understood that I didn't understand and I became obsessed with it. I dragged my father back about ten times. And the power of that experience made me curious about making movies.

I watched a lot of older movies and read what I could to learn about making films. So to be working on real a film and to be talking to real pros about how they did it... that was like being a kid in a candy store for me."

Keith also had a lady friend while on-location. "Her name was Joy Brown— you have done an absurd amount of homework—her family was friends with one of the reporters on the local paper and they did a little story. They thought it was cute. It was a little embarrassing because my love life was now in the local paper but it was a sweet memory in the end."

Cindy Grover (Lucy)

Like several of the kids in the cast, acting was big in the Grover family. Her father, Stanley Grover, was a favorite of Oscar Hammerstein and originated the role of Lieutenant Cable in the first national tour of the classical musical *South Pacific*. According to his daughter, "He was Josh Logan, Oscar Hammerstein and Irving Berlin's favorite leading man."

Cindy was in college when she was cast in *Jaws 2*, but she had a lifetime of experience behind her. "I started out in commercials. I probably did a hundred national commercials before I was ten. At eleven, I was hired for the television soap opera *Love of Life*, which I did for four years and I did a lot of episodic television after that. I was actually in college when I got a call to do *Jaws 2*. Ironically, I was actually **on** Martha's Vineyard on spring break from Middlebury College and I got a call from my agent saying they were trying to find me. I think I was recommended by somebody that had worked on *Network* (1976) (Cindy played William Holden's daughter in Sidney Lumet's Oscar winning film) I had been cast in *Network* sight unseen.

I had also auditioned for Joe Papp at that time so I'm not sure who recommended me. I got a call on Martha's Vineyard and they said they wanted me to do *Jaws 2*. I went and met with Shari Rhodes right away and got the part."

Though Cindy was hired by John Hancock she never filmed anything with him, spending her time on Martha's Vineyard rehearsing. But she remembers the difference between Hancock's vision and the finished film.

157

"There was so much footage that was shot of the kids having fun. Building characters. Building relationships. Building stories that were never used. But in the movie all of that great foundational stuff was not there. It was mostly about the shark and Brody and the family dynamic that was going on."

Cindy is part of one of the most iconic promotional photos ever released, showing her in the water as the looming fin of the shark passes by. The image is so intense that it has been advertised and sold on Ebay as an actual photo of a shark attack in progress.

"The famous promo shot came from a scene that I filmed as stunt woman *and* actress and it was very dangerous to shoot. The day we finally got it was gray and choppy and it was a very fine tuned operation to calibrate.

The vessel towing the pneumatic shark had a complicated compressor and controls on board and the circuit the boat made had to come only so close to the camera boat where I was shivering in between takes. I leapt into the water over and over to shoot the sequence. The boat had to make a loop towing the immense critter. The shark had to straighten out, then dive and then surface just enough to have the fin out, but all within the time it took the boat to navigate its route around the camera flat boat. We did it again and again and again. I was **so** cold, even in Florida! It was a nasty day when we finally got the shot. I remember Teddy Grossman, the stunt coordinator, who was a consummate professional in his staging of all our stunts, was particularly concerned.

He took time to work with me on the effect we were trying to create which required me to swim and then tread water in the pathway of the boat towing the shark and then judge correctly the distance behind the boat and the turn radius, while facing away from it and towards the camera, so that it appeared to the camera that the shark was making a beeline for me. Then I turn, hearing the warning shouts, only to turn into its path and to be hit, and grazed, at the midriff, by the shark. It took two or more days to get the shot as I recall, with so many problems of a technical nature on the first day and repairs needed to the pneumatic leviathan."

She continues to speak highly of Ted Grossman. "I definitely hold the memory of that time. It was a very difficult time and it was a big growing time for all of us. When I had to do really, really difficult stunts, like when I was in the water and the hydraulic shark would be towed around, Teddy was just so good at making you feel confident. I was already a water person but…he just took really good care of us. He would say, 'No, no, no, she doesn't need a double. She can do this.'

I'm treading water and trying to not get tangled in the cables and I'm also trying to look at the shark and not the camera, while still trying to judge where I am in relation to the shark. And then the shark would break down.

Some obligatory bloody midriff skin was shot when we filmed the episode again in the tank at MGM in the post production months."

Like the rest of the cast, Cindy also remembers some good times. "Some of my fondest memories include hanging out with the Gilpin family. Marc and his mother and I were close. And I was also quite friendly with the Owsley family, who really treated me like family. We were all so far from home and the Owsley beach house was a great place for us all to hang with a mom and pop and enjoy some family time.

I remember David had a girlfriend from Finland we all liked and we tried to speak Finnish! I remember with fondness how all us kids tried to keep each other warm or fed or occupied or play cards during the long days on the flat boats. Gigi Vorgan and I developed a sisterhood that continued for years until I moved away from California.

I remember Cameraman extraordinaire John Fleckenstein and the pitch pole stunt. He was shooting a scene from the back of my blue Prindle Catamaran of another sailboat pitch-poling to be edited into a scene and the travel of his camera would take the shot across Ben Marley and I in positions forward on the boat. When the scene had been set up and everything was ready for the boat to be pulled the shot we captured must have included my person. I was standing at the mast. When it was done I remember Jeannot radioed to Fleck, 'How was it?' And John replied, 'As Fate would have it, it happened between her legs.' And then, of course, Jeannot made some comment about the story of his life and everyone had a good laugh.

The puppy that David Elliot got mid movie was everyone's joy. We had some fun scenes in the bar in Destin and, of course, we did a lot of sailing. Lorraine was very kind. Jeff Kramer was fun. Funny and a gentleman. Frank Sparks and Ellen Demmy were both so protective of us kids. There were **very** protective. Very good people. David Brown was wonderful. He always took time to talk to me. I just loved him."

Mark Gruner (Mike Brody)

A veteran of more than sixty commercials and a few "Movie of the Week" roles, Mark had his SAG card by the time he was four. He was one of the actors hired by Jeannot Szwarc.

"I was hired as a recast. They probably interviewed a couple hundred guys and they brought six of his back for a screen test. One was a good friend of mine, Chris Knight from *The Brady Bunch*. We went to Florida and they put us out on boats. They took us out to the Gulf and the winds died and if you did not know how to sail you were S.O.L. I'd been sailing most of my life so they would send me back out to bring back the kids that couldn't sail.

Actors are professional liars. If you're up for a role in a cowboy movie and they ask you if you can a ride a horse you say 'Yes' and then you try to get a couple lessons in after you get hired. But if you lie you can get hurt or die. You have to remember that the ocean is a very unforgiving mistress, she doesn't care if you sink or you swim, so when you're out on the water you should know what you're doing."

With that in mind Mark talks about the infamous "saving Mike Brody" scene. "We probably spent three weeks in the water shooting the rescue scene. You have the shark, which weighs close to a ton, being pulled through the water for a distance of 200 or 300 feet. If you're not careful you can get hurt very easily."

But it wasn't all bad. "We spent nine months total making this movie, but we all made friends. Some among the cast and crew and some among the locals. I still have a few friends I still keep in touch with. . . several friends from the area. It was a monumental task undertaken by seasoned professionals at Universal. It was a very difficult shoot on location in the water. Romances were fast and furious."

Did he get along well with his movie dad? "They used to run the dailies—they would shoot one day, send the film out and it would be back in two days. Apparently one day Roy Scheider felt my close-up was bigger than his. Roy had a shit fit and yelled at Jeannot. Now Jeannot is not a big man but he and Roy got into a fist fight because my close-up was bigger than his. (laughs) Roy would sit out on the beach in his black underwear holding one of those collars that reflect the sun up into your face. Roy would sit there trying to get darker than me. Now I have an olive complexion, I'm already dark and tan. Roy wanted to be darker than me. Back then being tan was considered cool in society. There used to be a time when being fair skinned was. The times have changed. Now, the darker you are, the more time you have for leisure. The more time you have to spend out in the sun. Roy ran with that.

The studio took care of us. They would give us vitamin B12 shots and check us out when we would come back in from sailing to make sure we hadn't been sunburned. They would check our hands and feet for cuts and rope burns. Rope burns were pretty bad."

As a lover of the water, Mark's most enjoyable times were spent on the water. "You'd be sheeting in, flying the hull, skimming across the water and trying to dodge the other idiots in the camera boats. We'd have to pull up the tiller a lot and fly the hull, which is when you go up on one pontoon on a catamaran. You sheet in pulled tight and shove your tiller over and fly the hull. Gary Springer was really good at this.

There was one time where we launched a reporter from the Los Angeles *Times* overboard. We pitch pulled, which means we dug the front of the boat in. The boat went ass over applecart and we lost her. Nine hours later we find her hysterical in the bar yelling, 'You guys could have killed me!' We couldn't find her, we thought she was dead.

What happened was, we were sailing the boat and we were supposed to take her out on a tour. We told her it was really strong outside, weather-wise. She asked if we could fly the spinnaker and I asked her, 'Are you kidding?' When you do it the wind has got to be behind you. We call it "popping the chute." When you pop the chute, that's a spinnaker. **POW!** You take off.

What happened is that Gary, the girl from the Los Angeles *Times* and I were sitting in the boat when it pitch pulled. Gary and I are strapped in, we have harnesses on, but she was launched off like a potato chip through the air and landed face first into the surf. Gary and I are trying to get the boat righted by leaning towards the seaside pontoons. By the time we get the boat righted and turned around we notice the weather is getting worse and we can't find her. We were close to shore. We were so close that I thought we were going to break the mast off. The wind is howling and I say to Gary, 'I think we lost our chick!'

So she shows up nine hours later back at the Holiday Inn. She's threatening us, talking about how we almost killed her and everything else. No offense to her, but she really had no business being out in a boat. Of course, with the weather the way it was we did neither we. We were told to take her out so we did. So she washes up on shore and has to walk probably five miles back to the hotel. We started heading back towards Navarre and on the way back I say to Gary, 'Well, that's the end of our careers.' (laughs) At least we made sure she had a life vest on!"

Ben Marley (Patrick)

Another cast member from an acting family (Ben's mother is actress Stanja Lowe – his father, John, is best known as the studio executive who finds a surprise in his bed in *The Godfather* and his Academy Award nominated performance as Ali MacGraw's father in *Love Story* (1970).

"The first thing I ever did was a movie called *Welcome to L.A.* (1976), directed by Robert Altman's then protégé, Alan Rudolph. It was the easiest job I ever got and still one of the best times I ever had. And, of course, I got cut out of it. I played Sally Kellerman's step son and John Considine's son. I was so excited to get to act like the miserable teenager in a broken home and, instead of everyone one saying: 'Come on, don't be selfish…You're parents are doing the best they can' - they paid me!

I loved acting! That was about a week's work. I did a few tiny episodic roles after that and mostly went to acting class. Mainly cause in acting class I was the best actor in the world! Then I got *Jaws 2*.

Ask Ben how he got the role and he replies, "I'm still not sure. At least I'm not completely sure WHEN I got it. I had gone to Universal Studios and auditioned for it. I think I had read for Shari Rhodes and the director, John Hancock. And probably Dorothy Tristan. I remember the scene I read had something to do with a guy and a girl on the beach and some line about 'you can't get pregnant from just sitting down.' Something like that. Many of us found out during our six months plus in Navarre Beach, Florida that that was, in fact, not true. Kidding!

I also remember, in the actual audition—because I was a **REAL** actor,

I asked if I could do the scene laying on the floor. They said yes and I did. I never heard back from them.

Maybe more than a month later the phone rang. I was in my back yard jumping rope because I was an actor and you had to be in shape. Plus I thought I was **REALLY** fat at 5' 8" and 145lbs, a condition which they now have a name for. Body dysmorphia. I think it was Friday. The phone rang. I ran in and picked it up. It was my agent saying, "They want you to get on a plane on Sunday morning and fly to Pensacola, Florida to audition again with the director. You'll be there for a week. At the end of the week they will tell you if you got the part or not" So that's what I did. I remember getting off the plane and seeing everybody jumping into minivans to go sailing. John Hancock shook my hand and said 'get in.' To this day I am still waiting to hear whether or not I got the role or if they're sending me home on Friday."

Asked if he had a favorite scene that didn't make the cut, Ben instead recounts his favorite lines:

1. "Is it still there?," in reference to some beer that was supposed to be at Mike Brody's house.

2. "Timmy – Brooke!" I don't remember exactly but I imagine I was warning Timmy and Brooke about something.

3. "SHUTUUUUUUUUUUUUUUUUUUUUUUUP!!!!!!!!!!!!!!!!!" Nobody would shut up about the damn shark!

4. "LUUUUUUUUCYYYYYYYYYYYYYYYY!" Because, like a moron, while he was busy being all brave and stuff and slapping that god-damned cable with that toy paddle, Mr. Roy Scheider just happened to be doing it in an area that put my "girlfriend," Lucy, right smack between him and the shark. I think that was all fine. Though I do still think the sixteenth take of that particular scream was something a bit special and I do get sad at times that it didn't make it in."

As for fun stories he shares one he though was pretty funny: "We were shooting the end with the shark and the cable and the electric shocks and sparks and explosions, etc. and we were all absolutely freezing our asses off. They took us one by one, or pair by pair, stuck us on the rocks, threw water on us, and started rolling the camera while John Fleck would light and wave sparklers. Someone else held out a really, really big piece of tin foil, for the sparklers to reflect off of, course." And then there was Jeannot - about 5 feet from us yelling at the top of his lungs: "AAANNNDD DEEERE GOOOES DOOO SHARK!!! and we would scream-and he'd go "AAAAANNNNDDDD DEEEERREE GOOOOEEESSS ROOY!!! and we would scream-and he'd go "AAAAAAANDROYHEETSDOOO CABLE!!! AAANNND... You get it from there. I still think it's funny."

Susan Owsley McMillan (Denise) and David Owsley (Donnie)

Brother and sister boaters, Susan and David were originally hired to help teach the young cast members to sail. Soon they found themselves as cast members. David explains how they got the job:

"There may have been a local casting call. If there was we didn't hear about it and I would not have gone. Had never acted a day in my life. Still haven't. I am what I am.

A friend of mine from Pensacola, Tom Whitehurst—he competed in the Olympics sailing boats called, I believe, 470s. (Tom Whitehurst represented the United States in the 1976 Montreal Olympics, sailing International 470s. He placed 9th.) He had been suggested to the production by the Chamber of Commerce as a possible sailing instructor. They hired him and Ellen Demmy as instructors.

The Saturday before the kids were to show up to start lessons Tom went out to start putting the boats together that had been shipped in. He realized he was in over his head and called me to help him finish assembling the boats on Sunday so they would be ready on Monday. While we were working on Sunday Tom came up and told me there was a lady that wanted to meet me. She walked over to us on the dock and introduced herself as Shari Rhodes, the casting director. She was standing there with John Hancock and David Brown when I started to introduce myself. The first words out of her mouth were, 'Wow! You are way too southern.' Needless to say that kind of pissed me off so I replied, 'Too Southern for what?' She said, 'To be in the movie' and I told her I wasn't out there to be in her movie. I walked back out to the boat I was helping Tom with.

Later that day Shari was out on the dock where we all were and asked if I knew any girls that could sail catamarans. I told her my sister was the best in Pensacola but that she was just as southern as I was and probably not the least bit interested in being in the movie either. Shari kept at me that afternoon to please try to persuade Susan to come out and talk to her about it and that it was a non-speaking part so being Southern didn't matter.

I called Susan that night and talked to her about it and she said that, since she knew Tom, and if I would go with her, she would at least go out there and see what's up. Monday morning she and I went to the Holiday Inn and met with Shari. Shari jumped with joy that I showed up with Susan and said the higher ups had decided they wanted me involved and that they would make my part non-speaking. They really needed a couple (boy and girl) to sail one of the boats and with the two of us, with our experience on boats along with Tom and Ellen, there should be no problems teaching the kids how to sail quickly.

Shari told us what and how we would be paid and that we would truly be cast members, not extras. The part where she said what we would get paid got my interest and changed my mind about being in her damn movie, so they loaded us up and off we went to where they were doing a lineup of locals for the parts and, by some miracle, Susan and I were chosen out of that lineup.

That is how we got hired. We never asked for or applied for the job; they bought us.

I took Ricky Schroder on his first and many other rides on sailboats during that week, he was such a little kid then and he loved being on the boats verses being with his tutor or mom and sister."

Working behind the scenes, did David ever hear there was trouble with John Hancock? "Nope, never was aware anything was not working with Hancock. We taught sailing there for a few weeks then were all flown up to Martha's Vineyard to start filming. Filmed up there for three or four weeks and then were told everyone was going home and would be told when to come back. We were still getting paid so I assumed this is just the way things were done in this industry. The movie/union way of doing things was quite an eye opener for a kid from the non-union state of Florida."

Did he film anything under Hancock? "There was footage filmed of me in Martha's Vineyard as a double. I dressed as Brody's oldest son and sailed the green catamaran and also was dressed as the police deputy and sailed the boat that Ann Dusenberry was in after she was rescued. I don't recall if any of that made it to the film.

The Vineyard was quite vacant of people at that time of year so getting local help that knew about boats was difficult. I spent most days up there working with the crew, rigging the boats, etc. According to the local union in Massachusetts I had to be paid if I touched a boat other than as one of the kids so I was making a killing up there as production crew, a double and still getting paid as an actor. I liked it.

I was used also as a power boat driver while up there ferrying VIP's out to watch filming etc. One memorable trip was when then-Governor Dukakis and his wife were visiting John. I took them and Susan Ford, the daughter of President Ford, out on a boat as the Navy boys were out spinnaker flying off one of the Navy Yawls. I believe some of that footage is in the movie. It was a great month up there with no clue anything was wrong.

The whole process was fun – there was never a dull moment. I mostly hung with the crew, not the kids, as I was quite a bit older and had nothing in common with them. I really enjoyed them all and loved how well they all learned to sail and how fast they picked it up. Martha and Susie Swatek, Cindy Grover, Ben Marley, Susan and I mostly hung together. When I wasn't with them I could be found with the special effect guys, rigging the boats. We would have to come up with a way to flip the boats as if the shark did it. In fact, when the green tornado catamaran is flipped by the shark it was I who worked with special effects and tested the process many times before it was filmed. It was a real bummer when it came time to film the actual flip footage and they wouldn't use me as a double to flip it. They had to fly in stuntmen/women to do it since it was considered a stunt and the union said they had to. I wasn't in the stunt union, so I taught them how to do it. Strange way unions work. For the most part I was allowed to help most anywhere I wanted, so I stayed busy everyday doing something more behind the scenes verses in front of the camera.

There was a lot of footage filmed of Susan and I on the catamaran when the winds were high and the film crew was bored. Lots of footage of us sailing with the kids all out on their boats etc. If I recall correctly, when all the boats come sailing by the dive boat with the divers on board, I actually sailed by flying the hull over the edge of the dive boat as we went by. Many good shots, all on the floor somewhere in a cutting room."

Gary Springer (Andy Nicholas)

If anyone was destined for a life in show business it was Gary Springer, who is the only person you or I will ever know that had Marilyn Monroe as a babysitter.

Gary's father, John, was a press agent known as "The Guardian Angel to the Stars." Besides Ms. Monroe, his clients included Judy Garland, Elizabeth Taylor and Richard Burton. Gary had just been cast in a popular television series when *Jaws 2* came along.

"I had been cast as Chet Morton on *The Hardy Boys* TV series. In the books Chet was Frank and Joe Hardy's best buddy. Chet would get in trouble and Frank and Joe would get him out of trouble. When they started shooting the first couple episodes they really stuck to the books, so I had a lot to do in the first couple of episodes. But then came the part where the studios talk about things and figure things out and they deduced that the girls that were watching the show didn't really want to see anybody put Parker Stevenson and Shaun Cassidy. So I realized my role was getting smaller and smaller. I was getting paid for doing one little thing per episode. We shot on the Universal lot and one day I'm in the commissary having lunch and John Hancock, who I knew because my dad had represented a couple of his movies. He represented *Bang the Drum Slowly*. So I'm talking to John and he says to me, "it's really a shame that you're tied up doing this series because I'm doing a film for Universal and you'd be perfect for one of the roles. And, of course, that was *Jaws 2*. So I went to my agent and said, 'Look, the series doesn't want me. They're just writing stories for the two boys. I would love to do *Jaws 2*.' So my agent negotiated with Universal and I got out of my contract for *The Hardy Boys* and was signed to be Andy. I was ecstatic. It was great. I never thought about being an actor. I never studied it, and here I just had a TV series and I'm going to be in the sequel of the biggest movie of all time. It was just phenomenally fun.

When it came time to shoot I ended up driving my car back east because I knew I'd be gone for a few months. I had just found myself a nice little two-bedroom bungalow in Hollywood, which was really great. I had a friend of mine from New York who had moved out with his wife and I got them to stay in my house, so I had somebody take care of my house. So I drove across country. I planned to go to New York and stay a week and then go down to Florida, which was where we were going to learn to sail and everything.

So I was in Wisconsin because I giving a friend of mine's brother a ride back home and I get a phone call saying, 'Where are you,' and I said 'I'm in Wisconsin. You know that.' It was my agent and he said they needed me back in Los Angeles the next day. I told him I couldn't be back there tomorrow, I had to get to New York. So she called me back and said, 'Okay, you have to be back here on Monday'—this was like Friday—so I ended up driving 24 hours straight through from Wisconsin to New York, probably with medicinal help.

I hit a deer along the way in my white car so my white car was splattered with blood. I got to New York, pulled into my grandfather's house in New Jersey, where I was going to leave the car, and then my mom came out and picked me up. I had lunch with them and then I flew back on Monday. I showed up and asked what had happened. They said that the makeup guy for *Jaws 2* was asking if Gary Springer was around because they had to make a mold of his teeth. The production people called the agency, the agent calls me, I hurry back to California and the makeup people tell me they don't need me until next week.

We decided to stay in California for another week rather than go back to New York and then we headed down to Florida. I think I was the oldest of the kids. Ann Dusenberry might be a few months older than me. (Ann Dussenberry is, indeed, older). Dukakis, Tegan, Karen Corboy. Keith Gordon. David and Billy; they were all younger than me. And originally, in the Hancock version, Andy had the best part. Andy was the one that saved everybody. Andy was the wimp, that's why they wanted me to have braces and wear a hat so I'd look like Bill Dorky! (laughs) When the shark came Andy was the only one who didn't panic.

The scene with the helicopter? In the original scene Andy dives into the water and saves the helicopter pilot and brings him back to the boats. There was a part where the pilot lands and says to throw him a line and nobody moves and I have to start yelling at everybody, kind of like I do to Sean in the Jeannot version. So he was really a much bigger character, which I heard pissed off Roy Scheider incredibly.

But here we were, we were all having a great time. I was twenty-one or twenty-two years old. And here we all were learning how to sail with Ellen Demmy. We started out in mockup boats in a classroom then of course we all ended up on the Intercoastal Waterway sailing in Starfish just to get the hang of it. And we ended up being able to sail the boats we used in the movie."

Gary thinks there were a few different things that contributed to John Hancock's release. "There was one scene, I can't remember what it was, but we kept shooting it over and over and over. I liked John. I like his movies very much and I like Dorothy. I just don't know if he got it. Their script was a little odd and I know that Roy was not happy with the script because it really focused on the kids. The original script was more the kid's story.

I think that may have had something to do with it. I think some of the technical aspects of the film had something to do with it. There was one time where the kids were all supposed to be making out at the lighthouse. Tegan, myself, Nancy and Karen are making out. And we wound up on a Sunday afternoon going over to John and Dorothy's house. Dorothy had us all making out on the couch. She would say, 'Okay, move over here, move there' and I think the girls got a little upset about it and complained. There were really a lot of factors that happened.

I was on Martha's Vineyard when it happened but again, here I was, a twenty-one year old kid and I'm in *Jaws 2*. I've been to Florida learning how to sail now I'm on Martha's Vineyard sailing in Vineyard sound. It was great fun when we were down in Florida. I don't remember if Sarah Holcomb made it up to Martha's Vineyard. She might have left after a few weeks while we were still down in Florida but she was in the room right next to me at the Holiday Inn. I liked her she, was fun.

We all knew that the scenes we shot on the Vineyard weren't "right," and then we heard the production was shutting down. So I went back to New York again thinking, 'Oh dear - so much for that.'

So a couple weeks after I was back I got a phone call that said I had to go back to California. So we all gathered at Ann Dusenberry's house because she lived right down the street from Universal and we all waited there until it was our time to go meet the new people. It was like the sword of Damocles was hanging over our heads. All of us kids, Tegan and Nancy...it was like *American Idol* where they come back to the house shaking their heads saying, 'I'm out,' like they didn't win the gold ticket to Hollywood. So my turn came and I went and I met with Joe Alves, who'd been there from the beginning, and I met with the casting people and I met with Jeannot.

I remember we were down in Florida I went to get something for lunch and one day I'm sitting in the restaurant and Jeffrey Kramer came in and he sat down next to me and he said, 'You know, I don't think I'm made for this.' Because his part was literally nothing. Scheider was mad because it was all about the kids but Jeff's part was literally nothing so he said he was going to pass on it. I told him I was sorry and that it had been nice to meet him. We had a drink sitting there at the shrimp bar in the Holiday Inn.

Anyway, we were back in California and I meet with Jeannot and Jeannot basically says to me, 'You know, I shouldn't have you back. You were very tight with that whole first regime." Because, again, Andy was a much bigger role but he said, 'There's just something about you. I'm going to have you back.' Oh my God, I was so relieved. But he first said to me, 'I don't think I should bring you back.' I don't know the reasoning but he said 'I shouldn't bring you back but I'm going to.' So here I was elated again.

So they started up again and when we went back down to Florida we had some new kids, so the old kids had to start teaching the new kids how to sail. They basically gave us our boats and said, 'Go sail." So we would just go off on these sailing journeys, up and down the Panhandle, and I loved it. I could be on the boat every day. I just loved it sailing that boat. And we had a good time. Annie and Dukakis and David and Billy.

Of course Dave and Billy were more the antagonist of the movie so I would hang out more with the other guys. We were all friendly.

Then Jeff Kramer came back and he and I struck up a friendship. Even today Jeffrey is probably one of my two best friends in the world. I don't see him as much because he's in Los Angeles and I'm in New York but we talk constantly. It was such fun down in Florida because we were basically getting paid to sail and have fun. I mean, everything was going on but the movie because they were redoing the script, so we went on playing. And then they started filming.

It was such a great experience. It was long. It was slow. It was cold. There was the possible firing of all of us. But it was fun. For all of us, for all that we went through, the one thing that's great about it is that all of us kids are still friends. I mean, most of us were on that movie for eleven months and they're all still my best friends. We've all stayed in touch. And I think it's very rare that it happens like that. I mean it's been thirty-five, thirty-six, thirty-seven years now. We even had that reunion in California that Dukakis flew out for. . . that I flew out for. I mean, Cindy Grover came in from Hawaii. That was terrific.

We all have these stories together. I mean, we were all gathered around in the parking lot when Jeannot and Roy went at it with each other. I mean, it was pretty fun to see Verna Fields pulling on Jeannot and David Brown pulling Roy. I mean, they could have killed each other. And we all share these memories and the feeling of being part of this massive production.

And it also teaches you the fool hardiness of the movies. I mean they built that lighthouse from scratch and it was gorgeous but it was only used in one quick thirty-second shot. You've got to wonder how much money that cost. I mean it was a big f-ing lighthouse. And there's another reason why movies are so expensive. We had to bring in a crew from Chicago. We already had Michael Butler and his guys from California, but we needed a Chicago local so they had to bring them in and put them up and pay them per diem. It was the experience of a lifetime.

It's amazing how many fans the film has. One day my plumber came over to fix something and his wife is from Australia. When he found out I had been in *Jaws 2* he was like, 'Oh my God, that's my wife's favorite movie. She watches it constantly, she shows it to our four-year-old daughter.'"

Some of the kids found Roy Scheider friendly. Did Gary? "To be honest, when we were in Florida we didn't have a lot to do with Roy because it was obvious Roy didn't have a lot to do with us. It wasn't that we were being antagonistic, it's just that, well, he was Roy and we were us. In between takes he would take his shirt off and bring his sun visor out. It was just his way to bust balls. Than the A.D. would have to come over and say, "Roy, we're ready to shoot, could you put your shirt back on please?"

While Scheider may not have been friendly, there was one adult cast members the kids loved. "We all loved Murray Hamilton. The bartender at the hotel would leave a glass of gin and milk in the refrigerator every night for Murray to have with his breakfast. And he had to put up with Roy. Roy would come in in the morning and give Murray a new set of lines because these were the lines that Roy wrote and Murray would get so frustrated.

When I got into public relations I started promoting the Hampton Film Festival, which Roy always attended and he and I actually became good friends. I will say the job he did on the film was professional. He didn't want to be there but he was professional."

Besides the memories of filming, there is a very important reason that Gary finds the Jaws 2 experience so special. "I was driving down Pacific Boulevard in Los Angeles when I saw a friend of mines pickup truck up ahead. I pulled up next to him at a red light and told him I had just got cast in a movie and that I would get to go to Florida and Martha's Vineyard. The girl in his car said, 'I live on Martha's Vineyard,' and I said 'Great, give me your number.' A couple days later my friend gave me a yellow piece of paper with this girl's phone number on it. I put it in my bag and I'm sure I would've eventually called her at one point but by that time I was wrapped up with the cast and the crew.

Our very first night on Martha's Vineyard I was out to dinner with Lenora May and that girl was my waitress. She was actually waiting on John Hancock, Zanuck, Brown and Dorothy and she told them that she had met somebody that was supposed to be in the movie, she thought his name was Larry or something and he had curly hair. They pointed and told her that Gary Springer was sitting over there and that girl ended up becoming my wife. We were married for 26 years until she passed away in 2008.

The one thing I took away from this was the comraderies and the friendships that were built. We knew when we were down there that we were doing something special. I mean here we were, getting paid a lot of money, living in the Holidome and sailing. It was great fun it. It was the experience of a lifetime."

Martha Swatek (Marge)

Martha Swatek was used to being outside and was a natural fit to play Marge, the doomed, boat loving member of the Amity Kids. "At the time, my three sisters and I were world-class windsurfers. We competed in the 1975 Windsurfing World Championships in Ile de Bendor, France and the following year in the 1976 Windsurfing World Championships, which were held at Nassau, Bahamas. There were 465 competitors, Men's and Women's class competitions and 4 languages spoken at the pre-race meeting. Susie Swatek won first place; I won second place; Lori Swatek won third and the youngest of us, Cheri Swatek, was tenth place. It received International and US news coverage.

At home, the Long Beach *Press Telegram* ran a full page write-up of the competition and the Swatek sisters. The *Jaws 2* casting department saw/read this article and was impressed with the sailing achievements and a beautiful picture of Susie sailing. They contacted Windsurfing International to find out if the girls would be interested in auditioning for a role or being sailing doubles for the actors. Windsurfing International referred them to our parents and we got scheduled an interview/audition.

Waiting for our audition turn in the office building, we saw so many actors just horribly stressing out. I was not an actor or had taken any drama classes so going to the audition, I figured I would do my best and it would be good experience for job interviews. That gave me the confidence to talk to the director and others in the interview. After all of us sisters had a turn, they had Susie and I audition together. We had to make up a scenario and pretend act with impromptu dialog.

Much to our surprise, we got a call back and were hired two weeks later. They said that Lori was too old, she is the oldest; Cheri, the youngest sister, was too young, but Susie and I were the right age. Susie was hired as crew and as an extra and I as an actress. We signed a three-week contract. In two weeks we were on a plane to Florida to begin the film."

Martha talked about two actors that were later replaced: "I seem to recall that the actor that played Tina's boyfriend (Alan Stock) got sent home. As far as I knew, Ricky Schroder actually dropped out and, because he was to be with me on the boat, he was the only one of the first group that I followed career-wise after. We had spent some time together and I must say that I have never met such an intelligent young man who spoke with an adult vocabulary and at ease with all groups of people that he was around. It was such a pleasure to have met and hung out with him."

Did she ever sense any problems during the Hancock portion of the shoot? "I was not aware of any troubles with Hancock or anyone. The production staff did a great job keeping that sort of stress out of our/my days. I just observed, what seemed to be, hushed discussion about the movie. There seemed to be a lot of pressure on those in charge due to the sets, weather and costs. At the time I thought it wasn't my personal business and I did not ask or hear chit chat from the cast. Maybe others were more aware of the situation."

Martha is reminded about the Irish television rumor. Jeannot Szwarc has always maintained that there was no footage ever shot of Marge being eaten by the shark. Who better to ask then "Marge" herself? "You know what they say, that the director is always right! However, they did shoot four takes, two with blood in the water and two without. I screamed on the first take and was pulled down by my right leg and held under the overturned boat by the on-set water safety dive master and waited by underwater buddy breathing with him using a scuba regulator/tank.

I had lost all my air screaming on the first take and it was extremely difficult to get the first breath of air from the regulator. After the first take, I didn't scream again but just held my breath as I went under water. I was told later that the first two takes were the ones with blood but I never saw it in the water as it dissipated quickly and we had to wait underwater for around 3 minutes after each take.

I think there were about 4 different cameras taking the shot. The shark model that was used for my shots needed to be placed on a sandy ocean floor and at a depth of 30 feet. It was assembled on a platform that just springs forward (like a Jack in the box) and stops once it is at full length. If you were to see from the side camera angle, there was about 3 feet between the shark and me. Bruce (the shark) would travel upward at about a 45-degree angle and retract backwards at the same angle as I swam under the boat.

Since "old-school" film is 2-D, it just looks like I went into his mouth from a straight camera view. If one of the "blood" shots were used for the European release I can see why people may think I was in the shark's mouth. I was told after the film was released that the reason some of my scenes were cut and the "blood" shots were not used was to keep the PG rating."

As a lover of the outdoors, Martha has some great memories of the shoot. "Some of my favorite good times were racing the ocean dolphins with our catamarans. It was such a natural high to be out on the great ocean, screaming fast on our boats and interacting with such beautiful creatures. Fantastic! For a while there in Florida, people were shark fishing off the pier just short of a mile walk down the beach from us launching our boats from the sandy beach. Just a couple of tail flicks of a swim for a shark. On average the fishermen would catch six-foot long sharks.

We had to practice sailing daily for several hours in the morning or afternoon five days a week when not filming. The whole cast became very proficient at sailing. A few times we did have to go ashore as the sky would change from sunny and beautiful to black and raining in about ten minutes time. Occasionally there would be lightning strikes. You really have to hustle back to shore when the sky lights up. We laughed nervously as we made it to safety.

I was happy to have my sister, Susie Swatek, in a couple of the group scenes. She was hired as crew to help set up and take care of the boats for the actors. She is seen throwing a water balloon from the purple and blue sail boat and throwing darts in the Hogs Breath Bar scene. It was so nice to have my friend/sister supporting me and me her during this fantastic movie making adventure.

During the filming I adopted a beautiful stray cat that I named Tiffany I kept it in the hotel room with me and took her out for walks along the beach bluffs. I brought her back with me after filming.

I also remember seeing that the wardrobe department had fun too. They would prop the "burned body" from the boat explosion scene with a cigarette in hand in the make-up chair so that when tourists came to look around and peer in the window to see some movie making stuff they would see her and gasp!"

Billy Van Zandt (Sideburns/Bob)

Billy was a stage actor in New York City when he auditioned for *Jaws 2*. "Prior to *Jaws 2* I had only done theater. I went from high school to college, until it got in the way of auditions in NYC, then I quit when I began working steadily enough. My plays got me an agent in New York, and *Jaws 2* was, in fact, my first movie audition.

I remember spending the whole day at the Hilton (I think) doing improvs for John Hancock. I did monologues from *El Grande De Coca Cola*, which was one of the plays I had done, though it had **NOTHING** to do with the role I was cast in. It was a fun, long day.

Originally my character was going to be revealed as Quint's son. My opening scene was me on the ferry whistling the same sea ditty thing Robert Shaw sang about "fair Spanish ladies." I remember that clearly.

After John Hancock was released, did Billy expect any of his fellow actors to follow suit? "I had no idea the film was being recast. I was back home in New Jersey waiting for a call to return to the set. One day I was told to report back to work and when I did, I found a whole new cast of actors, except for Keith Gordon and Ann Dusenberry, maybe one more. Keith told me he had been flown out to Los Angeles to re-audition. I hadn't a clue. To my knowledge, I was the only one who didn't have to read for the new director. Why? Haven't a clue. I knew David Brown liked me so maybe that was the reason."

He also had no idea that Hancock was in trouble. "The four weeks we spent rehearsing with John Hancock were fun. Improv-ing scenes, rehearsing scripted scenes on taped out on the ground "boats", learning to sail, getting tan. I believe there was some concern about the "rehearsal make out sessions" between some of the actors who were playing boyfriend and girlfriend, but truly I had no idea there was any concern until it was over.

My take is Hancock's movie would have been great. It was dark and adult and followed the tone of the first movie. It definitely would have been an R, which I believe was the main concern in the transition. Everything in Jeannot's film was brighter and happier. And definitely PG, much to my disappointment, when they killed off my death scene. I think the only shot remaining from Hancock's footage is the first sign of the fin in the harbor outside the Holiday Inn. It's eerie and terrific."

How did he end up with the name "Bob Burnsides?" "I had a sizable role in the first version, in fact I was Robert Shaw's son. My first scene was on the ferry, whistling the same song he sings in the first film. They had me grow sideburns, as my name was "Sideburns." In the new version, Carl Gottlieb's script did away with the sideburns, the connection to Shaw, and changed my name to Bob Burnsides. Why Bob? Because in the first version I was to be eaten from the waist down and left "bobbing" in the water. It was a great violent scene. I was supposed to swim towards shore, then suddenly be pushed through the water until Roy took my hand and pulled me out of the water, only to discover it was only my upper half.

When that was deemed too violent, they had me on the pontoon of my boat kicking towards shore and had my legs chewed off. When that was deemed too violent, I was on top of the pontoon and the shark took me and the pontoon under water.

After watching the footage of the stuntman do my death, I asked to do it myself. David Brown said I could, but it had to be the last shot in Florida, in case I was killed doing it. So we did. Michael Butler, our DP, kept calling me Buster Keaton. They tied ropes around my waist, and put me on the pontoon. Then as the shark came down, they yanked me under water.

Then came the worry about the film's rating. Verna Fields fought for my death, but was told a certain number of deaths constituted an R rating and would kill box office. They had me climb ashore as a safety. I adlibbed 'Thank you, thank you, thank you.' I didn't know until I saw the movie on my hometown screen if I lived or died. I would have much preferred dying. It's an odd mismatch that I'm nowhere to be seen in the final shot. I guess I swam around to the back of Cable Junction."

Billy's brother is Steven Van Zandt, occasional actor (*The Sopranos*) and longtime member of Bruce Springsteen's E Street Band. This was a matter of concern for Billy on the morning of October 21, 1977. "One night someone was pounding on my hotel room door at one in the morning. I ignored it, thinking it was a prank. The next morning I got in the van to go to the location to film the stuff on the bay. And the second AD casually asked me, 'Are you related to the rock star Van Zandt that was killed in the plane crash last night?' Well, my rock star brother was out touring with Bruce and the E Street Band at the time. A time of no cell phones. In a panic, I ran back to the hotel to casually call my mother and father to see if it were true. A horrible moment. Turned out to be the guys from Lynyrd Skynyrd (among the six people killed in the crash were the band's lead singer, Ronnie Van Zant). The next day floral arrangements were sent to my parent's house. And my brother, coming back from tour, got to walk in to my parents' house and see his own funeral arrangements. I remember him joking about how small they were. 'That's all they thought of me??'

What memories did he take away from the film? "My first words of advice on making a film came from Murray Hamilton, who used to walk around with a lobster hand coming out of his sleeve, hoping people would try to shake hands with him. Feeling no pain, he came up to Keith and Tom and I one day to advise us, out of the blue—'Be careful. They'll kill you and they won't care as long as they get the shot.' That was my intro to Murray.

We all played backgammon nonstop, got to be quite expert at it, as we waited on the boats. And we all played a game called "Four Days to Zanzibar" It's a game Murray Hamilton taught us. Basically you speak in code across a crowded room describing a trip you're going on. And from the clues you give in the itinerary the other person guesses the famous person you're describing. "Four Days to Zanzibar" equaled Judy Garland. It was also the name of the game.

I also got to miss my grandmother's funeral. She had died over Thanksgiving weekend. And Tom Joyner refused to let me attend the funeral because I was needed on the set. I hadn't a clue I was entitled to say 'too bad' and stay out of town the extra ONE day, I was young. So I flew back to film instead. The shot they couldn't do without me? You see all the sailboats on the horizon. I'm apparently on one of those boats."

Gigi Vorgan (Brooke Peters)

Gigi Vorgan was on a hiatus from acting when she auditioned for the film. "I was in college. I was an acting kid. I'd been acting for years but I hadn't done anything for about three years. There always seems to be a time in young actor's lives when you're about 14 where they start using 18-year-olds who look younger for roles because then they don't have to follow the rules for working with younger actors. You have to have a teacher on set and a lot of other things.

When I was 18 the summer of my freshman year I got a call from my agent and he said if I could go down to Universal, first to screen test and then to meet with the producers and director of *Jaws 2* And I was like, 'I think I have time for that.' Three days later I left for Florida."

On the plane down Gigi realized she hadn't been given a character. "I didn't know who I was going to play, it was a surprise. I read with Gary Dubin, who I did not know, and obviously we both got hired and I was on my way there three days later. It was great. I was on summer vay-cay.

John Hancock was gone by the time I came on the film. What I remember being told was that his rehearsal and directing style was very odd. He was doing workshops with the kids and they felt his techniques were very odd or at least a little different than most peoples. He was doing a lot of things that you would do in the theater. They were not traditional film techniques.

Of course, I don't know what he did that got him replaced. I'm not sure. When I came on I joined the cast that had survived the transition to Jeannot and some that hadn't. I knew I was replacing somebody."

Was there any scenes she did that didn't make the cut? "There were the occasional snippets of lines in certain scenes. In the lighthouse sequence I think there were pieces of dialogue that were cut, probably for time. In the final scene there were other kids that were originally supposed to die. The way they shot it, they showed some kids getting eaten and also surviving. Apparently there were only a certain amount of deaths that they could have in the movie to get a PG rating. They didn't want to get an R because that would limit the audience. So whoever was listed in the script to die, they shot it both ways."

So what did they do for fun when the shark wasn't working? "Gary Dubin was killed off very early in the shoot so he would spend most of his time knocking around the hotel waiting for cover shots. There were romantic entailments. There were several romances among the cast and crew. Gary Springer met his wife on the Vineyard. I don't remember a lot of friction between anybody.

We used to have parties every Saturday night. The production company would have these parties every Saturday. It was a good way to blow off steam. Murray Hamilton would sometimes get up and sing with the band."

Was it hard to gather a beach full of extras? "There was a radio station that ran a contest. If you called in and answered a question, or maybe screamed "shark," you got to be an extra on the beach. It was pretty funny."

Donna Wilkes (Jackie Peters)

Donna Wilkes had a few film roles and commercials on her resume' when she first auditioned for the role of "Jackie" in *Jaws 2*. "Before *Jaws 2* I had done two small roles in movies. One was in *Almost Summer* (1978) which starred Bruno Kirby and Tim Matheson. The other was a small independent film with Keenan Wynn playing my grandfather called *Midnight Ryder*. Prior to that I belonged to a Musical Theatre Group from ages 4-11.

I came in to audition and read for the role of Jackie but I didn't get it Months later I was called in for another audition. I was a little confused so I thought it must be for some small part. I didn't know they were recasting the role I had originally auditioned for. So I auditioned, read with Ben Marley for the producers and director and finally landed the role."

Donna was never made privy to what had happened to John Hancock. "All I heard was bad angles and bad directing. I think it was a sore subject since some of the kids had gotten close to the first cast."

Much is made of Donna's hysterical screaming towards the end of the film. What filmgoers didn't know was that her screaming was her reaction to "Bob" being killed – a scene that was deleted from the finished film. "All I remember from that scene is being directed to be hysterical to the point of becoming comatose at the end."

At the end of the film, Chief Brody puts his jacket around Jackie and paddles off with her and Sean. So, were there any scenes left out that showed she was Mike Brody's "girl?" "There were no actual scenes shot – except maybe the one where I ask him if he always does what his parents ask him to do. Some flirtations and, of course, Mike sneaking out to meet me at the lighthouse. Yes, I was considered to be Mike Brody's "girl."

THE CAST

Now THAT WE'VE covered the "Kids," it's time to spend some time with the actors, extras and a certain hotel that starred in the film. They may not all have made it to the big screen but their stories must be told.

Ben Anderson (Sparky the Diving Instructor)

"I was working in the real estate business at the time and I heard they were looking for people to be used in the background of a movie. I went out to the hotel and filled out an application. Two things I put on my application stood out. I had taken scuba diving lessons and I was certified as a scuba diver so I let them know. Also, I added a few funny things. I told them, sure, I can do this and I can do that and I'm a scuba diver but my real talent is catching sand fleas at the edge of the surf and building sand castles. I was just joking around but the casting director read it and I guess she thought I might be kind of fun to work with so they called me up and asked me if I might be interested in auditioning for a speaking part. I went, 'Dang – heck yeah!' So I went in and I think there were eight or ten of us that were auditioning for these speaking roles and they ended up taking me and some guy just out of the Navy... we got the two speaking parts they had. He and I were on the diving side of it. My role was Sparky, the assistant scuba diving instructor. There was a scene in the movie where the kids are all going out and there was a dive scene on the back of the boat and they got an actor from California (Barry Coe) to play the guy who gets scared underwater. But before he goes down he taps me on the shoulder and says, 'Now Sparky's gonna take you down today.' I'm the one whose hand takes the mask off of his face after he is scared by the shark and says, 'Get us in, for Christ's sake!' So I ended up with about four lines in the movie,. There was one scene I shot with Roy Scheider and Lorraine Gary on the dock.

Of course, the funny thing is that I went from being in the background and making minimum wage to a speaking part that, because of the rules of moviemaking, made me an actor who received benefits, like a driver. They weren't sure if they should put me on a daily contract or weekly one because they weren't sure how long it would take to shoot the scenes so they decided to put me on weekly, which met instead of being paid minimum wage, which was probably less than two dollars an hour, I got bumped up to 830 bucks a week. And of course, when we filmed out on Navarre, they were insistent that I had a union driver to drive me but I lived close enough that I told him I'll just meet you there. I ended up working four weeks under contract. At the end of it all I ended up with about $3200 and that's what I used to buy my wife's engagement ring."

Captain Jerry M. Baxter (Helicopter Pilot)

Captain Jerry M. Baxter was a Vietnam veteran who kept flying helicopters after the war. He was known around Pensacola not only for his unique crop dusting business but for his time spent on the Calypso with the great Jacques Cousteau. "I had been off on the Calypso with Jacques Cousteau and there had been some articles in the paper and stories on the local television station. When the people from Universal were planning to do the movie they went to the Chamber of Commerce and they asked if they knew of anybody that had a helicopter. The Chamber told them they did and they gave me a call. I flew down and talked to them and we struck a deal."

Captain Baxter used his own helicopter in the film. When he learned the helicopter's fate, he went to work. "It was my helicopter in the film and when they told me what they had planned I built a mockup helicopter that looked like mine using scrap parts; gears, rotors, and things like that. This way they could do all of the crashing necessary without damaging mine." When filming was finished the production took the mock-up helicopter back to California where it sat on display at Universal Studios.

Asked how he got into flying and how he ended up working with Jacques Cousteau, Captain Baxter replies, "I got into helicopter flying in Vietnam when I was in the Army and when I got out I started my own business. What happened was Cousteau and the Calypso were coming from St. Petersburg on their way to New Orleans and they were going to do some filming in the gulf on their way to South America.

On the way to New Orleans their helicopter pilot pulled a dumb ass trick and untied the ropes securing the helicopter to the deck, which meant when a big wave hit it washed the helicopter overboard. When they put to shore here they contacted the Chamber of Commerce and they told them about me. They called me and I came down and interviewed. We struck a deal and I met them in New Orleans with my helicopter, spare parts, and maintenance tools—everything I needed for when we went off on the cruise."

Captain Baxter was a part of one of the film's deleted scenes and describes it like this: "There was a scene where I rescued Marge and we share an air bottle underwater and then I bring her up. They cut a lot of stuff out because I did a lot of shots with the kids that wound up on the cutting room floor." Fans of the film also love his chin whiskers. "I never had a beard in the old days but once I started flying for Cousteau he suggested I grow one. He said it would look good so I went ahead and grew one and trimmed it up and I've had it ever since. I was filming with Cousteau down in Mexico and we set up camp on an island that was being used as a bird refuge. It was extremely hot and the bugs were so bad that I got so many bites and began running an extremely high fever. That sickness turned my beard white! Here I was in my early 30s with a snow white beard and according to the ship's doctor it was because of all the poison from the bug bites in my system."

Besides the beard, Captain Baxter takes on more thing from his experience on *Jaws 2*. His nickname is "shark bait."

Jeannie Coulter (Speedboat Driver)

Driving a speedboat was just another day at the office for Jeannie Coulter. As she tells it, "I was a stunt woman and they interviewed about five-hundred girls at Universal Studios. We had to read the scene and do all the acting in front of everyone and I really didn't think I was going to get it so I didn't think about it."

At the time Ms. Coulter was the stunt double for Farrah Fawcett (and, later, Cheryl Ladd) on the television show *Charlie's Angels*. "I had been offered a job on the production of the film *Cannonball Run* (1980) doubling for Farrah Fawcett then that same day I received a call telling me that I had to leave for Florida the next day. I told them I couldn't do that because I've got two children. I accepted the job but I went down two days later but I had to turn down the job on *Cannonball Run*. Sadly the girl who took my place on *Cannonball Run* got injured and was paralyzed from the neck down" (Stuntwoman Heidi Von Beltz was critically injured when the car she was riding in was struck by a van. The van driver did not make the move he was supposed to and hit the car. To film inside the car, the vehicles seat belts and restraint system had been removed.)

Talking about her career, Ms. Coulter says, "I grew up in the movie business. My sister was the star of the television series *National Velvet*. We were put in the Children's Screen Actors Guild and did a lot of background scenes and stuff in TV shows. "But as I got older I didn't think I was good enough or secure enough to pursue a career in acting so I did stunt work. I was always athletically inclined so I started doing that and I really loved it and I kept getting really good parts in different movies and TV shows through the years."

On her work on *Jaws 2*: "It was a three-month process. It was really difficult shooting in the water. One time they moved the shark closer to the boat and when the shark attacked the boat it almost flipped it over. My ankle got caught during the scene and I ended up tearing up my knee. I was in a cast from my hip to my ankle the rest of the shoot. They would have to saw the cast in half when it was time to shoot.

It was very difficult to put together because the shark is hitting the boat with force, tipping it almost over, and it was hard to get it right. In the fire scenes you'll notice I'm not wearing a fire suit. I'm wearing Nomex (a flame and heat resistant substance). It was hard to control the fire and I had my eyebrows and eyelashes burned off. It was quite difficult because we were out in the middle of the weather and the wind and the waves. Everything affected shooting. They always tell you the worst place to shoot is on the water and it's really true."

Ms. Coulter is also part of a deleted scene: "They did film a scene of me dying but they told me it was just too morbid. You know I'm in the boat and I'm on fire and I just lay there and die. But it was fun. Jeannot would always tell me, 'Go into the sparklies, go into the sparklies,' when I was driving the boat. But I didn't know where the sparklies were because he was on shore looking at the sparklies and I was on the water. But I did do my best to drive into the sparklies. It seems like we spent weeks doing that."

Marshall Efron (Deputy Batliner)

A well-known writer and comedian, Marshall Effron (and his partner, Alfa-Betty Olsen) had created the Emmy award winning PBS program *The Great American Dream Machine*. He had also appeared in director John Hancock's Oscar nominated film *Sticky My Fingers...Fleet My Feet* as well as his feature films *Bang the Drum Slowly* and *Baby Blue Marine*.

Mr. Efron talks about his short time on *Jaws 2*, "I had been in a couple films with John. We were still in rehearsals when John was fired. When John was fired I knew I was fired too. We did drive around with the local police.

While at the police station a very interesting thing happened. A man walked in and asked 'What time do the riots begin?' At least that's what the policeman I was with thought he had asked. Apparently he had seen me get out of the police car and he was actually asking 'What time do the rides begin?'

"I enjoyed Navarre Beach. This was my first and only trip to Florida." When asked if he was ever told why Hancock was let go he replies, "I heard they were dissatisfied with the dailies."

But the experience wasn't all bad. "I was down in Florida for quite a while and I ended up trading my hotel room with Roy Scheider. Roy did not like the side of the hotel his room was on so we traded rooms."

Christine Freeman (Terry the Waterskier)

You wouldn't think to look in Missouri for a championship water skier but that is where Christine Freeman is from. "I learned to waterski when I was about four and just took to it."

Ms. Freeman had worked with stunt coordinator Ted Grossman on the film *Freaky Friday* (1976) and when he saw that a skier was needed for *Jaws 2* he gave her a call.

"I was a member of the United States water ski team in 1971 and 1973 and we competed internationally. The water ski world is a pretty small world and once you get to that level everybody knows everybody. I had moved to California and I was at graduate school at UCLA studying to be a nurse when I got a call from a guy I knew at the San Diego Waterski Club. They were working with Walt Disney to set up all the waterski scenes in the film and they were looking for somebody who was about the size of Jodie Foster at the time. It was a lot of fun because I always wanted to be an actress though I never pursued that route. I went to Martha's Vineyard in the spring of 77 for two weeks but never skied.

Originally it was storyboarded that was I going to be skiing with another person; that the shark was supposed to chase us and knock me off my skis but I would be able to grab onto the other guy and then climb up on him. I know there was an interruption in the filming but I was never told why. I was told that once they moved the production to Florida they would call me back. We never filmed on Martha's Vineyard and I was never sure why but eventually they sent me home and then called me back to Pensacola in October. I know we were there almost until Christmas. . . at least two months. It was fun. It was a vacation for me.

188

One reason for the length of time was because they had trouble matching shots. One day it would be pretty outside and then the next we'd get dark and cloudy outside. Plus, the boat they were pulling me with wasn't exactly an ocean ready craft so they had to have really calm water for it to be safe, particularly for the boat so it wouldn't just fall apart.

For the shot where they filmed me skiing and the fin coming up behind me they had a fin on a plank which was sunk into the water and being pulled by another boat which you don't see. They would pull the fin and as their speed increased it would rise to the surface. They would vary the speed and that's how they got the up-and-down effect of the fin.

They originally wanted to film it where I would fall and then be treading water and looking towards the boat. They wanted to film it where I was floating in the water and the shark would just come up behind me and take me down. They had divers and scuba gear down below and they would jerk me down under the water. Unfortunately when the shark would come up on its ramp out of the water it would just stop and sit there hanging in the air. They couldn't get it to work so I spent two days floating in the water in December. It wasn't very comfortable."

How does she feel about being part of the iconic *Jaws 2* poster? "My mother had both the *Freaky Friday*" and *Jaws 2* posters framed and they're in my house. People are so impressed that I'm in the movie but they don't realize that the hardest part for me was waiting to set up the shots. I am an administrator now at my company and a couple years ago during one of our meetings somebody puts a slide of the poster in a presentation and it popped up on screen. It was good for a laugh. My daughter, when she was younger, would watch that scene in the movie and she hated it because she couldn't figure out where I was."

Susan French (Grace Witherspoon)

Born in California in January 1912, Susan French was a late-comer to acting, debuting on an episode of *The Alfred Hitchcock Hour* at the age of 53. She had uncredited appearances in *The Sting* (1973), *Airport 1975* (1974) and *The Hindenburg* (1975) before appearing in *Jaws 2*.

Lorraine Gary on set

Lorraine Gary (Ellen Brody)

If Lorraine Gary's husband had been anyone but the head of a major film studio she could have had a remarkable career. Hired by Steven Spielberg for the role of Ellen Brody in *Jaws* based on her performance

190

in *The Marcus-Nelson Murders*, the television film that gave birth to the popular television series *Kojak*, she almost lost that role when it was discovered that producer Richard Zanuck had offered the role to his wife, actress Linda Harrison. The story goes that, when Zanuck came to him with this problem, Mr. Sheinberg picked up the phone and called producer William Frye, who was at the time beginning production on the film *Airport 1975*. "Bill," Sheinberg said into the phone, "you've got another passenger on your plane," and soon Ms. Harrison was airborne!

When asked if she had any reservations doing *Jaws 2* Ms. Gary says, "The only reservation I really had was that I had just been accepted to law school. This was my second acceptance. The first time I couldn't go when I was younger. I had just gotten accepted to a local law school in California and I was planning to go and then *Jaws 2* came up. So I never did go."

On set she had some reservations because originally the character of Ellen Brody was not fully written. "It was not a substantial role and I worked with Dorothy Tristan to try and flesh out the character. You have to remember back then women didn't have very active roles in these types of films. This was right before Sigourney Weaver and *Alien* (1979). That film was kind of a breakthrough where a woman would actually be the star in something action-packed"

Speaking of stars, like most on the set she did not get along with Roy Scheider. "The truth is we did not really love each other in any way. The relationship was stony. I think he felt that he was the star and no one else was."

When asked about her favorite scene in the film she points to the scene where Brody has just been fired and has had a few drinks. "The one where Roy comes home drunk was a lot of fun because a lot of that was improvised and improvised scenes are my favorite."

Many of Ms. Gary's favorite memories occurred off the set. "Once we got to Florida I remember serving a lot of lamb curry. We would have people over for dinner or throw a party and I always served lamb curry. Which is a very funny thing to do in such a hot climate but I had just learned how to make it. I lived in a house that was owned by the then Governor of Louisiana, Edwin Edwards. He, of course, went to jail but he's out now" (laughs). (NOTE: In 1997, after serving four non-consecutive terms as Governor, Edwin Edwards was charged with bribery and, after being found guilty, spent nine years in prison and was released in 2011. Never accepting responsibility for his misdeeds, he ran for Congress in 2014. He lost.)

"It was a very old house and when the lightning storms came, I would get very scared. . . a little afraid. David Brown was always so lovely to me. When we would have the occasional dinner he was always so charming. I also remember having the finest bluefish ever prepared by Joe Alves while we were on Martha's Vineyard. It was the finest bluefish I've ever had in my life. Barbecued."

Lorraine Gary with extra Andy Vasiloff

April Gilpin (Renee, the "Shark Tower" girl)

April Gilpin accompanied her mother, Sandra, to Florida where her brother, Marc, was starring as Sean Brody. One day she was called into action: "I was in Florida with Marc and our mother to be looked after by mom while the shooting was done. On the day of my scene, right before it was shot, they realized they needed a girl to do the scene and I think my mother said, 'What about April?' The director and a couple of other people pulled me aside and asked me to say the line. Jeannot then said, 'Ok, you've got the part – let's go!' I remember that Joe Mascolo

192

made me cry on the first take. I said my line and he yelled, 'Shut up!' Everybody told me it was a joke but I was terrified."

Murray Hamilton

Murray Hamilton (Mayor Larry Vaughn)

A Tony award nominee for his work on Broadway, Murray Hamilton was probably best known for his role as Mr. Robinson in *The Graduate* (1967) before his performance as Amity Mayor Larry Vaughn in *Jaws*.

While filming *Jaws 2* Mr. Hamilton learned that his wife, former actress Terri DeMarco, was facing a severe medical situation and asked to be released from the picture. Not wanting to lose Mr. Hamilton, the film's co-producer, David Brown, had the shooting schedule arranged so all of Mr. Hamilton's scenes were filmed first. This was done and Mr. Hamilton went to be with his wife, who recovered.

Mr. Hamilton's son, David, accompanied him to the Florida location of *Jaws 2* and shares some of his memories:

"Whenever possible mom and I would join dad on the set. We were with him the entire time he shot the original *Jaws*. And whenever a film shot in the summertime and I was out of school, that's where I'd be. Dad always struggled, as many actors do, with the idea of putting quality against making a nice living. He knew the film was a bad idea. He had a very nice moment in the first movie where he finally realized what a schmuck he'd been and says, 'My kids were on that beach too.' Just the fact that this was *Jaws 2* and the same thing happens and he reverts back. . . it was so stupid that it almost ruined that great moment in the first movie. He hated that aspect. He just didn't think it would be very good. He knew they couldn't get Dreyfuss back, but they did get Scheider. They also offered him more money than he had ever made in the history of his career as well as his name above the title which had never happened in his career. That was hard to pass up.

Being a kid at that time was fun. I actually have a tooth from each shark. The one from *Jaws 2* is soft. They had to change it from the hard teeth on the *Jaws* shark because it had almost killed Robert Shaw when it bit through his harness. Of course, to me, the shark in *Jaws 2* looks stupider because of it (laughing). I had fun though. Most of the cast were teenagers but I was just a little too young. I was fourteen. If I had been seventeen I may have been able to hang out with them on their down time. I did become very friendly with Keith Gordon. He and his parents would often come over to our house for dinner.

My most vivid memory was during the filming of the opening scene around the hotel pool and for some reason Roy Scheider just had a melt-down and really, in my mind, inappropriately began berating Jeannot Szwarc, calling him a TV director who didn't know what he was doing. I remember him walking back and forth like he was holding court, like he was Clarence Darrow, just berating and slamming this poor guy. And my dad never forgave Roy for that."

Jeffrey Kramer (Deputy Jeff Hendricks)

Jeff Kramer was a local boy from Martha's Vineyard when he was cast as Deputy Hendricks in *Jaws*. An actor living off island, the story goes that when a casting call went out on the Vineyard his mother sent in his headshot along with a note explaining that, to save the expense of a hotel room, Jeff could stay with her! Jeff talks about his involvement with *Jaws 2*.

"I'd gotten a call that they were going to do a sequel and I got a call to show up. John Hancock was going to direct and when I showed up they gave me a script that he had basically rewritten so that my character was hardly in it. I looked at the script and I said to myself, 'What am I doing? Am I crazy?' My part had been cut in two and they gave the other guy half my lines. We were the comic relief. I had a small enough part to begin with and I didn't want to do it that way. I didn't like it. I didn't like the way it had been rewritten and even though I needed the work I told them I just couldn't do it.

And I went home. I left. I told them, 'I don't want to do this. You should hire someone else because you don't need ME. This is nothing like the character that I played. You have me as part of a Mutt and Jeff comedy show,' which is not what I wanted to do and I left. I remember flying out with Christopher Knight (Peter Brady on *The Brady Bunch*) who had been there auditioning and I remember meeting Rick Schroder's mother in Florida.

So I ended up going home and then a few weeks later I get a call that said John Hancock is no longer on this project and that there is a new director named Jeannot Szwarc. I'm also told that Jeannot has asked 'Where's the guy that played the deputy? I really like the original guy,' and that's how I ended up back in the film. And Jeannot has become one of my oldest and best friends. I got married in his house and he's the godfather to one of my kids. (Keeping it in the *Jaws* family, another one of his children's godfather is Richard Dreyfuss).

On the release of John Hancock, Kramer has this to say: "So when I came back I heard that the footage was terrible. It just didn't work. Sometimes there were three units shooting at the same time and they wouldn't get a decent foot of film."

Kramer also had problems with Roy Scheider on this go-around. "Sometimes I would come to the set early and Roy would tell me that he had rewritten the scene and it wasn't necessary for me to be in it. So I'd look over to Jeannot and David Brown, who was a consummate gentleman and they would look back at me and they would cover their mouths like they were joking and they would put me back in the scene. I don't think Roy was happy. I know he didn't want to be there but I think contractually they made him. The joke was that people had to be restrained from urinating on his Mercedes. He would throw temper tantrums in front of 400 people. I mean, we were there for months and

I don't think he ever bought anybody a drink. They had to put cones around his Mercedes. And of course there is the whole story of him and Jeannot rolling on the floor and choking each other. It was well documented. It was even in *People* magazine. David Brown used to say, 'I've worked with all the greats and Roy isn't one of them.' He was just so unpleasant on this one. On the first film, on *Jaws,* he was such a nice guy. He just didn't want to do this and he was very unhappy. He sat in the sun in his G-string for so long that they had to color correct him in the mix.

The joke on the set was if any of us ever went to prison we would get six months off because we did *Jaws 2.*"

The Navarre Beach Holiday Inn

Joseph Mascolo (Len Petersen)

Joseph Mascolo was a well-known character actor when he was chosen to replace Dana Elcar in *Jaws 2.*

"I was doing a play and the director was friends with David Brown. David had told him they were looking to cast the part and he told them he thought I would be very capable. He asked me if I wanted to go to Florida and I said, 'Sure, I'd love to do that.' He spoke to David and on his recommendation of my work they hired me. That's how I got in."

A Holiday Inn T-shirt (from the collection of Jim Beller)

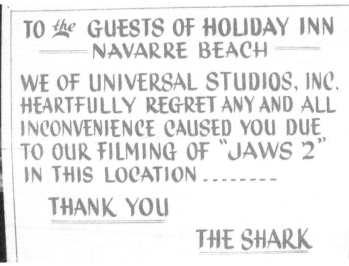

TO *the* GUESTS OF HOLIDAY INN
NAVARRE BEACH
WE OF UNIVERSAL STUDIOS, INC.
HEARTFULLY REGRET ANY AND ALL
INCONVENIENCE CAUSED YOU DUE
TO OUR FILMING OF "JAWS 2"
IN THIS LOCATION . . . .
THANK YOU
THE SHARK

One of the signs that let guests know they were sharing their hotel
with "The Shark"

197

Jeffrey Kramer

Mr. Mascolo is unsure as to why John Hancock was released. "My understanding is that they weren't happy with the tone of the picture. That's what it amounted to. So they brought in Jeannot. But I was hired after the fact."

As for his favorite scene, "I love the scene on the beach where I'm leading people around and Scheider is up in the tower looking for sharks. That was fun because we literally had the whole beach packed with hundreds of people there. It was just fun doing it because it was almost like I was running a parade!"

Tom Rosqui (Deputy Hendricks)

A Joseph Jefferson Award nominee as Best Actor in a Principal Role in 1974's *The Sea Horse*, Rosqui was a long time theater associate of John

Hancock's. He was best known for his performance as Rocco Lampone, one of Michael Corleone's capos, in *The Godfather Part II*.

Joseph Mascolo and Fritzi Jane Courtney

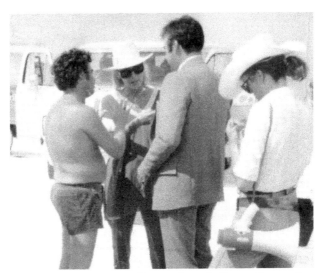

Joseph Mascolo and Lorraine Gary confer with director Jeannot Szwarc.

Joseph Mascolo and Lorraine Gary confer with director Jeannot Szwarc.

Roy Scheider and Gigi Vorgan

Roy Scheider about to mount the shark tower.

Roy Scheider and Jeannot Szwarc on the beach

Roy Scheider (Police Chief Martin Brody)

An Academy Award nominee for Best Supporting Actor for his role in *The French Connection* (1971), Scheider achieved stardom as Police Chief Martin Brody in *Jaws*. Following *Jaws*, Scheider signed a three-picture deal with Universal. He followed up *Jaws* with a co-starring role as a closeted hitman opposite Dustin Hoffman and Laurence Olivier in *Marathon Man* (1976), a Paramount film. In May 1977 he starred in William Friedkin's *Sorcerer*, the first film under his Universal contract. The next film under the contract was to be *The Deer Hunter*, with Scheider taking on the role of Merle (later Michael), played by Robert DeNiro in the finished film. During pre-production a major plot point was changed and Scheider left the project, citing "creative differences." With Scheider still owing Universal two films, and the studio wanting him to make *Jaws 2*, a deal was struck whereby the studio would count *Jaws 2* as two films and the conclusion of Scheider's contract.

Colin Wilcox (Dr. Lureen Elkins)

Colin Wilcox was 28 when she made her feature-film debut as Mayella Ewell in the classic film *To Kill a Mockingbird* (1962) She worked steadily in episodic television and appeared in such films as Mike Nichol's *Catch - 22* (1970) and James Bridges' *September 30, 1955* (1977) prior to being cast in *Jaws 2*.

Call him "Cheeks" Brody!

THE CREW

This chapter highlights the people that created, supervised, directed and captured the magic behind the camera.

Joe Alves (Production Designer/Associate Producer)

Along with Carl Gottlieb, Joe Alves is the *Jaws* alumni that fans most love talking to. Here are his memories from *Jaws 2*.

Before even being hired on the film he was thinking about a sequel.

"I was working on *Close Encounters* in Mobile, Alabama when I met a girl who rescued Great Danes. She had a couple of Great Danes and she said 'Let's go to the beach and run them.' I said it sounded like a good idea and she suggested going to Pensacola so we went. We saw that whole stretch between Pensacola and Destin. There was nothing there.

Just an incredible stretch of beautiful white beaches and I thought, you know, if they ever decide to do a *Jaws 2* this would be perfect. Number one, because it's so pretty. Number two, we wouldn't have the boat interference that we had on *Jaws*. When I scouted Martha's Vineyard for *Jaws* it was in the winter and there were no boats out there. But once summer came, there were an incredible amount of boats from that came from Hyannis to the Vineyard and back and forth so I thought this would be incredible if they decided to do it.

On *Jaws* I had to make the shark because the special effects department said it would take a year and a half to make. We made the shark for about $250,000. By the time I came onto *Jaws 2* from *Close Encounters* they had already started making the shark at the studio and they had already spent a couple million dollars. Because *Jaws* was such a successful movie they could put a lot of charges onto *Jaws 2*, which they were doing. They had hired John Hancock and he started to work on the script with Dorothy Tristan. At the time, Steven was cutting *Close Encounters*. They asked me to do *Jaws 2* but I had some questions about doing another *Jaws*. I met with Steven and he wasn't very excited that they were doing a *Jaws 2*. He thought it would take away from the original film. And he said he'd really like me to do *1941* (1979), which he was preparing. But I told him that Zanuck and Brown had offered me an associate producer position. It doesn't sound like much but Zanuck and Brown never had associate producers so it was almost like being a line producer. It was a big step. I would also be production designer and direct second unit. So I went back to Steven and he said he would offer me the same thing and I said, 'Fine I'll go with you,' but then he told me he didn't have a deal yet. He was still finishing up *Close Encounters*. I got a lot of pressure from Zanuck and Brown to do *Jaws 2* so I did that. I came on board. And I met with John Hancock. He had already started things but Zanuck and Brown wanted me very involved with it, and that was fine. I got along with John fine. That's how it happened. Later on, after they fired John, Dick Zanuck asked me if I would go and talk to Steven about doing *Jaws 2* if he was available. Because of my association with Steven he thought I might have some influence. And Steven said he would do it for $1 million, which then seemed like an incredible amount of money. He really wanted to do *Jaws 2* as the USS

Indianapolis story instead of a sequel. So that's what happened. He said he would do it for $1 million and 10% and of course they thought that was outrageous, which it might have seemed at the time.

So I came on board and we decided that we would use Martha's Vineyard for all the walk and talk stuff in town and on the wharf and then do all the water stuff in Navarre. So I was jumping back and forth between both locations in trying to deal with the effects people in Navarre because we still didn't have much shark wise. I think we had the traveling shark and a fin on the vineyard but none of the major shark stuff was going to be done there."

When asked about the turmoil after Hancock was let go, Alves recalls: "It was a very awkward time. There was thinking that Verna Fields and I were going to take over. But the Directors Guild said you can't do that. You can't take a cameraman or art director or whatever and have them replace a fired director if they are already working on the picture." (NOTE: This is known as the Eastwood Rule. In 1976, during the production of *The Outlaw Josey Wales* (1976), director Phillip Kaufman was fired and the film's star, Clint Eastwood, took over in the director's chair).

"Now both Verna and I had done some second unit work on *Jaws*. I actually did a big scene with the boy on the raft with the shark. Steven gave me a couple of good scenes. So it seemed like a logical thing.

First of all, I think John thought I was responsible for him getting fired and I tried to make it really clear I had nothing to do with that. I was in Florida when it happened and I was really surprised. Here is the one problem I had with John and that's that he was multi-focused. I don't think he really realized how enormous a project it was. As he was preparing for *Jaws 2* he was also directing a play with Tennessee Williams. I got to meet Tennessee Williams, which was great, but I said to John, 'You know there's really so much we have to get ready for.' And then we went to Navarre he got all involved in building this pier and I said, 'John, why are you getting involved in that'?

Meanwhile we are going back and forth to locations. When we got back to the Vineyard I had a great time with John and with Michael Butler surf fishing for bluefish. We had a lot of fun on Chappaquiddick. John was a really fun guy. But in certain respects I don't think he realized the immensity of the problem. In the first couple days of shooting he called me down to the pier and says he's going to wrap. Now, as the associate producer, I had some input and I said, 'John, it's only 3 o'clock, , , you've got a lot of light left.' He said he was having a little trouble. Everyone has a little trouble. I said, 'John, you're having a little trouble **now**? We haven't gotten to the hard stuff. You can't wrap at 3 o'clock.' I called Tom Joyner down and we had a big discussion about John wanting to wrap so early... I mean, we still had three or four hours of light left. Having done the first *Jaws*, Tom and I both realized that things weren't going to get easier. I mean we still had the sailing and the other shots to do. Basically he started falling behind and Zanuck asked me if I would start doing some pickup stuff... second unit stuff. And I did a considerable amount of it.

John had a different visual concept of the movie then I had but I went along with it because he was the director. He wanted it to look really dark. He wanted the boats to be painted dark colors. He wanted to see broken picket fences. It's like the whole island came apart because of the shark and he wanted to show the disintegration of the island because of the previous shark incident. But it gave the movie a really sort of down look. Even the kid's boats couldn't be bright colors. Everything had to be dark. I wasn't crazy about that and I don't think Dick Zanuck was crazy about that but that is how John visualized it. In any case, I did the second unit stuff and then I had to go down to Florida to coordinate setting up the stuff for Bob Mattey's crew.

When Tom Joyner and I went down and scouted we found this huge stretch of beach and right in the middle was the Holiday Inn, which was great to stay at because we could be totally isolated from a lot of activity. But it needed a pier so we built a pier. So I'm down in Navarre coordinating with Bob Mattey when I hear John Hancock got fired. I had absolutely nothing to do with it. I went back to LA to talk to Verna and asked her what we were going to do. She said that Ned Tanen (the President of Universal's Motion Picture Division) wanted to shut it down. I thought that since Lorraine Gary was Sid Sheinberg's wife that maybe he would be interested in keeping it going. Of course Roy Scheider didn't want to be there but he had a contract. Roy was a nice guy but he was very difficult.

Anyway, when I talked to Verna there had been talk about her and I doing it but that wasn't going to happen and I said, 'You know, there is a director that I worked with on *Night Gallery* that I really like a lot.' I thought he was the best director of all the young directors we had on *Night Gallery*. I thought Jeannot's work was the most clever. I knew he had just done a movie called *Bug* (1975) which I hadn't seen in a while, so Verna went and watched *Bug*. *Bug* had come out when *Jaws* had come out and Jeannot and Steven used to share an office when they were just young directors at Universal. Jeannot had actually seen the script of *Jaws* laying around.

I called Ned Tanen and said I'd like to talk to him because they're canceling *Jaws 2*. He said to come up so I did. He asked me if I wanted to direct it and I told him I guess that's not going to work out but I told him that I had a director that I like and Verna likes and we think we can start up again. So they interviewed Jeannot and they made a deal. We brought back Carl Gottlieb and we had him rush to redo whatever Dorothy Tristan had done. So we went to Navarre and worked like crazy to start up again.

The studio was now so involved they were spending money like crazy. They weren't really involved in the first one but now that the second one... since the first one was such a success they were thinking they were going to make more money. So what happened was we had to catch up. I asked Bill Gilmore if he would do some second unit and he did. He did most of the second unit on Martha's Vineyard. The drive-by stuff. Stuff that established Brody and his wife on the island, Bill Gilmore shot that stuff.

At that point I was down in Navarre filming some of the second unit pickup shots. There were a couple shots left over from Hancock. I think there was one with a spinnaker where a boy is riding a spinnaker and bouncing up and down on the water and we shoot the shark's point of view of him splashing down. John shot that. I also had to get busy making sets so that Destin would look like Martha's Vineyard. The police station, things like that, we had to make things up. Before Jeannot started shooting we recast a lot of John's people. I really liked Keith Gordon and I'm glad they kept him. He's really turned into a fine director. So we got all the kids together and we had a discussion and we told them that they

STORY BOARDS
"Shark vs Helicopter" – 9/28/1977

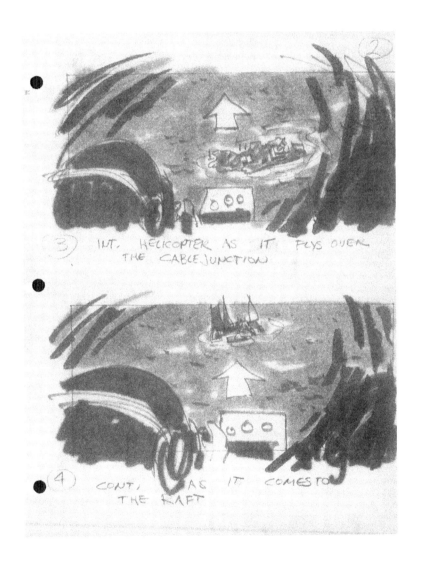

③ INT. HELICOPTER AS IT FLYS OVER
THE CABLE JUNCTION

④ CONT, AS IT COMES TO
THE RAFT

211

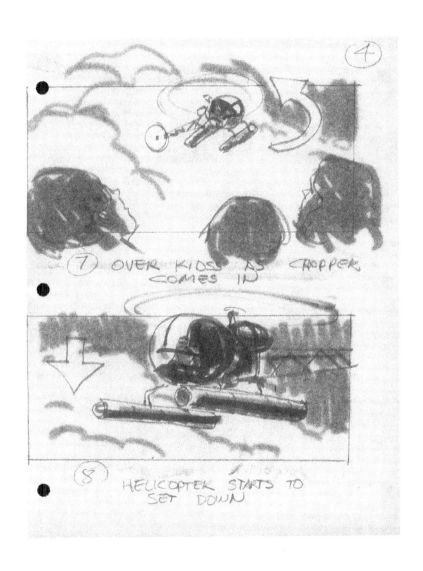

213

⑤

⑨ LONG SHOT - HELICOPTER AND RAFT
IT IS STARTING DOWN

⑩ CHOPPER LANDS ON THE WATER

214

(11) INT. HELICOPTER - RAFT IN BG.
PILOT STARTS OUT OF CHOPPER

(12) PILOT THROWS A LINE
TO THE KIDS

⑦

⑬ KIDS CATCH THE LINE

⑭ THEY TIE THE LINE TO THE RAFT

8

15 PILOT GETS BACK INTO THE
CHOPPER

16 LONG SHOT AS CHOPPER TURNS
AND STARTS OUT

217

218

(19) LINE STARTS TO GO TIGHT

(20) UNDER WATER P.O.V. AS
LINE STARTS TO GO TIGHT

23 INT. HELICOPTER

24 IT STARTS TO LIFT OFF

221

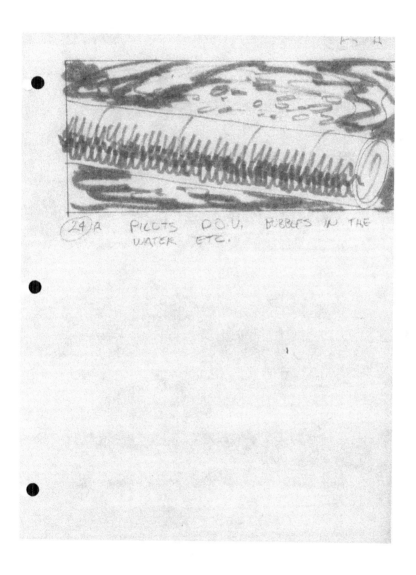

24) A PILOTS P.O.V. BUBBLES IN THE WATER ETC.

222

223

27 PILOT REACTS TO SHARK

27 A P.O.V. OF SHARK
WITH THE PONTOON IN

224

(14) A

(28) INT HELICOP... PILOT REACTS TO SHARK

(28) B   BLADES SPEED UP

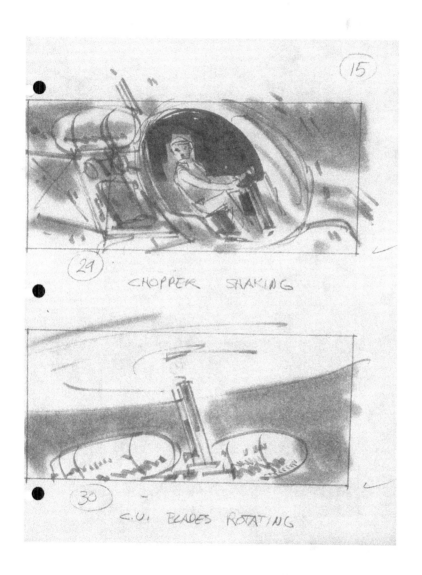

CHOPPER SHAKING

C.U. BLADES ROTATING

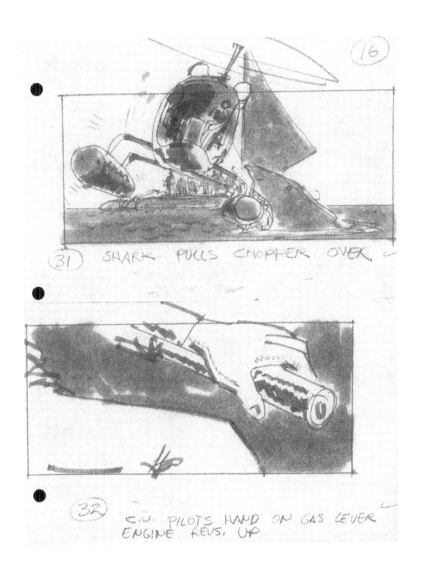

31) SHARK PULLS CHOPPER OVER.

32) C.U. PILOTS HAND ON GAS LEVER
ENGINE REVS. UP

227

(17)

(33) MED, C.U. PILOT⁺ BEING SHAKEN
JACK & FORTH

(34) OVER KIDS — SHARK AND CHOPPER
IN B.G. — CABLE JUNCTION IN FAR
B.G.

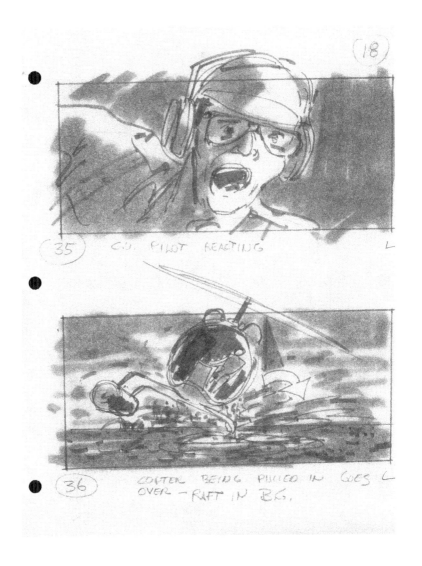

35   C.U. PILOT REACTING   L

36   COPTER BEING PULLED IN GOES L
OVER — RAFT IN BG.

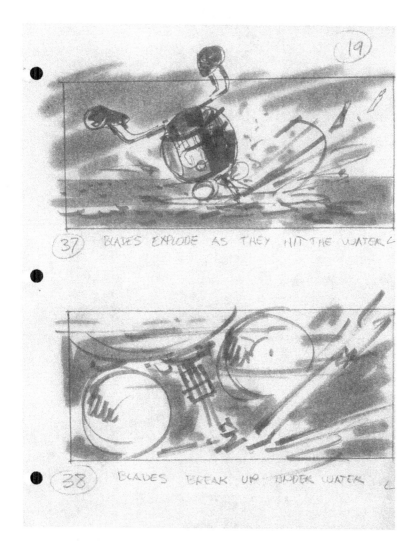

37 BLADES EXPLODE AS THEY HIT THE WATER

38 BLADES BREAK UP UNDER WATER

39) PIECES OF
THE BLADES RIP INTO THE SAILS

40) KIDS REACT AND DUCK

231

41 SMALL BLADES HIT THE WATER
AND BREAK OFF

42 BLADE HITS A MAST AND
BREAKS IT

43) KIDS REACT

44) UPSIDE DOWN MOVE IN   PILOT INSIDE HELICOPTER (UP SIDE DOWN)

233

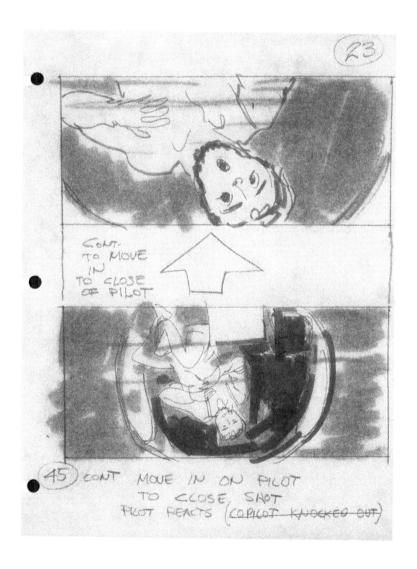

23

CONT.
TO MOVE
IN
TO CLOSE
OF PILOT

45 CONT MOVE IN ON PILOT
TO CLOSE SHOT
PILOT REACTS (COPILOT KNOCKED OUT)

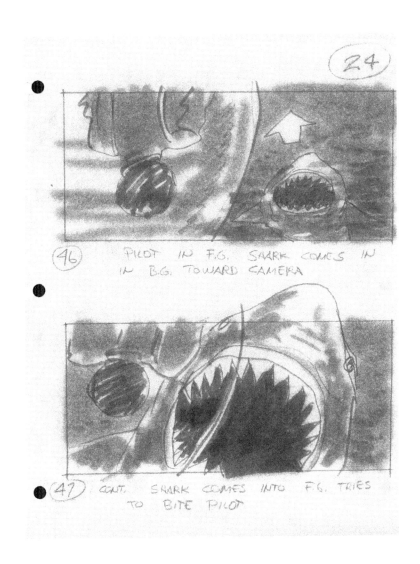

(24)

(46) PILOT IN F.G. SHARK COMES IN
IN B.G. TOWARD CAMERA

(47) CONT. SHARK COMES INTO F.G. TRIES
TO BITE PILOT

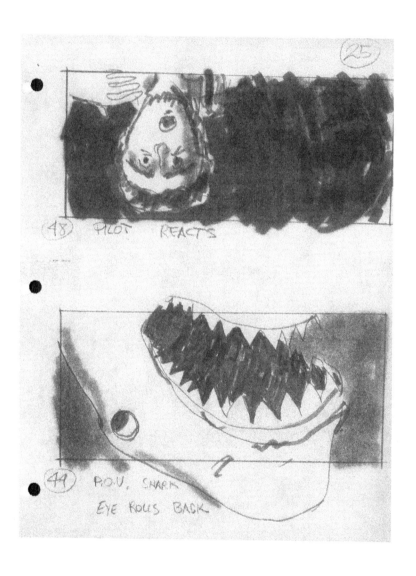

48 PILOT REACTS

49 P.O.V. SHARK
EYE ROLLS BACK

236

50 SHARK SMASHES INTO
PLASTIC — IT CRACKS
WATER RUSHES INTO HELICOPTER

51 C.U. PILOT — HE SCREAMS

237

(27)

51 A SHARK TURNS AND
SWIMS AWAY

51 B PILOT GRABS AN AIR BOTTLE
PUTS IT TO HIS MOUTH

57c PILOT SWIMS OUT OF THE CHOPPER - UNDERWATER

(52) KIDS REACT

(53) D.O.U. AS THE HELICOPTER PONTOON SITS ON THE SURFACE

240

should know we wanted a happier look, brighter boats, so I repainted them all brighter colors. We told the cast and crew to forget about what had happened and to just go out and have a good time. Because I wanted to give it a real Vineyard look I built this huge lighthouse at the end of the island near Pensacola where they also found the orca, the killer whale. That was a big construction job."

When asked if it was Hancock's vision or actual work that got him fired, Joe says, "I would not imagine it was because of the look of the film. Again, I never got involved in that decision but whatever happened it caused them to shut down the movie.

We also had to build cable junction from scratch in Pensacola. It was built entirely out of fiberglass rocks and they floated it to Navarre and got about half way there when they encountered a waterspout that just destroyed it. We were finding fiberglass rocks on the beach for miles and we had to rebuild it. Once we got it out there and had it established we figured out how to kill the shark. You would need a big cable to go from there to the mainland so that worked out pretty good. The reason we had to build the island is because we couldn't shoot on an island because the platform for the shark had to sit 30 feet below the water.

I was on location from April 1977 to January 1978. In January, David Brown came to me and said they needed some more shots of the police boat crashing on the rocks because we didn't get that footage. It was very hard. In some respect it was harder than the first one because even though we had better water we also had waterspouts. I remember in one shot Ann Dusenberry is comatose because Eddie had just gotten eaten by the shark. There was a shot afterwards of her just going crazy in the boat after seeing the kid getting killed. So as I am shooting she looks behind her and says, 'Joe there is a waterspout coming'! I say 'Okay' but I've got to get this shot before we lose the light. She said, 'I can't do this - it's too scary,' so I told the prop man to give her a bottle of brandy. So they went out there and gave her a couple shots of brandy and she settled down. We got the shot and we headed back to shore."

Of Alves' favorite shots in the film, two of them involve the shark. "I love the way Jeannot set up the shot where Marge is taken. You just see the shark come up and then when he's gone so is Marge. It was very subtle. Up. Down. Gone. And seeing the reaction of the boy. I think that worked.

One of the most amazing shots is when the shark is coming and they're trying to pull Mike Brody into the boat and the shark scrapes alongside the boat. The timing of that worked so well and it could've been very dangerous if it hadn't. I mean it was so close. When they pulled that kid out that shark was right there. I guess if you look close enough you can see the shark's mechanism in its mouth when it goes by but it does it so quickly and it is edited so well that you don't really notice. Today you would go back with CGI and fix those little details. Same thing on *Jaws*. If we'd had CGI we could've gone back and gotten rid of all the little boats in the background that ruined the shots. Steven didn't want anything in the background because you wanted them to be isolated. Sometimes we had to wait an hour for a sailboat to get past the horizon but today we could shoot the sailboats and then go back and wipe them out. It's an entirely different filmmaking process today but that's what it was and we dealt with what we had.

For *Jaws 2* we shot so much more action because the studio kept getting involved. They wanted more shark. And when we actually cut the film — Neil Travis was the editor — they left out a lot of the action stuff. It was cut and then recut. Jeannot cut it much tighter and then Verna came in and supervised a cut that brought in more of the action."

In regards to Roy Scheider and his constantly evolving tan: "Roy was always on the beach with that reflector on his face and Michael Butler asked me to tell Roy to take it easy because there was no continuity. The sand was so white that it was hard to photograph him. We all went and talked to him. Me, Jeannot, David Brown, Verna. And we all told Roy that he really needed to stay out of the sun because we were having problems. He would nod his head and say, 'Yeah, yeah, yeah' and the next day he would out in that little skimpy bathing suit and his reflector back at it. I never had a problem with him. He was a really nice guy. There was some pressure between him and Jeannot. Jeannot wasn't used to doing an effects movie and he was a little impatient. He would say 'Camera ready?' and the effects department would say 'We're not ready yet.' On a movie like *Jaws* or *Jaws 2* you do a lot of waiting because you have so many elements to deal with. You have the boats. You have the water. You have the effects. All of that stuff, and it sometimes takes hours to get everything together to get a simple shot."

Bill Badalato (Unit Production Manager)

A production manager and film producer, Bill Badalato had worked with John Hancock previously on the film *Let's Scare Jessica to Death*.

"John and I started out together. It was his first feature film and mine as well. He and I have been friends for decades. I also worked for him on *Bang the Drum Slowly*."

Asked why he stayed on the production after Hancock was fired, Mr. Badalato says, "When I stayed on it was very stressful because John was responsible for getting me that job. So when that all happened I just felt terrible because he had gotten me the job and now he was leaving but the reality was that I was the production manager for the Florida shoot and I could not have just left. It would've been totally unprofessional. Since then John and Dorothy and I have been through a couple of movies together so everything worked out.

John was a very bright filmmaker but I don't think the studio was happy with what was coming back in the dailies. It was a very political movie… it was very politically charged. You're trying to follow up Steven Spielberg and you have a lot of his people. You have Joe Alves, of course and then you have Verna Fields who some didn't perceive but was a very powerful person and then the usual players from the studio. It was a very tangled web.

Of course all this is hindsight but when I look back I can see it was a very political and politically charged atmosphere. You've got the head of the studio's wife in a co-starring role, you have the production designer who received a lot of credit for the first movie. John is the interloper. He's the new guy on the block so his work is looked on with a lot of scrutiny. He may have had some ideas that they didn't want and that's what contributed to it.

It was a very difficult situation. The movie was a grind to make. A very, very difficult grind and I think, and I'm saying this in retrospect, that the location wasn't the best and of course you had problems with the million dollar sharks. I mean the movie was made with various pieces of shark from all over the place, and that was thanks to the ingenuity of the special-effects department, but the reality is the shark was never tested properly. It was never tested in saltwater and sometimes that's the culture of making movies but this went on and on and on and on. It was like a lifecycle. Babies were born, people died, there was a suicide, and we started shooting in cold weather. Today, of course, with visual effects, we would have none of those problems. Even today I pay a lot of attention to water movies and the difference today is amazing.

I find it amazing when I compare what it took to make *Waterworld* (1995) versus what it took to make *Jaws 2* and then you look at movies now like *Life of Pi* (2012), it's an entirely different world. It was quite a production challenge

The shark issue was enormous. They spent millions of dollars on that thing. Universal was very hands-on and I don't think some of the production people were as savvy as they needed to be. I don't think there was enough production savvy people before all this happened. It's a different game now, more people get involved in a different way.

Getting back to Verna, she had a very proprietary feeling about the project. I had an assistant named Maxine Manlove and Verna took a liking to her. One day she noticed Verna's perfume and she asked her what it was called and Verna told her 'Power!' Which I thought was absolutely great. I know Verna had a lot to do with the John situation. A lot of editors feel responsible because they do contribute greatly, some more than others, and I do think that was going on there a little bit. Editors often have to find the movie and I think most directors learn after editing that their movie is never really what they thought they shot. A movie on the page may not look right and the performance may not have been right and on the other note sometimes the dailies are spectacular but when you put them together things suck. An editor is very important.

I mean everybody's important but it really just depends on where your ego is. If you think your indispensable chances are you've got a real problem. If you're confident that you're doing your job then that's great but if you think the movie can't go on without you then you're wrong.

I really learned a lot from *Jaws 2*. I'm a boots-on-the-ground kind of guy and any movie I approached after that I definitely made sure that any mistakes I observed I corrected. Nobody gets up in the morning and says they're not going to do a good job at work. That's not how it goes.

John is also a musician and I think he brings an operatic quality to his work. I think had he stayed on he would've made a good movie."

David Brown (Producer)

Born in New York City, David Brown worked his way up in the film business, landing as an executive at 20ᵗʰ Century Fox. It was there he met Richard Zanuck and the two formed the Zanuck/Brown Company. Among his early films: *Sssss* (1973), *The Eiger Sanction* (1975) and, of course, *Jaws*.

Michael Butler (Director of Photography)

The son of Academy Award winning special effects wizard Lawrence Butler, Michael Butler discusses his work on *Jaws 2:*

"I was interviewed by David Brown and Dick Zanuck.. As a stunt cameraman I had worked on *Tora, Tora, Tora* (1970) for Zanuck's father, Darryl, at 20ᵗʰ Century Fox. I grew up at Columbia Studios. My family has been in the motion picture business for 108 years. My father was an illusionist and special effects genius. He was responsible for creating what is now known as the Green screen. It was a tri-Met process for which he won the Academy award for *The Thief of Bagdad* in 1940. So I had a background in special effects, which is what appealed to them. I was also young.

After I met with David and Dick they introduced me to John Hancock, the director. We got along well. He was very personable. But in talking to him I realized that he wanted to make *Jaws 2* an artistic film and I kind of swallowed deeply when he said that.. We all wanted to make it as best we could but John had no experience in filming a special-effects picture, let alone dealing with sailboats in the ocean or a mechanical shark, which will try your patience to say the least.

I met with Joe Alves and we quickly became good friends. He could see that I had the background and the energy needed for the picture. I did speak with Bill Butler (no relation – the cinematographer on *Jaws)* and the one thing he told me was that continuity was going to be a terrible issue because even under normal weather conditions on the ocean the tides... the wind... everything becomes a problem.

They brought Bob Mattey back, who had made the shark for the first film, and for some reason this shark was made out of steel. I asked him if he knew what happens when you mix steel and salt water and he told me he thought they were putting this one in a tank. I was like, 'What? You did the first movie didn't you? You should know they're not going to put it in a tank.' So you can imagine that once we were finished with the picture we had to keep waiting for the shark elements to work properly. And that was taxing.

The problem with John became apparent during the first week of shooting, during the scenes with the children and the sailboats. He really had no concept of what to do with the sailboats or how limiting they were. He also wanted to add atmosphere, which is done in a lot of movies but not on the ocean because of the wind and what have you. He kept falling behind schedule. You've seen his movies... he's a fine actor's director but this was a movie that pleaded for a completely different kind of director.

After dailies Joe and David and Dick would talk to me for a long time. Usually in cases where they fire the director they usually fire the cameraman as well but that didn't happen. Mr. Brown made it perfectly clear to me that I wasn't going anywhere. But I liked John. In the end they didn't make it as nice as they could. They picked them up at location one morning and they didn't even tell him. They just drove him to the airport where his bags were already waiting. It was one of those kinds of situations... it was basically ugly. I think it was unfortunate. The way Dick and David did it was a cowardice move. They didn't even give him a chance and speak to him. I mean, come on, they couldn't sit down with him and say 'Look, to be honest we think you're over your head. This is not the kind of picture you should do.' I felt so bad. I was sitting in the car as we were supposedly driving to location and I knew exactly where we were going and the look on poor John's face when we arrived at the airport and there's a guy holding his suitcases. He kept saying 'What, what, what?' and I told him 'John you got to talk to the producers.'

When the production was shut down for almost a month I thought Dick Zanuck was going to have a nervous breakdown because the film was costing Dick and David directly. At one point they talked about Verna directing it or Joe directing it and then they finally settled on Jeannot. He had done a lot of television work for the studio; he was very well schooled and he was very receptive to listening and taking suggestions when he felt he was out of his realm."

One popular shot in the film came about when Mr. Butler put cameraman John Fleckenstein on the back of the shark. "It was my idea to put them on top of the shark. We had special rigging made and cut down an ARriflex camera as small as we could and the way we filmed it gave a direct point of view from the shark. John I went to high school together. He was a bass player in a band and my father ran the Optical Department at Columbia and so we had an opportunity to get John into the union. John came to work for me first as my assistant and then my operator for many, many years until he retired. My brother David was an aerial cameraman, he worked on the picture as well.

There was one funny scene where the shark is supposed to attack the rubber raft with Keith Gordon on it and when the shark bit down all of his teeth came out. It was such a stressful shoot that any time we could have a hilarious moment it was great because it allowed us to laugh once in a while.

Jeannot was intent on showing much more shark than the first one and he was able to because, and I can't believe I'm saying this, because this shark occasionally worked much better than the first one. Which wasn't easy because it was made out of metal and sometimes it would just freeze because the metal had gotten so corroded. It was a challenge, it was an immense challenge, but thanks to Joe Alves' tenacity and skill they made it work. He was definitely the driving force. He had done the first one together with Steven Spielberg so he knew exactly how frustrating it would become. I thought for a time after we shut down that they were going to give the picture to Joe but apparently they couldn't. You think he would've been first choice since he made the first picture and he was a production designer and he had a cameraman that he trusted. Me."

Ellen Demmy (Sailing Instructor)

Along with Susie Swatek, Martha's sister, Ellen Demmy taught the Amity Kids how to sail like professionals. The "kids" loved her so much

247

that they insisted she have a part in the film. In one of the scenes shot at the Hog's Breath Inn, beautiful and blonde Ellen can be seen as a bartender dealing with the unruly teenagers. "Hey, Ellen," Gary Springer asks, "did you know that this is the only dump in town where the garbage man delivers?" According to Ellen, she was to reply, "What?" However, to save the cost of paying her for delivering one line, the studio cut it.

John Fleckenstein (Camera Operator)

John Fleckenstein left the exciting world of rock and roll in order to one day sit on the back of a shark!

"Michael Butler and I had been good friends since childhood and his father owned the Optical Department over at Columbia. I'd always wanted to get into the business and the way you do that is you join the cameraman's union. There was one in California, one in New York, and one in Chicago. And then each union had three groups; group one, group two, group three. Everyone in group one had to be working before group two and then everyone in group two had to be working before group three. When everyone was working and they still needed someone, that's how you got in. It was a father-son deal just about. I was in a musical group when I got out of high school called Love with Arthur Lee and Johnny Echols. I played around with them and we created a big following on the Sunset Strip. We recorded our first album with Elektra. We were the first rock group that Elektra records ever recorded. I had recorded half of the album when Michael called me and said they couldn't get anybody, now was the time, come on over and we'll get you started. You work for three months and then you're in. So I quit the group and I went to work. This would happen several times. I would have to quit the group and go to Columbia to work in the optical house. After a year or two I wanted to work in production. I was still in group three. One of my friends called me and asked me to join a band he was in called the Standells. So I left the studio and went to work with the Standells. We toured for about a year and a half and then one day Michael called me and said he was in Hawaii doing a picture called *Tora, Tora, Tora* and asked me if I wanted to get back in. So I left the Standells and got back into the picture business, which is where I stayed for the next 30 years. I got the job on *Jaws 2* because of Mike. We've been together so long.

Being a camera operator on *Jaws 2* was a unique deal because you had to be a certified scuba diver, which I was. Filming in the water was very, very difficult shooting and being the camera operator on that was different than being a camera operator on most any other film. When we started filming we had a rig that Nelson Tyler had created that kept the camera level. When you're on the water everything is moving so when you put your camera on sticks everything is still moving around. We tried Nelson's creation but it just didn't work right so after about four weeks of shooting we decided to do the film handheld. That was the end of sticks and everything and we did the rest of the film handheld.

One morning I came out and they had a saddle on the shark. It was the tow shark. I would ride it as it went up and down. All of the shots of the kids zooming around in their Hobie Cats, those were all handheld. I was in a harness much like a mountain climbers harness. I could adjust it and I could hang off the sides of the boats and get the shot. I would just hang off the side and use my feet as a fulcrum to keep my balance. That's how we got a lot of the shots on those little watercraft.

I don't really know what they didn't like about John Hancock's footage. I know he rehearsed the kids a lot. I remember one incident very early on when Zanuck and Brown were there. We were filming in Edgartown and they were on the set. It was a beautiful sunny day but John had decided for some reason not to shoot and I remember that Zanuck and Brown were very upset about that. Like any movie we had such a large crew and any down day was mucho expensive. I don't think John even knew he was going to get fired. What I heard is that one day instead of taking him to location they took him right to the airport. They cleaned out his house, packed him up and took him right to the airport.

So production shut down for about a month while they went looking for another director. At that time we were scheduled to leave Edgartown and go to Florida where we were scheduled to shoot in Navarre Beach. I had already rented a beach house down there as had Michael. A lot of the crew was scheduled to stay at the Holiday Inn. A lot of the guys went home and I stayed there.

One of my favorite scenes to shoot was a shot from below. One of the grips built a boat that I could be lowered into. The end was like a big cement mixer that would keep me out of range about 5 feet below the water with an air bottle and we used this for the water skiing scenes. One day I had gotten the shot but Michael and the key grip John Black got into an argument and they left me down underwater. I had no contact with anybody. I was starting to run out of air so I grabbed my five-minute bottle. I loosened the 80 pounds of weight we used to keep me down out of sight and I just went out the back of the boat. I dropped the weights and when I popped up the boat was about 60 yards past me and I can see Michael and John still talking. Eventually they did come back and get me.

Jeannot had very little wide-screen experience. When he would look through the camera he would call it the "slit." David Brown came up to me one day after the dailies and said that Roy Scheider felt that he was not getting as big a close-up as Lorraine Gary was when there was two close-ups. Lorraine seemed larger on the screen. So Roy wanted a meeting. David Brown asked me if I'd ever been to New Orleans. I told him 'No' and he said, 'you're going to love it - your leaving tonight.' They were going to have the meeting in the morning and David wanted to get me out of there. Roy and I were actually very friendly because a lot of times when I was shooting him the director wasn't even on the set. Roy and Lorraine also had another conflict. He was quite tan while she would never go out in the sun. They may have argued about that as well while I was in New Orleans."

Susan Ford (Special Photographer)

The 19-year old daughter of the 38th President of the United States, Susan Ford was a former journalism student at the University of Kansas when she was hired by Universal to take on-set and behind the scene photographs during the production of *Jaws 2*. Some of her photos can be found in Ray Lloynd's book, *The Jaws 2 Log*.

Carl Gottlieb (Screenwriter)

A member of the improvisational comedy group The Committee and an Emmy award winning writer for his work on *The Smothers Brothers Comedy Hour*, Carl Gottlieb was asked by his friend, Steven Spielberg, to add some humor to the script for *Jaws*. Spielberg also cast him as

John Fleckenstein (far right) and the Standells.

John Fleckenstein rides the shark for the cover of *American Cinematographer.*

251

Extra Andy Vasiloff and Special Photographer Susan Ford.

Newswire Photo sent to all major newspapers on July 21, 1977 featuring
Special Photographer Susan Ford snapping a shot of Roy Scheider.

Meadows, the publisher of the local paper. When the studio decided to make *Jaws 2* they gave him a call.

"They offered the job to me at scale and I turned it down. I thought it was insulting, especially after the performance of the first film, so I told my agent to tell them no, I wasn't doing it. But I also said, 'They'll be back and it'll cost them' and, sure enough. . . . (laughs) I remember after they started shooting I would go by Universal and visit Verna Fields in her office. Sometimes she would invite me to watch the dailies. I know Joe Alves had shot a lot of second unit stuff because they wanted to establish Amity as the town again and they had just started principal photography with John Hancock directing some of the teenagers. There just seemed to be so many horrendous mistakes in the dailies. It was like he was doing things directors shouldn't do. Everyone was shaking their head, saying "oh my God we're in trouble!" It's a big deal when they fire a director and it's a huge expense. You can't replace a director with anybody who's already on the production so Joe Alves was not allowed to step in. You couldn't have any production executives step in so Verna couldn't take over. I wasn't a director. I wasn't skilled enough to do it at that time. I was just beginning my movie career. So they all asked, 'What are we going to do?'" I was asked if I could have a story idea so I started wracking my brain while they looked around the Universal lot for a director. And they found Jeannot Szwarc.

Jeannot had shared a bungalow with Steven when they were both directing television there. He was a television guy who had done a movie or two but he was really skillful. They knew him as being an on time, on budget kind of director. After the first film they were very nervous about time and budget, even though nothing was Steven's fault the first time. They knew it was an effects heavy picture so they needed a director who knew what he was doing. So they settled on Jeannot and I came up with a storyline that would keep everything going and be more about kids in jeopardy, which was a high concept effective film idea.

They had a one-week hiatus built into the schedule for relocating the whole company from Martha's Vineyard to Florida. They decided to make it a two week hiatus so they could find a new director and get a handle on the script and get me started writing. First I had to write what they were going to film when they resumed in Florida, which I think was the orca scene, the killer whale scene. After that I could basically go back to the beginning of the movie and rewrite the whole thing. So I flew to Florida. I got set up in a hotel room where the company was filming.

Everyone else is waiting to start and I'm holed up in my room typing away. And every time I go out for a break or just to get some air or wander down to the coffee shop someone from the crew—there were like 120 of them staying there, and they would do this with innocence, they weren't trying to bug me, they would ask 'How's it going, Carl?' I'd walk another 50 feet and I'd hear, 'How's it going, Carl?' I'd walk into the coffee shop and someone would ask, 'How's it going, Carl?' So I'd get the coffee to go so I could get back to my room because I didn't want to hear that question.

They got into trouble, they fired the director and they shit-canned the script. I had to come up with a whole new concept and I got paid a lot of money. At least three times what they offered me the first time.

I mean nobody got a dime from the first one. Bill Gilmore, the executive in charge of the production, had been there for years. The studio had always told him if they had a success everyone would share in it. Here comes *Jaws*. Bill Gilmore is the hero. He was the production manager, line producer, production executive… he really got the picture through. And they gave him a big screen TV. The studio can be very chintzy."

Of course, some things in the script were already set so Mr. Gottlieb worked around them. "In the *Jaws 2* script I had kids. I had the island. I had the big fish. There was a lot of things that had already been built so I couldn't undo it. I did have to figure out a way to get all the kids out on the water and in trouble. That was the hardest thing. Basically, before they hired me, I had to show them what I would do to make it right and they all agreed it was a good idea. I invented the notion that there was a cruising culture for teenagers on the island. Kind of like the kids who used to go out in their cars on Saturday night. So I said, 'What if they do that with boats,' and it turned out to be the right thing.

Did Roy Scheider have any input on his character? "Roy hated doing the film. He was there by contract. He didn't have a choice. He didn't want to do it so I just made him the reluctant hero. As always."

Ask him which of the scenes contributed to the script were his favorite and he names two, beginning with the death of Eddie. "I like the moment where the shark drags him towards the boat. He just gets his hand up on the side. The shark bites him and his hand is gripping the boat so tightly it breaks the wood off. I also liked the helicopter crash. The helicopter crash was based on an experience I had when I was making the movie "M*A*S*H" and we had a helicopter crash on the set. Nobody was hurt, it wasn't a big fiery crash. They were filming a lot of helicopter landings and takeoffs. All of us in the cast had the afternoon off because we had filmed in the morning. We had lunch and then we just waited around. I think they only had the helicopters for a few days so they were doing all the landings and takeoffs. At one point one of the helicopters took off and I think they said the choke was set too rich… the mixture was too rich. You could hear the engine lagging. It wasn't going "chop-chop-chop" the way they normally do. It was more like "ka-chop, ka-chop, ka-chop." Everybody looked up and said, 'Well, that's not right,' and then the helicopter, instead of lifting off got up maybe 50 or 100 feet, angled towards the ground and crashed into the trees.

What I remember is the way the helicopter blades went flying. I'd never seen that in a helicopter crash in the movies. It's always a fiery ball. So I made a note to myself that if I ever film a helicopter crash I'm going to have those blades flying like they do. So when I had the opportunity in *Jaws 2* I suggested to have the shark eat the helicopter.

I remember being outside of a theater showing *Jaws 2* and this kid came out and talked to another kid who was in line getting ready to see the movie and he said, 'Wow, that Jaws man—people used to call the shark 'Jaws'—that Jaws eat a helicopter!' Those two action moments are my favorite. They were scripted. They existed as words first and the director visualized them and they were two very effective moments."

One of Gottlieb's quandaries when writing the first film was that he would often have to cut his character, Meadows, out of scenes because he wasn't necessary to the story. Did he ever think of giving Meadows a cameo? "Yeah, I would've liked to have done that but I had so much else to do that I think I would've been seen as overreaching. I think Jeannot or Joe or the producers would've come to me and said, 'Carl, there's a lot more to do.'"

Ted Grossman (Stunt Coordinator)

Best remembered by *Jaws* fans as the doomed estuary victim, Ted Grossman was brought back to work on *Jaws 2*.

"I was the stunt coordinator on *Jaws* and they brought me back for this one. I only did *Jaws* and *Jaws 2*. I didn't bother with the others. (laughs) Hell they're probably still making them, I don't know."

On shooting the death of Eddie: "I know there were a couple things we did that probably ended up on the bottom of the film editor's shoe." When asked if the stunts were more dangerous he makes a good point. "There are a lot of things you do that you don't think are dangerous but a person can fall off their chair and break an arm. I was doubling for Gary Dubin for the scene where he's supposed to be in the shark's mouth and he gets slammed into the side of the boat. We had a speedboat pulling me and if they didn't trigger the release in time I'd still be down there! So many things can go wrong on a set. When I first got in this business David Sharp, who is like the Babe Ruth of stuntmen, was leaving the business as I was coming in and he asked me if I was going to keep doing this and I told him I wasn't really cut out to do anything else. And he told me if I keep doing it the law of averages say something is going to go wrong. Whether it's a mechanical failure or something caused by somebody you are working with, something will go wrong and you have to be hopefully prepared for it. There was a stuntman who worked for Marlon Brando a lot that was doing a film where he and two other people had to run out of a bank. The director wanted it a little more spectacular so he had them set the bank on fire so that they could run out and jump over the fire. It was really simple. Anybody could have done it, you're only jumping two feet. It was nothing but the director wanted a little extra something to make it more exciting. Someone had left some oil on the floor and when they all ran out he slipped on it, landed on his head and was paralyzed from the neck down. That was it. Sometimes these things happen, sometimes they don't. But it's just like life. You could step off a curb and look the wrong way.

It was such a long shoot you wonder who decided 'let's go make another movie on the water?' Remember *Waterworld*? That was a disaster but I'm sure it looked good to the people that were sitting in an office in a comfortable chair. The logistics on both *Jaws* and *Jaws*

2 were a nightmare. When you're on the water and you have to move boats around and things like that it just takes a long time because once you get them moved then the light is not right or you have people in the background on sailboats drunk throwing beer cans at you. It's not like doing a stunt with a car. When you finish you can be back in front of the camera in thirty seconds. It's easy to set up. But when you are out on the water it's a whole different deal. Putting up with all the elements."

Ted and Roy Scheider were good friends and often hung out on their time off-set. "I know Roy loved the sun. No matter what the temperature was he would go out on the beach and sit there with his sun reflector. It's almost like he was addicted to it. One night Roy and I went to Pensacola to have dinner and as we were walking towards the restaurant three girls were walking towards us and as soon as they passed us they stopped. One girl said, 'Oh my God, it's Al Pacino!' (laughs) And Roy turned around and said 'I'm NOT Al Pacino.' I said, 'Come on AL, let's go eat dinner!' As we walked away the one girl said, 'See, I told you it was Al Pacino.' They were telling him who he wasn't. He was such a good guy."

John D. Hancock (Director)

Kansas City born and Harvard educated, John Hancock earned an Academy Award nomination for his short film *Sticky My Fingers...Fleet My Feet* in 1971. This led to his first feature film, the still scary horror film *Let's Scare Jessica to Death*. He followed that up by directing Michael Moriarty and a still unknown Robert DeNiro in the baseball themed drama *Bang the Drum Slowly*. It was a friend of his that recommended him for *Jaws 2*.

"Dorothy was friends with Howard Sackler, who had been instrumental in suggesting the Indianapolis speech in the first film. He had been asked to write the sequel by Zanuck and Brown. I knew Dick Zanuck. He was a fan of the short film I did. I had done a picture called *Let's Scare Jessica to Death* that had a lot of scenes where the audience screamed, which I think he and David Brown liked. I was having trouble getting the pictures that I wanted to make made and when they offered me this I thought, well, maybe if it makes a lot of money I can do something I want to do. I really liked the first picture so I took it on.

257

I thought Howard's script was very dark and I tried to find someone to flesh out the characters. I tried to get Nancy Dowd, the woman who wrote *Slapshot* (1977) to look at it but she wasn't interested. Dorothy was a writer so I let her take a look at it.

Parallel to all of this time working on the script was the animosity of Sid Sheinberg. Originally Dick Zanuck's wife was to be in the first film but apparently Sid overruled that. Sheinberg would take me aside and explain to me how important it was that this time Lorraine go out on the boat. I went to Dick Zanuck and he said, 'Over my dead body.'

If you have worked in a bureaucracy where you have had several bosses, it's clear that you have to try to give them each what they want. I had never had several bosses. I had always worked for myself. I ran my own theater so this was something I was unfamiliar with. I didn't know how to do it so I decided that I had to choose between the two. The one guy is a lawyer that I don't particularly like and Dick Zanuck obviously is a person I like. I liked his pictures and I respected him as a filmmaker. So when we turned in the next draft without Lorraine on the boat Sid Shineberg would never meet my eyes in the commissary again.

When we started rehearsals there was an actress that I didn't feel was right and I replaced her. It turned out she was an executive's girlfriend. Verna Fields was another element. Very friendly, very supportive. She had recommended the editor that I hired. Verna was a cancer survivor and cancer survivors tend to get very determined. She had been so valuable on the first picture that I think she felt she should have been hired to direct the second. She had become a vice-president at Universal because of her great work but now she was always lurking. She would look at the dailies and say, 'I don't understand what John is trying to do here. For the life of me, I don't know what he's doing.' So now here is a sensational film editor who can't figure out how to cut something. It just built and built and built. And of course the shark never worked and we had to shut down. So one day the Universal jet landed on Martha's Vineyard and that night Dorothy and I were on our way to Rome."

Hancock also felt that members of his crew had let him down. "Another element of it all, which is very important. During pre-production there's a whole subterranean battle that takes place between the production manager and the director that gets hired. And I've learned that subsequently the director has to win most of those battles. Joe Alves did a great job in the first film and when I spoke to Steven Spielberg he told me to trust Joe Alves. So I took all the people that had worked on the first picture instead of insisting on my own crew. So I was there kind of by myself and that's never a great moment when you're a director. You're surrounded by people that owe their jobs to "not you." So I really got ground up, especially between Zanuck and Sheinberg in reference to Lorraine's role (when reminded about the plot of *Jaws: the Revenge*, he laughs. "She finally got to go out on the boat!"). For a time after I was fired Verna was directing. Sid Sheinberg and Robert Aldrich, the head of the DGA, got into a shoving match at the Polo lounge because he told Sid 'You're not going to replace a DGA director with your vice president.' But in the end she got her way.

We were very proud of the script. We worked very hard on it. Zanuck and Brown loved it. Sid Sheinberg, not so much. (laughs) Than I made another mistake. The story out was that we had separated over "artistic differences." Dorothy and I are in Rome and the *National Enquirer* tracks us down. They asked me what happened and I said, 'The shark ate me," and I think Sheinberg, who was known as a sharp lawyer, took it personally.

I really think they didn't want a picture with a different look. I think they wanted the same thing. Which is normal. It's a sequel and you want to have all the advantages of the first picture. Had I known going into it what a fantastic director Steven Spielberg was I would never have taken the job because it was such a tough act to follow. It wasn't clear yet at that point, even after he had done *Duel* (1971). I got typed as a warm and human director but I always wanted to do an action film and I saw *Jaws 2* as a way of changing that label.

Steven Spielberg was very helpful and he actually had some wonderful ideas. I was very impressed with his work on the first film, specifically his way of threading a series of shark non-scares, making it seem very ominous."

When asked if any of his footage survived the final print, he notes 'There's a shot or two. The scene of the fin coming up in the harbor, which was something Spielberg had suggested, was mine and there's another sequence. We were going off to film something else and I

259

saw a boat that was dipping people in the water and I thought, 'Gee, that's another shark scare.' They kept a couple scenes but they got rid of my cast."

Questioned as to whether the experience on *Jaws 2* hurt his career he is quick to answer. "Of course. I mean, I still got jobs but it was very hard for me to be able to make the pictures I wanted to."

He turns his attention to the crew again. "I had a production manager named Tom Joyner and his job one day was to clear the harbor of boats so the kids could set sail on their little adventure with no other boats around. He failed badly. So what do you do when a trusted lieutenant fails you? You can refuse to shoot and maybe cause someone to lose their job or you go ahead and shoot and I went ahead and shot it. Of course Verna is watching dailies and she keeps pointing out 'John there's a boat here, John there's a boat over there.' Also remember this was before video assist. There was a sequence where the camera operator cut people's heads off and I was furious. I mean, I wanted to fire him. But then I got fired before I had a chance to fire him. The heads were cut off!

At that time dailies were always tense because you sat there wondering if they got your shot. I mean the operator tells you he's got it but does he? Which is why I love video assist." (NOTE: Video assist, the process of setting up a video camera with the film camera so the director can review what he's just shot, was invented by Jerry Lewis).

Asked if he's ever seen the film, he replies "I've seen the picture. Do I like it? No. It seems to have no story and I was a little unhappy with the cast.

Before we went down to Florida to start rehearsal Dick Zanuck called everybody into his office and asked, 'Does anybody have any reason why we shouldn't proceed"?' and as I look back on it now I should've said 'I'm not that secure with this cast.' I also should have said that before we left I wanted to see the shark work. But taking that position and stopping everything would've been counterculture to the way I've always worked. I've always trusted the people around me. I should have spoken up on both of those points but I didn't. I mean, I read with Steve Guttenberg, who may not be the greatest actor in the world but who I thought had a lot more charm then Gary Springer. And if he hadn't decided to take another project I would've hired him instead of Gary."

Martin and Ellen Brody (Roy Scheider and Lorraine Gary) relax with a drink.

Police Chief Brody (Scheider) gives Reeves Vaughn (David Elliot) a ticket.
Only after Carl Gottlieb took over the script duties did Elliot's character
become Larry Vaughn, Jr.

Mike Brody (Tegan West) and Andy Nicholas (Gary Springer) head towards their boat with Sean Brody (Ricky Schroder) tagging along behind.

Mike and Sean Brody (West and Schroder) take some time out to go sailing.

Mike (West), Andy (Springer) and Lucy (Karen Corboy) on the water.

Mayor Vaughn (Murray Hamilton) confers with Deputy Hendricks
(Tom Rosqui)

Tom Joyner (Production Manager)

The production manager on *Jaws*, Tom Joyner happily joined the *Jaws 2* team.

"I was working at Universal Studios. Universal is so busy they tended to keep us working and since I had done *Jaws* it was just a natural selection to go do *Jaws 2*. Myself...Joe Alves...there were several people that made the transition. John Hancock was already on board when I came to the project. Joe Alves and I did some scouting and we put the budget together. We settled on Navarre Beach and was in the process of settling in down there. We thought it would be better for the sailboats to be down in Florida as opposed to on the Vineyard. On *Jaws* we had such difficulty trying to keep a clear horizon and keep it under control on the Vineyard.

Whatever happened with John Hancock was above my pay grade. I think there was something happening during the rehearsal period. The way John was working with the young kids that apparently went awry. I really don't know the details.

Another reason we chose Navarre Beach was because it had the perfect rising and lowering of the tides. They had to put the shark in about 30 feet of water to have it operate so we had to find a place with a proper depth that would work. It was a new shark but it basically worked the same way. We had to have a barge on which to operate, it was pretty much the same design to my recollection.

One thing that was interesting happened to our boat coordinator, Fred Zendar. We had a whole fleet of motorboats anchored on a tether line. They were Boston Whalers and they were about 100 yards offshore. Every morning everyone would go down to the docks to get in their boats. One day a storm whipped up. The waves were just enormous and the boat guys were panicking because they didn't know how to get the boats. All of a sudden here comes Freddy with a surfboard and he jumps on the surfboard and paddles out. He got to the boats and proceeded to bring them onto the beach. He'd bring one in, paddle out and bring in another. He'd drive them right up onto the sand.

Chris Mueller, Jr. (Model sculptor)

With a career that began with working on various horror films at Universal Studios, most famously sculpting the title character for *The Creature from the Black Lagoon* (1954). He moved on to Walt Disney, where he worked on such Disneyland attractions as The Haunted Mansion and Cinderella's Castle (if you look close enough, you can see the Gargoyles). He also sculpted the giant squid for the studio's *20,000 Leagues Under the Sea* (1954).

Sol Negrin (Director of Photography – Martha's Vineyard Re-shoots)

A veteran of television, Mr. Negrin was responsible for the photography during the Martha's Vineyard re-shoots.

"I had worked with Jeannot when he was doing the *Kojak* series and he asked me if I would go to Martha's Vineyard because they had to reshoot some of the film. It was October and we were concerned about it because everything they had shot previously in Florida was finished. But, they needed to shoot on the island as background for certain scenes because pretty much everything that had been shot originally had been scrapped. The concern was the weather. We ended up having to put leaves back on the trees. (laughs) I worked with Joe Alves, who was the second unit director, and we had Roy Scheider and a couple other people come up from Florida to shoot those sequences.

We shot everything within 10 or 12 days, whatever needed to be shot over again. We were very fortunate that the weather was still in the 70s that particular year so it didn't get too cold. They basically had to open the island back up for us because a lot of the places were closed because it was after the summer season.

The only problem we had on the set was that my gaffer, Milty Moshlak, had a heart attack on the job. He stayed in the hospital there for quite a while and didn't come home until Thanksgiving. He died right after. He worked for me on a lot of things, especially *Kojak*. He was my key gaffer. It was a tough shoot because what they been able to do in a month originally we had to do in 10 or 12 days. It was a grind all the way through."

Director of Photography Sol Negrin supervised the reshoots on Martha's Vineyard in October 1977

(l-r) Cameraman Leo Ledowitz, Assistant Cameraman Maurice Brown and Director of Photography Sol Negrin catch Chief Brody (Scheider) as he leaves his office.

Edmund Papp (Photographer – Destin *Log*)

Edith Blake was the photographer who brought the making of *Jaws* and *Jaws 2* daily to the readers of the Vineyard *Gazette*. The readers of the Destin *Log* had Ed Papp.

"I was a shareholder in the Destin *Log* newspaper and I was the paper's official photographer and sometimes I wrote stories. When you're running a brand-new newspaper you do a little bit of everything. My job was getting stories and this was the big story in Destin."

Unlike most sets, he was welcome. "They wanted to be good neighbors and they wanted to be congenial with everybody, especially those in power, and the newspaper is a little bit of power. The studio was very nice to us and we had invitations to come down any time. The main gathering point for the location was less than a block from the newspaper. It was called Captain Dave's restaurant and it was just a matter of a hop and a skip to go down there.

Since I was around so much I became friendly with David Brown. His wife, Helen Gurley Brown, had come down to interview the director. While this was all going on they were getting ready to blow up the shark so David Brown asked me if I would escort Helen out to the location which was about 2 miles out on the water. So Helen and I were taken off to this big floating platform. We chatted while they were setting up the shot. I took some photos and soon I was getting phone calls from everywhere, even *Time* magazine. It seemed like everyone wanted to know how the shark died. Of course as a guest of the studio I couldn't send them my photos. *Time* magazine made a very nice offer but I had to turn them down. It just seemed like everyone wanted to know how the second shark died.

Two observations from that day: while we were on the set David Brown would keep looking back and up at Helen and you could just see how much in love he was with this woman. She would keep stealing glances down at him because he was down below us where the cameras were. I was really struck by that. I was also struck by the fact that there were maybe 100 people involved in this process and they all moved around like ants. Everyone knew where they were supposed to be, it was like poetry in motion. We had to wait for the proper lighting, they couldn't shoot the scene until it was close to the end of the day... until it was dusk... because it had the match the footage shot the day before. The window to match the light was critical. There were three false starts. One because there was a boat which I think was full of paparazzi that got into the shot right before they were about to push the button so they had to try again. Soon you are hearing 'Okay, were going again. Quiet on the set.' They got ready and then suddenly overhead there appeared this big lumbering aircraft. It flew right over us so they had to wait for that. And the third time everybody's ready, everything goes and the batteries don't work. The electric charge doesn't set off the explosives. And by now everybody's gone into panic mode because they're losing the light. The director of photography is just going ape-shit screaming, 'We're losing the light!' But again, like a busy anthill, everything gets put into motion and the shot goes perfectly. Everybody's laughing and clapping, everybody's having a good time. So after that Jeannot Szwarc came up to our platform and started talking to Helen Gurley Brown and she interviews him. But the interview doesn't last long because apparently there's one more shot to get so Jeannot cannot talk to her for too long. After he left she came over to me and she was just livid. I mean she didn't know me. I was just this little peon but she had to vent to somebody."

Mr. Papp wasn't the only photographer on the set. Did he ever meet Susan Ford? "I met her when she came down. She was a fellow photographer and she was very cordial. Hello. How are you? You're a photographer – I'm a photographer. Things like that. She was very shy... very quiet and didn't say a lot unless you were talking to her.

One thing I noticed is that the production couldn't spend enough money. I'd heard a rumor that Universal had made so much money on the original *Jaws* that their tax bill was outrageous. Apparently they were told that if they put that money back out into the economy they wouldn't have to pay those taxes. I don't remember where I heard it but that studio couldn't spend money fast enough. I remember one time I was on the set and I was standing behind Joe Alves, who was setting up a shot on the Captain Dave's boat dock area. He's looking inland and he's picturing in his head what the camera will see. He spotted a small sailboat that was on a boat trailer in the background and he said to his assistant 'I wonder if that sail should be up or should be down?' So first they put it

268

up and then they put it down then he said to put it back up. I was told that every time the union member lifted that sail or put it down it was forty-five bucks and he must've lifted it and raise a half dozen times. Up and down. Up. And. Down Remember back then forty-five bucks was a lot of money."

Did he ever work his way into the movie after spending all of that time on set? "I was in three or four scenes in the film in the background. Heck my car made more money one week than I did. They needed it in the background. It was an AMC Pacer and they put a Massachusetts license plate on it and used it for a couple of days. I'd say the way they just threw money away was amazing.

There was one scene where Roy Scheider pulled up to the dock to go to the police boat and there were a group of extras just walking back and forth and I was part of the group following him with the camera at my back. And me, being the ham I am, began wondering how I might get my face pointed towards the camera. As Roy Scheider passes, behind him there are two beautiful girls in bikinis. They call action. Roy gets out of the truck and begins walking towards the camera while our group is walking away from the camera. Roy Scheider passes me and here come the two girls in bikinis. When they walked past me I turned around and licked my lips! The director yelled 'Cut, cut, cut...who told you to turn around?' I always remember that day as the day I brought a whole production to a halt."

Sid Sheinberg
(President and Chief Operating Officer of Universal Studios)

As the head of Universal Studios, Sid Sheinberg turned the studio into one of the most powerful, and profitable, in Hollywood. Among the films produced under his reign: *The Sting, American Graffiti* (1973) and, of course, *Jaws.* He had also taken an interest in an un-tested filmmaker and helped groom his career. His name was Steven Spielberg.

Did he have any reluctance in suggesting a sequel to *Jaws?*

"These days, of course, once a movie becomes a hit people think about making a sequel to it. Back then it was a rarity. We had no reluctance."

269

As for Spielberg returning, "We knew at the beginning that Steven wasn't interested but we did contact him when we had to replace the director. I asked him if he had an interest and he said he did. But he asked that we delay the start of the picture and that was something we didn't want to do so the question of him directing wasn't really an issue."

When asked to pinpoint the problems the studio had with John Hancock, Mr. Sheinberg commented, "Once filming began we just felt like he didn't have the experience necessary to make this kind of a picture. He was a relatively new director. In seeing some of the dailies we kept trying to convince ourselves that he was good for us but then, in seeing more dailies, we realized we were endangering a very big asset. So it was a combination of the dailies and our belief that he didn't have the experience necessary to make the film we wanted."

As the Father of the modern-day, blockbuster sequel, he offers this: "There's a big difference in putting out some sequels as opposed to other sequels. It depends if the first film was an original film or if it was just a film by the numbers. I think in the case of *Jaws* that it was the significant originality. I think Jeannot did an outstanding job in keeping that legacy alive."

Jeannot Szwarc (Director)

The time is the 1970s. In a bungalow office on the lot at Universal Studios sit three directors. One is Steven Spielberg. One is John Badham. And the other is Jeannot Szwarc.

Born in Paris, Jeannot began directing on American television in the late 1960s. He worked on such shows as *Marcus Welby, M.D., It Takes a Thief, Kojak* and *Night Gallery*. In 1975 he released his first feature film, the horror film *Bug,* based on the novel *The Hephaestus Plague.* He was aware that *Jaws 2* was being made but never expected to get a phone call. "What happened was that Joe Alves and I had worked very well together on *Night Gallery.* Joe called me and asked if he could come and see me and he brought me a script and I read it.

On replacing John Hancock he is very diplomatic. "I don't know exactly what happened with John Hancock. I wasn't there and I don't want to speculate on it. They were looking for somebody who could take over the project quickly and who could work well under a lot of pressure and Joe had seen me do that. I then met with Zanuck and Brown and then I had a meeting with Ned Tanen at Universal. It all came together quickly."

Since Steven Spielberg had reached out to John Hancock did his old office-mate give him a ring? "I never spoke to Steven. My understanding is that Steven would have done the film if they could have waited six months and if he could rewrite the script completely, but the studio couldn't do this. I also know he was working on his own film at the time so I understand him not calling. You have to understand this happened so quickly. One day I'm in a meeting and three days later I am on location.

I felt if we concentrated on a major sequence we could use that time to rewrite the script. We brought back Carl Gottlieb to rewrite the story for us. Carl fleshed out the kids. I also noticed that the deputy wasn't there and I asked, 'Where's the deputy, I liked him.'"

John Hancock felt there were too many chiefs and not enough Indians on his set. Did Szwarc feel the same way? "Once we began shooting there was very little studio interference. They, of course, would see the dailies and they seemed confident in what they were seeing."

When asked if things did indeed get physical with Roy Scheider, Mr. Szwarc is once again a diplomat. "Whatever happened is between Joe Alves, Verna Fields, Roy and I. Roy was not happy. He didn't want to be there and he felt that he wasn't being treated like a star. His new movie had just come out and he had spent a lot of money on the ads." (NOTE: The film being mentioned was director William Friedkin's *Sorcerer*, in which Scheider plays a man on the run from the mob who finds himself in the middle of a South American jungle. The film itself was as snake-bit as Scheider's character. As the film followed four different characters in various parts of the world, a majority of the opening reel was in foreign languages with subtitles, causing many in the audience to leave, thinking the entire film was the same way. Also, the film had the misfortune to open right before a little film set in a galaxy far, far away opened called *Star Wars*. Scheider had also personally paid for full page ads to run in every major city newspaper on opening day, touting his performance).

Besides the elements and the shark, Szwarc also found himself battling something else during production. "One day we were shooting and there suddenly appeared what seemed to be clouds of butterflies. Very beautiful clouds of butterflies. They were very beautiful but they were very frustrating and I can still remember thinking, 'How can I create this scene with all of these butterflies.'"

Dorothy Tristan (Screenwriter)

Dorothy Tristan has always been creative. As a model she appeared on the cover of *LIFE* magazine. As an actress she had co-starred opposite Jane Fonda in *Klute* (1971). She also liked to write. So when her husband, director John Hancock, asked her to take a look at the script for *Jaws 2* she was happy to oblige. "John was having trouble trying to flesh out the characters. Howard's original script was very dark. So I took a look at it and made some suggestions. John liked them and asked me to do a draft. He showed it to Zanuck and Brown. They liked it and I was hired."

One thing she did was name one of the characters Reeves, after a person she knew personally. "He was a wonderful fellow. Nothing like the character. The only thing they have in common is the name."

The novelization of the film *Jaws 2* is "based on the screenplay by Howard Sackler and Dorothy Tristan." In the novel, the shark is revealed to be female. "Yes, it was intentional to make the shark female. We saw it as "The Return of the Mate" for vengeance. I had killed a big rattlesnake in Malibu once, John's mother teased me that the mate would come and get me – and it did! Or at least another big rattlesnake showed up outside my office. He was quickly dispatched with a hoe."

On working again with her *Klute* co-star Roy Scheider, Dorothy frowns. "Roy never seemed to like me much." When she said this, Mr. Hancock chided in with 'Well, that's because he used to have breakfast every morning with your ex-husband.'" (Film Editor Aram Avakian)

When asked what scenes of hers that survived the film she's most proud of she cites two; "The first is the water skiers. And I love the way we killed the shark!"

John Williams (Composer)

After winning the Academy Award for his original score for *Jaws* it was almost a necessity that John Williams return for *Jaws 2*.

Richard Zanuck (Producer)

The son of studio executive Darryl F. Zanuck, Richard Zanuck followed his father into the business and produced his first film when he was only 25. He met David Brown in 1970 when both were working at 20th Century Fox. The two formed a partnership that turned out films like *The Sting, Sugarland Express* and *Jaws*.

Don Zepfel (First Assistant Director)

Don Zepfel was a veteran of four Universal productions, including *MacArthur* (1977) and *Which Way is Up?*(1977) when he joined the *Jaws 2* team.

"The production was a bit snake-bit sometimes but we pulled it together. I was with the picture the whole time. I started as the second A.D. and Scott Maitland was the first A.D. I was down with the kids when they were learning to sail in Florida and I was up on Martha's Vineyard for the three or four weeks we were there. I was laid off when they shut down and I went and sat on my wife's family farm in Virginia waiting on news if the movie was going to start up again. I got the call and we went back down to Florida and shot through Christmas. I was on the picture through March 1978 when we were doing re-shoots in Catalina so I spent almost a year on the movie.

I had worked as second assistant director with Scott Maitland on the movie *MacArthur* with Gregory Peck. Scott had been hired as the first assistant director on the movie and he took me along as second A.D. Scott had done most of the film until he cracked a vertebrae while stopping the camera boat from crashing into a sailboat. He stuck his legs out to keep the boats from crashing and somehow he cracked his vertebrae. He went on working for several weeks after that but sometimes in the afternoon his legs would start to tingle and he would shut down. I would take over in the afternoons but finally we convinced him to go to the doctor and the doctor told him he needed to lie flat on his back so with him out of action I got bumped up to be the first A.D. But Scott continued to work with a broken back for weeks after he was injured.

For the reader as curious as the authors, Mr. Zepfel explains that it is that a first assistant director does: "The first assistant director is like the executive officer. He's actually the one who calls 'Roll camera' while the director yells 'Cut.' He's a logistics guy. You make sure the actors are where they're supposed to be. He's the one that calls 'Quiet on the set' and makes sure that all the actors are there, that the cameraman is ready, that the sound man is ready. That makeup and hair have done their touchups. Then he checks to see if the director is ready. And when the director is ready he calls 'Roll camera.' He's the one that organizes it and he's right there next to the camera the entire shoot. He's never more than 50 feet from the director and the director of photography. He has a walkie-talkie and he calls the second assistant director to go get actors or go get props and whatever else is needed. He's the main communications guy and the guy that prepares the daily schedule."

Mr. Zepfel was on the production when John Hancock was released. "I don't know the reasons he was fired but I have my own theories. He just wasn't the right guy to direct this movie. He was more of an actor's director if you want to call it that. And this was a heavily physical shoot. He had a vision for a shot of sailboats that could not be accomplished and he was not one who understood the mechanics of sailing.

When the sailing advisor would say, 'No, the boats can't sail in that direction because the wind is blowing from a different direction,' he would get upset about it. He just didn't seem to understand sailboats and large logistics. I think he's a fine director with small groups of actors but this was a film that was spread out over the ocean.

It was not a script with people just talking a lot. They were all over the place. I just don't think at the time he was cut out for a movie this complex. I think that's why he got it. Nobody ever told me exactly why. I think they hired him because I think originally they wanted to make it a more personal movie. That's what happens a lot. You have a large action movie but you hire director who has a small, intimate touch so you get a new look on the movie. I have a feeling that's why they hired him. I mean, he had done *Bang the Drum Slowly* and some other films that were really good movies. I just think he was the wrong director for this movie."

Things were just as turbulent after Hancock left, but in a different way. "While we were shooting in Navarre Beach a hurricane came in over Labor Day weekend. I had actually gone to New Orleans with my

274

wife because it was a two-day weekend. We'd been shooting six days a week so when you have two full days off you take advantage of it. We were sick of the place so we went to New Orleans for the weekend.

During that weekend a hurricane came ashore. It damaged the shark platform, sank one of the tugboats and cable junction was pulled free. We had to go retrieve it from out in the middle of the gulf. Then they ran into a waterspout that turned the shooting barge completely around, which was kind of scary.

There were weather issues because we were there the wrong time of the year. The movie was supposed to be shot in June, July, and August in Florida and ended up being shot in August through December. By the end the actors were wearing wetsuits underneath their bathing suits because it was freezing out on the water.

It was a very arduous picture for all these kids because they were out on their boats a lot of the time. At the beginning of the shoot it was pleasant and fun, but when it gets to be 30° out in their bikinis. (laughs) They would all wear down parkas, take them off at the last minute and act like they were happy. It was a tough movie for the kids that were sailing. Getting sunburned and getting beat up by the waves. It was not easy for them."

Of all his recollections, Mr. Zepfel reveals what may be his funniest. "Ricky Schroder was only on during the Martha's Vineyard shoot and then he was replaced by Mark Gilpin. Before filming Ricky had been the Kodak photo kid with this beautiful blonde hair. He did a lot of Kodak commercials. To make him look like Brody they had to dye his hair brown for the movie. And after they let him go they tried to dye his hair back to blonde and apparently it wasn't very successful. When you dye blonde hair brown, and then you try to go back to blonde, you can often end up with various shades of green or orange! I just know his mother wasn't very happy about it. Of course she was unhappy because, one, he been let go and, two, his value as a child actor had been decreased because he had green hair. Of course he went on to be a great actor and had a great career but *Jaws 2* is not one of his highlights."

CATCHING UP

AFTER ALL OF THE READING you've just done, I'm sure you're curious as to what happened to all of these fine people (and hotel)? Wonder no more.

Joe Alves

Prior to the release of *Jaws 2* Joe Alves was nominated for an Academy Award in the category of Best Art Direction – Set Decoration for his work on Steven Spielberg's *Close Encounters of the Third Kind*. Though he lost the award to the team that worked on *Star Wars* he bested that primarily British crew when he received the BAFTA, the British equivalent of the Oscar, the next year. He later served as the production designer for such films as *Escape from New York* (1981), *Freejack* (1992) and *Drop*

Zone (1994). In 1983 he finally got his chance behind the camera when he directed *Jaws 3-D*. The film remains the highest grossing 3-D film released in the 20th Century.

Fans of Mr. Alves' work can order signed reproductions of his *Jaws* storyboards, as well as illustrations from his other films, like *Close Encounters of the Third Kind,* by visiting www.joealvesmovieart.com.

Mr. Alves lives with his wife in California.

Ben Anderson

His movie career behind him, Ben got into the real estate business, operating Anderson Realty USA. In his professional career, Anderson became a State Certified General Real Estate Appraiser for both commercial and residential properties. He also earned a license as a Real Estate Broker and Real Estate Auctioneer. Having served on numerous committees of the Emerald Coast Association of Realtors, including President, he has also worked at the state level as the District Vice President of the Florida Association of Realtors, which consists of 150,000 members. Furthermore, Anderson was asked to serve as the Director for the National Association of Realtors which is one million members strong. In August 2011, Anderson was appointed the Tax Collector of Oskaloosa County, Florida, a position he still holds.

He and his wife, Karen, have three grown sons and four grandchildren. They reside in Florida.

Bill Badalato

Following *Jaws 2* Bill Badalato served as production manager for such films as *Night Hawks* (1981), *Top Gun* (1986), *Broken Arrow* (1996) and *About Schmidt* (2002). He also re-teamed with John Hancock as production manager for *Weeds* (1987) and *Prancer* (1989). He has also served as Producer or Executive Producer for films like *Top Gun, Hot Shots!* (1991) (and its sequel), *Men of Honor* (2000) and 2004's *Around the World in 80 Days.*

Captain Jerry M. Baxter

Captain Baxter is enjoying retirement in Pensacola, Florida.

David Brown

Following *Jaws 2*, Mr. Brown continued to produce with Richard Zanuck, turning out films like *The Verdict* (1982), *Cocoon* (1985) and *Driving Miss Daisy* (1989), which won the Oscar for Best Picture.

In 1988 he formed his own production company, The Manhattan Project, Ltd. and went on to produce films such as *A Few Good Men* (1992), *Kiss the Girls* (1997), *Deep Impact* (1998) and *Chocolat* (2000).

Mr. Brown passed away on February 1, 2010. He was 93.

Michael Butler

Michael Butler went on to serve as Director of Photography for a trio of films directed by Hal Needham: *Smokey and the Bandit II* (1980), *The Cannonball Run* (1981) and *Megaforce* (1982).

He currently resides in Oklahoma.

Karen Corboy

It's been quite a long time since Karen has been involved in acting. She worked as a registered rep in the brokerage industry, and also as a realtor. She earned her Bachelors in Business Management degree and currently works with customer service at a large manufacturing company. Karen has a son and a daughter, a grandson and two bulldogs. She still lives close to Chicago.

Ellen Demmy

Ellen lives happily with her family in Florida.

Gary Dubin

Best known as Danny Partridge's friend Punky Lazar on *The Partridge Family* before doing *Jaws 2* Gary Dubin has continued to work successfully in film and on television ever since.

John Dukakis

John continued to act for another five years after *Jaws 2* and was in several feature films, guest starred in many television shows and was a recurring character during the first two seasons of *Family Ties*. After "retiring" at the end of 1984, he went to work on Capitol Hill for John Kerry, who had just been elected to the United States Senate. He was a legislative assistant there until he left to campaign for his father in the 1988 Presidential campaign. He then went back to show business and

A "special edition" prepared for Ellen Demmy by her family

Karen Corboy

Gary Dubin, proudly wearing Eddie's death shirt.

became the business manager for the just-about-to-break New Kids on the Block and worked with them for several years before he left to run Paisley Park Records, Prince's Warner Brothers record label. He then segued into management when he co-founded Southpaw Entertainment. The firm's first client was Boyz II Men and they subsequently managed Janet Jackson, Blackstreet, Vanessa Williams and other urban acts. In 1999 John left Southpaw to go run the music division of Will Smith's Overbrook Entertainment Company. In 2007 he moved back to Boston and joined Hill Holliday to run a new division focused on branded entertainment which lives at the nexus of entertainment and marketing. It's been a great run and John looks forward to being in Boston for years to come. He's been married twice and has four amazingly wonderful kids ranging from ages 5 to 26. He is currently leading his agency's work on behalf of the bid committee that is seeking to bring the Olympics to Boston in 2024.

G. Thomas Dunlop

Tom Dunlop is the author or editor of five books dealing with subjects on Martha's Vineyard. He is a writer for Martha's Vineyard Magazine and the Vineyard Gazette, where with John Wilson he co-produces the Historic Movies of Martha's Vineyard project, a pioneering effort to save and present films of the Island dating back to 1920 and before (vineyardgazette.com/historicmoviesofmarthasvineyard).

His books include:

Vineyard Gazette Reader: An Anthology of the Best of the Island Newspaper, 1970-1995 (co-editor with Richard Reston. Vineyard Gazette, 1996)

Morning Glory Farm and the Family that Feeds an Island (Vineyard Stories, 2008)

Schooner: Building a Wooden Boat on Martha's Vineyard (Vineyard Stories, 2010)

The Chappy Ferry Book: Back and Forth Between Two Worlds — 527 Feet Apart (Vineyard Stories, 2012)

Reflections on Martha's Vineyard (essays for the Vineyard Gazette) by William A. Caldwell, edited by Tom Dunlop. Vineyard Stories, 2015)

Ann Dusenberry

Ann was under contract to Universal Studios as a "contract player" when assigned to *Jaws 2* and continued to work under the Universal umbrella for another three years. The contract system ended in 1980 and Ann continued to work in film and television for the next ten years. In 1986 she had the great privilege of working with Lucille Ball on her last network series. The ratings were low and the show wasn't making the cut. The critics were <u>really</u> tough on Ms. Ball. Ann found it heartbreaking and began to get discouraged and jaded. Another three years went by and she began studying with a great acting teacher. However, the fun had gone out of it as the roles she was being offered were not inspiring her.

Ann decided to go back to school and enrolled in a Masters program to study psychology. Shortly after school started she met composer Brad Fiedel and his daughter, Alixandra. She graduated in 1992 and began accruing hours for her license to become a therapist. She and Brad married in the spring of 1993 and their daughter, Zoe, was born at the end of the year. She became a stay-at-home mom, raising two beautiful daughters with a loving, supportive, creative and passionate best friend. She never became a therapist but feels she's learned a lot "on the job."

In the past decade she has charged back into the theater, which is where it all began for her, acting, directing and producing theater locally. She recently co-produced and directed Brad's one-man show, *Borrowed Time*, which will go on tour the beginning of 2016.

Marshall Efron

After leaving *Jaws 2*, Marshall went back to work with John Hancock, appearing in his film *California Dreaming* (1979). As the 1980s began he found himself one of the most sought out actors to provide voices for animated programs and films. Among his credits: *The Smurfs*, *The Biskitts* and *The Transformers* on television and such popular films as *Robots* (2005), *Ice Age: The Melt Down* (2006), *Horton Hears a Who!* (2008) and *Despicable Me* (2010).

David Elliot

David worked as a cab driver in New York City, a professional boxer in Los Angeles, and attempted fur trapping in the Yukon before taking a job as a carpenter, where he found he had an aptitude for building things. He quickly became one of Hollywood's top Construction Coordinators in feature films and was elected to the Executive Board of I.A.T.S.E Local 44. Because he gets bored easily, David also earned his Private Pilot's License with an instrument rating, and started working nights and weekends for a Private Investigator, which eventually led David into his third career. After earning his Private Investigator's license, David opened PIHollywood.com, specializing in the enforcement of judgments and eventually was elected President of the California Association of Judgment Professionals, where he wrote the curriculum and taught the Judgment Enforcement Fundamentals course that is now a requirement of the organization. Then, missing the creative aspect of his earlier life, David started to write. He fooled around with it for a number of years before enrolling in the UCLA Fiction Writers Certificate Program, where he developed *Shining Target* for his graduating project, and was nominated for the Kirkwood prize. Currently, David is working on the second manuscript for the Richard Braddock series, as well as a collection of short stories exploring unusual social environments. David is ecstatically married to the renowned artist Gabrielle D. McKenna-Elliott, whose work may be viewed at http://gabriellemckenna.com. When not working on their creative projects, David and Gabrielle enjoy raising her son, playing hockey, skiing, and exploring the world on their bikes, running, hiking, kayaking, paddle-boarding, rock climbing.... as well as just living quietly in their cozy home.

His first novel, *Shining Target* was released in July 2015 by Willow Tree Press. Anyone who wants more information about the book is encouraged to visit DavidElliottAuthor.com.

John Fleckenstein

After *Jaws 2*, John joined DP Michael Butler on the Peter Fonda film *Wanda Nevada* (1979). He also served as cameraman for Steven Spielberg's *E.T.* (1982) and *Flashpoint* (1984). In 1986 he graduated to

Director of Photography on *The Men's Club*, which starred Roy Scheider. He also served as the Director of Photography on the *Flipper, Any Day Now* and *Women's Murder Club* television series. In 2009 he rejoined the Standells (as John Fleck) and continues to tour with the band today. For more information head to: http://www.standells-official.com.

Susan Ford

Susan Ford stayed behind the camera and worked as a photojournalist for such publications as *Newsweek, Ladies Home Journal* and *Money Magazine.* She currently serves as a trustee of the Gerald R. Ford Presidential Foundation.

She and her second husband, Vaden Bales, reside in Tulsa, Oklahoma. Ms. Ford was contacted by the authors and politely declined to be interviewed.

Christine Freeman

After she completed filming the scenes involving the water skier she returned to graduate school at UCLA to complete her Masters of Science in nursing. Upon completion she continued living in the Los Angeles area where she embarked on her career as a nurse practitioner. In 1985 she relocated to Colorado Springs, Colorado where she continues to reside. She has a daughter who will graduate from high school in 2016. Her daughter learned to water ski but would never watch *Jaws 2.* When she was very young she could not figure out what happened to her mother after her "death" when she was standing right in the room with her.

Her nursing career has been very good to her and she is currently the service line director for women and children's services for a large health system in Colorado.

She continues to water ski when she has a chance on the lake where she learned in Missouri. Snow skiing, wind surfing and fitness have always been a very important part of her life, and Colorado is the perfect state for people who love the outdoors and nature.

Although her success in competitive water skiing was substantial as a world title and record holder, her friends and co-workers are most

285

impressed with her *Jaws 2* work. She still gets people telling her that they "Saw her on TV last night," when the film runs during shark week.

Acting continues to fascinate her and she recently just completed a voice over acting course and her first demo tape this past year.

Susan French

Ms. French re-teamed with Jeannot Szwarc on his next project, *Somewhere in Time* (1980). Though she only had one line, which consisted of four words, it may be the most important line in the film. She went on to appear in such television shows *as Quincy M.E., Dallas, Little House on the Prairie, L.A. Law, Moonlighting* and *Picket Fences.*

Susan French passed away on April 6, 2003. She was 91.

Lorraine Gary

If ever there was an actress who deserved to do more it was Lorraine Gary. Because of her marriage to Sid Sheinberg, in the author's opinion, her job opportunities were limited. Which is a shame. She was so closely scrutinized that MCA/Universal stockholders actually questioned her salary for *Jaws 2.* Following *Jaws 2* she turned in a brilliant comedic performance in Steven Spielberg's *1941* and shined again as George Burns' daughter in *Just You and Me, Kid* (1979) After almost a decade off she returned as Ellen Brody in the final film in the *Jaws* series, *Jaws: the Revenge.* On a brighter note, writers Bob Gale and Robert Zemeckis named Marty McFly's mother in the *Back to the Future* films Lorraine in her honor.

After retiring from acting Ms. Gary became a literary agent for three years and after that began working at non-profit companies. She has happily done volunteer work for the past three decades. In 1995, together with her husband, Ms. Gary received the Simon Wiesenthal Center's Humanitarian Award. She currently is a Board Member and Chair of Policy and Strategic Communications for the Feminist Majority Foundation, producing and directing videos detailing the battle for women's rights. This is a very important topic for Ms. Gary and she hopes her fans visit the organization's web site: www.feminist.org. To view her videos, just type "Lorraine Sheinberg" in the search section.

Lorraine and Sid Sheinberg live in Los Angeles and will have recently celebrated their 59th Wedding Anniversary as you read this. They have two sons.

Marc Gilpin

After shooting *Jaws 2*, Marc Gilpin was signed by Verna Fields to appear in Alfred Hitchcock's next scheduled film, *The Short Night*. Sadly, Mr. Hitchcock died before production could begin. He and Ricky Schroder would cross paths again a year later when Marc and Ricky were both under consideration for *The Champ* (1979). Marc had initially been chosen for the pivotal role of "T.J." but, as he was about to fly out to Los Angeles to sign his contract, was called and told the studio decided to go with Ricky as he more resembled Jackie Cooper, who had played the role of the young boy in the original 1931 film. Marc was later signed for an extended arc on Schroder's popular television series *Silver Spoons*. However, after the first episode, he was released, presumably at the request of Ricky's mother, who was still unhappy with Ricky's being released from *Jaws 2*.

Marc went on to star as young John Reid, the youngster who would grow up to be the title character in *The Legend of the Lone Ranger* (1981). He would work steadily for the next decade, mostly in television, including the 1985 made-for-television film, *Surviving*, which also starred Ellen Burstyn, Marsha Mason, Paul Sorvino and River Phoenix.

Marc currently works as a freelance artist and recently joined the board of the non-profit animators' guild, "A Bunch of Short Guys". The largest animation guild in Texas, ABOSG fosters a community of world-class artists and storytellers.

Keith Gordon

Of all of the final "Amity Kids," Keith Gordon went on to have the most successful career in front of the camera. Following *Jaws 2* he played the young Joe Gideon in Bob Fosse's Oscar winning *All that Jazz*. He then worked with director Brian De Palma on *Home Movies* (1980) and the classic thriller *Dressed to Kill* (1980). He also showed his lighter side opposite Rodney Dangerfield in *Back to School* (1986) after returning to scare people as the owner of the title car in *Christine* (1983).

In 1988 he went behind the camera, writing and directing *The Chocolate War*. His next film, 1992s *A Midnight Clear*, is regarded as one of the greatest films about World War II ever made. Film critic Alan Jones, writing for the *Radio Times*, called it, "A powerful tragedy full of surprises and visual style." His other films include *Mother Night* (1996) and *The Singing Detective* (2003).

Gordon continues to direct today, helming acclaimed episodes of such recent television shows as *Dexter*, *Masters of Sex* and *Homeland*.

He and his wife, actress/producer Rachel Griffin, live in California.

Carl Gottlieb

A favorite figure for *Jaws* fans all over the world to speak with, Gottlieb continues to work both in front of and behind the camera. He directed the Academy Award nominated short *The Absent-Minded Waiter* written by and starring Steve Martin, and co-wrote Martin's first feature film, *The Jerk* (1979). He also appeared in the film in the memorable role of "Iron Balls" McGinty. Other films written or co-written by Gottlieb include *Which Way is Up?*, which was inducted into the "I Love Black Movies" Hall of Fame as the Funniest Black Movie Comedy EVER, *Caveman* (1981), which he also directed, *Doctor Detroit* (1983) and *Jaws 3-D*.

Gottlieb turned his experiences on the set of the motion picture *Jaws* into the book *The Jaws Log*, which today, four decades later, is STILL the best-selling book about the making of a film. He also co-wrote *The Little Blue Book for Filmmakers: A Primer for Directors, Writers, Actors and Producers* with Toni Attell and *Long Time Gone: The Autobiography of David Crosby*, with David Crosby.

A long and respected member of the Writers Guild of America, at press time Mr. Gottlieb currently serves as the Guild's secretary/treasurer. He lives in Los Angeles, California.

Ted Grossman

Ted Grossman went on to serve as a stuntman or stunt coordinator in some of the most popular films ever made, including *E.T.*, *Star Wars:*

Episode VI: Return of the Jedi (1983), *Indiana Jones and the Temple of Doom* (1984), *Cocoon* and *Indiana Jones and the Kingdom of the Crystal Skull* (2008).

Cindy Grover

In 1979, Cindy appeared with Leigh McCloskey in the short-lived but well reviewed television series *Married: the First Years,* which also co-starred her father, Stanley, and Gigi Vorgan.

She currently lives in Hawaii.

David Hamilton

Murray Hamilton

Everyone's favorite Mayor, Murray Hamilton later appeared in *The Amityville Horror* (1979) reteamed with Steven Spielberg for *1941* and played Captain Rutherford T. Grant on NBC's popular series *B.J. and the Bear.* A fine singer, who early in his career recorded an album, Murray's biggest regret was that he never got to do a musical. Sadly, Murray Hamilton passed away on September 1, 1986. He was 63. He was survived by his wife, Terri, and his son, David.

There was never a question that David would follow in his Dad's footsteps so for the last three-plus decades he has done just that. David has performed primarily in musical theater, both regionally and in New York, and has been a member of the Children's Theater Company "The Fanfare Theatre Ensemble" since 1983.

John D. Hancock

After departing *Jaws 2* John Hancock went on to direct 1979's *California Dreaming,* which co-starred Dennis Christopher, Glynnis O'Connor and Dorothy Tristan. In 1987 he directed the critically acclaimed Nick Nolte film *Weeds* which he co-wrote with Dorothy and two years later he helmed the popular Christmas-themed film, *Prancer.* He also worked in episodic television during the next two decades, working on such shows as *Hill Street Blues, The Twilight Zone* and *Cracker: Mind Over Murder.* John is still making movies today. In 2015 he directed *The Looking Glass,* which Dorothy wrote and starred in.

John and Dorothy live in Indiana.

Sarah Holcomb

Sarah Holcomb co-starred as the Mayor's daughter who accompanies Tom Hulce to the Toga Party in *Animal House* (1978) and followed that role with a dramatic turn opposite Robby Benson in *Walk Proud* (1979). In 1980 she appeared with Madeline Kahn and Rita Moreno in the film adaptation of the popular off-Broadway comedy "Happy Birthday, Gemini." That same year she slipped on an Irish accent as Michael O'Keefe's girlfriend, "Maggie" in "Caddyshack," which would prove to be her last film. In that short time she proved herself a fine actress, a gifted comedienne and, more than three decades later, still has a very loyal fan base.

The authors contacted Sarah but she politely declined to be interviewed. Sarah currently lives happily with her family.

Holiday Inn – Navarre Beach

The Holiday Inn went on to serve the visitors to beautiful Navarre Beach, Florida for another 27 years. One of those visitors was a young man named Joel Salsbury. His family were frequent visitors to the hotel, both during the filming of *Jaws 2* and afterwards. They visited so often that Joel ended up working there. As the years went on, Joel devised an ideal Labor Day Event: A screening of *Jaws 2* in the famed Holidome, which became an annual event for some time.

Sadly, the Holiday Inn was destroyed in September 2004 when it found itself in the path of Hurricane Ivan.

As this book went to print, it was announced that Holiday Inn was preparing to build a new hotel on the spot of the old one. The new Holiday Inn – Navarre Beach is scheduled to be open in 2016.

A commemorative T-shirt for one of Joel Salsbury's annual "Jaws 2" Labor Day parties held at the Navarre Beach Holiday Inn.

Tom Joyner

Following *Jaws 2*, Tom Joyner went on to serve as the Unit Production Manager for films like *More American Graffiti* (1979), *The Blues Brothers* (1980), *Tender Mercies* (1983), and *Predator 2* (1990). He also got into the producing game, serving as Executive Producer of the Mark Harmon comedy *Worth Winning* (1989) and *That Old Feeling* (1997), which starred Bette Midler and Dennis Farina and was directed by Carl Reiner.

Mr. Joyner is happily retired and living in Los Angeles.

Lily Knight

After she left *Jaws 2*, Lily headed for the lights of the theater. In 1983 she made her Broadway debut opposite the great Geraldine Page, giving an acclaimed performance as the titular character in *Agnes of God*. For the past two-plus decades, she has been a staple of television, appearing in such shows as *Law & Order*, *Homicide: Life on the Street*, *ER*, *Joan of Arcadia*, *Big Love*, *American Horror Story* and many more. She has also appeared in films several films, including *A.I.: Artificial Intellegence* (2001) and *The Singing Detective*.

She currently lives with her husband, actor Steve Hofvendahl (*From the Earth to the* Moon), on an urban farm in Altadena, CA and has a recurring role on the television show *American Crime*. As this book went to press she was preparing to do a film called *The Role Model*. She is active in Los Angeles theatre, most recently appearing in a play called *A Small Fire* at the Echo Theater. She has created and toured three shows with a group called "Ensemble Galilei" and is currently creating the next show, *Galileo and his Lost Marbles*, with the band and actors Bob Berky and Adrian LaTourelle.

Jeffrey Kramer

Jeff Kramer went on to appear in films like *Halloween II* (1981), *Heartbeeps* (1981) and *Clue* (1985) as well as such television shows as *M*A*S*H*, *The Incredible Hulk* and *Happy Days*.

He went on to move to the other side of the camera, serving as the Producer or Executive Producer of popular television series like *Ally*

McBeal and *The Practice*. In 1999 he won two Emmy Awards when those shows were named the year's best Comedy and Drama, respectively. Though he wasn't asked to reprise his role in *Jaws: the Revenge*, there was a script that he was keen on doing. "There was a script that I thought would be fun that Joe Dante was going to direct called *Jaws 3/People 0*, but I think the studio felt they couldn't laugh at this industry that they had created. (The script was written by Matty Simmons and John Hughes).

Jeff now runs his own production company and lives in Los Angeles.

Ben Marley

Ben Marley is still acting. His credits include the television productions *From the Earth to the Moon*, *The Pride of Jesse Hallam*, *Off the Minnesota Strip*, *Skyward* and the films *Apollo 13* (1995), *The Cold Reader* (2008), *The Last War Crime* (2012) *and the upcoming Territory* (2015). A writer as well, Ben has a number of projects in the works but mostly enjoys time spent with his dog, Smoke. He preceded "Flo" as the spokesperson for Progressive Insurance but would not wear the white jumpsuit.

Joseph Mascolo

Mr. Mascolo went on to appear in many television shows, including *Lou Grant*, *Hart to Hart* and *Hill Street Blues* as well as popular films like *Sharky's Machine* (1981) and *Heat* (1986), both of which co-starred Burt Reynolds. In 1983 he made his first appearance as Stefano DiMera on the daytime soap opera *Days of Our Lives*. 32 years later he's still there, having appeared in almost 1500 episodes.

Mr. Mascolo and his wife live in Los Angeles.

Lenora May

After leaving *Jaws 2*, Lenora headed to Los Angeles, where her first job was a guest appearance on *Little House on the Prairie*.

She's continued to act, starring in many television films and pilots, among them *Living Proof*, *Hobson's Choice* and *Fantasies*, while guest starring on such popular programs as *ER*, *Medium and Desperate Housewives*. Most recently she has appeared on *Grey's Anatomy*, *Scandal and Switched at Birth.* She also has a recurring role as Dr. Chernoff on *Mistresses.* She has appeared in over 50 commercials and still performs on the stage. Her most recent role in a play was at the Santa Monica Playhouse playing an Italian mama in *Raise Me Up.* As a producer, she is currently developing two feature films: *Spillville,* a historical drama about composer Antonin Dvorak, and *Beginning,* a romance/drama based on a true story. Her two children complete the picture. Lenora is married to Emmy award winning writer Craig Heller (*General Hospital, As the World Turns*).

Lenora May

Susan McMillan

Susan still lives in Pensacola with her husband. They have two grown sons. She and her family are still into sailing and loving the beach.

Chris Mueller, Jr.

Chris Mueller, Jr. passed away in Los Angeles on August 3, 1987.

Sol Negrin

Mr. Negrin went on to work on several popular television programs of the 1980s, including *The White Shadow*, *St. Elsewhere* and *Dear John* as well as serving as an additional Director of Photography on the Eddie Murphy comedy *Coming to America*.

He currently lives in New York.

David Owsley

David Owsley

David still lives in Pensacola, is retired and now "doing my own thing for me." His life revolves around the water, woods, nature and doing good for others, especially special needs children.

Edmund Papp

After leaving the newspaper business Mr. Papp headed south to Key West, where he currently writes stories about mermaids and sea sirens with connections to Greek mythology for his *Daughters of Poseidon* sci-fi series. For more information on this project, head to www. mermaidhunter.com

Nancy Sawyer

"Working on *Jaws 2* was an amazing experience. I adored John Hancock and Dorothy Tristan. Working with these two talented and supportive people gave me such confidence at a young age and they both truly inspired me. Although the unfortunate scrapping of the original *Jaws 2* movie did set me back in many ways, I still haven't given up. After years of raising children and despite struggling to survive in recent years I haven't forgotten who I am inside or where my gifts lie. I never forgot about acting, not for one day or even one minute. It's always been who I am since both before and after the *Jaws 2* experience. Nothing could ever change that. I've been working to make up for lost time, now that my youngest child is finishing high school. After some small parts in film and TV and studying at the Lee Strasberg Theater and Film Institute, (once in my teens and again in 2011), I know that it's still all there within me, heart and soul, only stronger. I'm prepared for and look forward to all the good work that lies ahead in the future."

Roy Scheider

Despite his reluctance to do the film, Scheider was very positive to the members of his fan club when he wrote them in early 1978 – "Just finished sound looping on *Jaws 2*. Looks like a winner and there's certainly enough of yours truly to go around!"

Nancy Sawyer

Following *Jaws 2* Scheider went on to enjoy a great career. His next film was *Last Embrace* (in the same note to his fans Scheider praised the film's young director, Jonathan Demme). He then took the second role he would forever be identified with, that of Broadway director/choreographer Joe Gideon in Bob Fosse's *All That Jazz.* For his performance, in which Scheider not only acted but had to sing and dance, he received his second Academy Award nomination, this time for Best Actor. He continued the 1980s with such popular films *as Still of the Night* (1982), *Blue* Thunder (1983), *2010* (1984), *52-Pick Up* (1986) and *Listen to Me* (1989).

On February 11, 1989 Scheider married actress Brenda Siemer. He continued to work, appearing in films like *The Russia House* (1990), *Naked Lunch* (1991), *The Rainmaker* 1997) and *The Myth of Fingerprints* (1997). He also had a starring role in the television series *SeaQuest: DSV.* Roy and Brenda had two children, son Christian and daughter Molly, who they adopted. His new family allowed Roy to slow down his work schedule, so he spent the children's early years only doing the occasional film or television role.

Much has been made in this book about Roy and his suntan. For the record, Roy was very sick as a child and was unable to go out and play very much. He became very heavy. When he was eleven he was given the "all clear" and began what would become a lifetime of physical fitness. To Roy the child, overweight and sitting indoors most of his young life, being thin and tan meant you were healthy. Sadly, it was his love of the sun that killed him.

On February 10, 2008 – the day before what would have been his 19th Wedding Anniversary – Roy Scheider died of multiple melanoma at the University of Arkansas Medical Sciences Hospital in Little Rock, Arkansas. He was 75.

Ricky Schroder

Of all of the "Amity Kids," Ricky Schroder is certainly the most well-known actor to come out of the production.

Following his release from *Jaws 2* Ricky went on to gain stardom when, at the age of 8, he co-starred opposite Jon Voight and Faye Dunaway in the remake of the 1931 film classic, *The Champ*. Though he criminally (the author's words) was not nominated for an Academy Award for his performance, he did win the Golden Globe as the New Star of the Year in a Motion Picture – Male. At age nine, he remains the youngest winner ever of a Golden Globe.

He went on to co-star opposite William Holden in the film, *The*

Earthling and appeared in several television films. In 1982 he began a five season run as the star of the highly popular television series *Silver Spoons* and made new fans when he co-starred with Robert Duvall and Tommy Lee Jones in the mini-series *Lonesome Dove*. He also appeared in the follow up *Return to Lonesome Dove*, where he once again played the son of Jon Voight. He also had recurring roles in such popular television programs as *NYPD Blue*, *Scrubs*, and *24*.

In 2004 he became hyphenated as the writer-director of the film *Black Cloud*. His other directorial credits include the television films *Hellhounds* and *Our Wild Hearts*. His US Army themed reality television series, *Serving Strong*, on which he serves as Executive Producer, is scheduled to begin its third season in January 2016.

Ricky currently lives in California with his wife and four children. His oldest son, Holden, is named for his *The Earthling* co-star.

Sid Sheinberg

Sid Sheinberg could be remembered for any one achievement and it would be more impressive than most. You could cite the fact that he championed the work of a young director named Steven Spielberg. Or the fact that, by greenlighting *Jaws 2*, he is the father of the blockbuster sequel. Finally, you could add that in his three decades as the head of Universal Studios he helped bring to fruition some of the most popular (*Jaws*, *E.T.*, *Jurassic Park* (1993)) and important (*Schlinder's List* (1993)) films ever made.

After leaving Universal he went into business with his son, Jonathan, creating the production company called The Bubble Factory. As he approaches the age of 80, he is still there in his office every day.

Skip Singleton

After leaving *Jaws 2*, Skip went on to Ole Miss which he attended on a tennis scholarship. After graduation, he began his first career in tennis, playing and living in Europe. He returned to Northwest Florida to teach and run a tennis operation at a resort. He went on to become the country's youngest Master Pro and was also named Florida Pro of the Year. He is also the author of three popular books on the sport. At age 35, Skip embarked on a new career by going to law school to study intellectual property law. Upon graduation, he worked at a large law firm in Washington, D.C. as a trademark lawyer. After some years, he left the law firm to start his third career in real estate founding the firm DC Living Real Estate, LLC with his wife, Debbie, and serving as the Principal Broker. Skip and Debbie also founded the non-profit DC Design House, Inc. that runs the annual DC Design House charity event to benefit the Children's National Health System.

Gary Springer

Following *Jaws 2*, Gary appeared in the films *Hometown U.S.A* (1979) and *A Small Circle of Friends* (1980)
He is living in New York City and still having fun in the movie biz.

Alan Stock

Alan is currently happily living anonymously in California.

Martha Swatek

Martha has been a high school teacher in Long Beach for the last 26 years teaching Fashion, Clothing and Nutrition. She is married with one son. Her first grandchild was born last year.

Jeannot Szwarc

Following the enormous success of *Jaws 2*, Universal was more than happy to allow Jeannot to make a film he was passionate about, the romantic *Somewhere in Time*. Starring Christopher Reeve and Jane Seymour, the film has a fan base as loyal as the fans of *Jaws*. Every year the Grand Hotel on Mackinac Island has a special *Somewhere in Time* weekend, where fans can return to the days of Richard Collier and Elise McKenna. He followed this film up with *"Enigma* (1983), *Supergirl* (1984) and *Santa Claus: The Movie* (1985).

His television work includes *Ally McBeal, The Practice, JAG, Heroes, Smallville* and, most recently, *Scandal, Castle* and *Bones*.

Mr. Szwarc lives in Los Angeles.

JAWS 2 REUNION

In mid-March 2012, Tom Dunlop notified Billy Van Zandt that he was going to be visiting California. One phone call led to another and on March 24, 2012, the very first "Jaws 2" reunion was held!

(l-r) Billy Van Zandt, Jeffrey Kramer and Lorraine Gary

Billy Van Zandt and Donna Wilkes

Lorraine Gary and Jeffrey Kramer

John Dukakis, Gary Springer and Joe Alves

John Dukakis, Susie Swatek, David Elliot, his date and Tom Dunlop

Dorothy Tristan

Dorothy appealed the film's screenplay credits to the Writers Guild of America but was denied a screen credit. Despite the fact that the novelization of the film states that it is "based on a screenplay by Howard Sackler and Dorothy Tristan," she never received any royalties from the book.

She returned to acting following *Jaws 2*, appearing in the films *Rollercoaster* (1977), *California Dreaming* and *Down and Out in Beverly Hills* (1986). The latter film made her the only actress to appear on-screen, in different films, with all three leads from "Jaws" – Roy Scheider in *Klute*, Robert Shaw in *Swashbuckler* (1976) and Richard Dreyfuss in *Down and Out in Beverly Hills*.

With her husband she wrote the film *Weeds* and the television film *Steal the Sky*. Dorothy also wrote the screenplay for John's 2000 film *A Piece of Eden* (2000). In 2015 she not only wrote and starred in the film *The Looking Glass* but released her autobiography, *Joy Street*.

She and John Hancock will celebrate their 40th wedding anniversary on December 29, 1975.

Bryan Utman

Bryan worked steadily in the decade following *Jaws 2*, appearing on *The Waltons* to start 1980. He also had recurring roles in two series – *Herbie the Love Bug* and *Seven Brides for Seven Brothers*.

He currently works as a nurse, "taking care of many sick folks and helping them to be strong again."

Billy Van Zandt

After *Jaws 2*, Billy has gone on to become one of the most-often produced playwrights in the world, starring in twenty-three of his own plays, Off-Broadway and around the globe. He's also appeared in the films *Taps* (1981) and *A Wake in Providence* (1999) which he also co-wrote.

Billy has written and produced over 300 hours of television comedy, earning an Emmy nomination for his work on *I Love Lucy: The Very First Show*, a People's Choice Award and NAACP Image Award for *Martin* and a Prism Award for *The Hughleys*.

304

He splits his time between California and New Jersey. For more on Billy and his work, head to www.vanzandtmilmore.com

Gigi Vorgan

Gigi Vorgan followed up *Jaws 2* with a role opposite George C. Scott and Peter Boyle in *Hardcore* (1979). Gigi also appeared in the films *Caveman, Summer School* (1987) and *Red Heat* (1988). On television she was seen on such series as *Fame, Alfred Hitchcock Presents* and *Knots Landing,* where she had a recurring role.

Today she is a New York Times bestselling author who has co-written seven books with her husband, Dr. Gary Small. She has two kids in college and lives in Los Angeles with her husband and their labradoodle, Rocky.

Tegan West

After *Jaws 2,* Tegan went on to appear in film and television until the new millennium. Roles in shows like *Wonder Woman, Hill Street Blues* and *Cheers* and films like *Hamburger Hill* (1987), *Sleep with Me* (1994) and *Grace of My Heart* (1997) kept him busy before the cameras until 2005. That year he went behind the camera, co-writing the feature film *The Cave* (2005). He continues to write for both live action and animated projects and makes his home in Los Angeles.

Colin Wilcox

Colin Wilcox continued to appear in films (*Marie* (1985), *Midnight in the Garden of Good and Evil* (1997)) and television (*Christy, American Gothic*).

Ms. Wilcox passed away on October 14, 2009. She was 74.

Donna Wilkes

Following *Jaws 2,* Donna continued to act in film and television. She had a recurring role in the short-lived Maclean Stevenson series *Hello, Larry,* and also appeared on shows like *T.J. Hooker, Father Murphy,* and *Gimme a Break.* In 1984 she played the title role of "High school honor student by day/Hollywood hooker by night" Molly "Angel" Stewart in the film *Angel*. Donna continues to act today and enjoys meeting with her fans at various convention events.

John Williams

Quite simply, John Williams is the most popular film score composer EVER! As this book goes to print, he has earned an incredible 49 Academy Award nominations, second only to Walt Disney. He has won the Oscar only five times, though it should be noted that often he would be competing with himself, with two scores nominated, and would split the vote. In fact, from 1968—the year he received his first Academy Award nomination, through 2014—a span of forty-six years—there have only been fourteen years where he didn't receive a nomination.

He has scored every one of Steven Spielberg's films except for *The Color Purple* (1985). His best known scores include *Jaws, Star Wars, E.T., Jurassic Park, J.F.K.* (1991), and the Harry Potter films. At press time Mr. Williams was finishing up his score for *Star Wars: Episode VII – The Force Awakens* (2015).

The authors contacted Mr. Williams but, due to his work schedule, he was unable to participate in this project.

Richard Zanuck

Following *Jaws 2*, Mr. Zanuck married Lili Fini and the two of them began producing on their own, including Lili's directorial debut, *Rush* (1991). They also produced *Driving Miss Daisy*, taking home the Oscar for Best Picture. Mr. Zanuck's other films include *Mulholland Falls* (1996), *True Crime* (1999) and several films by Tim Burton, including the remake of *Planet of the Apes* (2001), *Big Fish* (2003), and *Alice in Wonderland* (2010).

Mr. Zanuck passed away on July 13, 2012 at the age of 77.

The authors contacted Mr. Zanuck but sadly he passed away before he could be interviewed for this project.

Don Zepfel

Mr. Zepfel continued to work as the First Assistant Director on films like *Love at First Bite* (1979) and *The Nude Bomb* (1980). He then served as either the Unit Production Manager or Production Manager on many projects, including *Zoot Suit* (1981), *Weird Science* (1985), *The Mummy Returns* (2001), *Terminator: Salvation* (2009), and *Thor* (2011).

Back Row: Billy Van Zandt, Martha Swatek, David Elliott, Tom Dunlop
Front Row: Ann Dusenberry, Donna Wilkes, Gary Springer, Joe Alves, Gigi Vorgan, Ben Marley, back of Jeannot Szwarc's head.
Foreground Jeffrey Kramer.

Back Row: Sid Sheinberg, Martha Swatek, Lorraine Gary, Joe Mascolo, Gary Springer, Tom Dunlop, Cindy Grover, Jeannot Szwarc, Ann Dusenberry, Billy Van Zandt, Susie Swatek, Carl Gottlieb, Allison Caine, Jeffrey Kramer. Peeking over Carl's shoulder: John Dukakis and Ben Marley.
Front Row: Donna Wilkes, Gigi Vorgan, Joe Alves

FROM THE SET

A cup from the Holidome party scene (courtesy of Ms. Janet McArdle)

Cast and Crew T-shirts (from the Collection of Jim Beller)

Cast and Crew T-shirts (from the Collection of Jim Beller)

Cast and Crew T-shirts (from the Collection of Jim Beller)

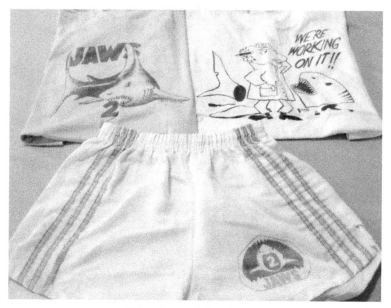

More Cast and Crew Wear.

The ORCA nameplate (from the Collection of Chris Kiszka)

The Divers Camera (from the Collection of Chris Kiszka)

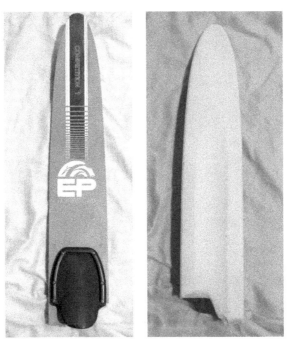

The Water Skis (from the Collection of Chris Kiszka)

THE FANS

On July 1, 2011 the authors stood on a corner of Main Street in Edgartown, Massachusetts chatting with Tom Dunlop. Inspired by the recently released book, *JAWS: Memories from Martha's Vineyard*, the three began jokingly discussing a similarly themed book on *Jaws 2*. By the end of the discussion the laughing had stopped.

We are very grateful to our friends who have supported us over the past four years. We feel it is only right to allow them to share a few words on why they enjoy the film *Jaws 2*. To them we say "thank you" from the bottom of our hearts.

Jill Hubbs – Navarre Beach, Florida: *Jaws 2* is the quintessential thriller movie - drama, action, a little romance, a lot of terror, and great music that stirs the fear of the unknown in the ocean... The killer that lurks beneath... Sssshhhhaaaarrrrkkk! I loved *Jaws 2* for all of that and also because I was a "Hello Girl" in the opening party scene! (Filmed in Navarre, Florida - right in my own back yard in Pensacola, Florida...) Best. Movie. Ever!

Tom Dunlop – Edgartown, Massachusetts: I love *Jaws 2* because, thirty-seven years later (after throwing in the invention of the home computer, the Internet and social media), you can find out that something you worked hard on as a callow youth still means something to the folks you made it for.

Elizabeth Kelly – New York: I liked *Jaws 2* mainly for the more shark footage and also for the inclusiveness of the teenagers fending together for survival. Also that the pernicious carcharion burnt to a crispity crunch and also for the meticulous musical score.

Kurtis Nash: *Jaws 2* was the first film in the series I saw at a very young age and I was immediately hooked on *Jaws*, the oceans and sharks. The reason I am such a big fan of *Jaws 2* is because of the familiar feel it has to the original and of course the return of Roy Scheider.

Ian McLean – Sydney, Australia: Three quirky, unique and favourite motion pictures where the solid rapport of the talented casts shine through – *Jaws 2, Supergirl* and *Santa Claus* - all guided into life by the same director, Jeannot Szwarc. Coincidence?

Barnaby Marriott – Brighton, UK: *Jaws 2* enthralled me as a kid, and I would watch the videotape over and over again. There was something that struck a chord with me at that age, the shark terrorizing the young characters! The film has continued to enthrall me to this very day – it's as wonderful as the original film with endlessly quotable dialogue and iconic scenes.

John Richard Burke: *Jaws 2* for me worked brilliantly from the beautiful cinematography to John Williams incredible score, especially 'Ballet for Divers,' which echoes the behemoth beneath the waves.

Nolan Philpott – Norwich, UK: *Jaws 2* had the familiar feel of *Jaws* with a finale that is, for me, as thrilling at the first. My favourite aspect of the film? The score by John Williams. Love it.

Jon Donahue – Orlando, Florida: I was a Skipper at the JAWS attraction at Universal Orlando. Every time that shark bit into the power cable and fried, I thought of *Jaws 2* - a worthy sequel to one of the greatest movies of all-time! ...and a dream job!

Dustin McNeill – Greensboro, North Carolina: Unlike the wonderful original, *Jaws 2* hurried to the first reveal of the shark and liberally featured it for the rest of the film. As an impatient, shark-loving child, I always appreciated that.

Colin Wilby – Chorley, UK: The only worthy sequel to Steven Spielberg's masterpiece, shared the thrills and spills of the original. Featuring some great footage of Bruce once again menacing the shores of Amity Island. It felt like a natural continuation of the *Jaws* story.

Karen Francis – Surrey, UK: *Jaws 2* is one of those rare things: it's a sequel that works. Yet again you are left rooting for the main characters. You really care about them. There are plenty of shocks, blood and elements of humour...and one of my favourite characters ever...Brody! This is a timeless classic and I love it!

Steven Schraub: A sequel to my all-time favorite, *Jaws*, was well worth the anticipation. *Jaws 2* proved itself all on its own. With Roy Scheider at the helm and the music of John Williams, the results were extraordinary.

Phil Gallagher – UK: I have to say I love *Jaws 2* because it focused on the island and its residents more, had an electrifying score and the genius move of burning the shark made it look nastier.

Ryan MMc – The North, UK: I love *Jaws 2* for many reasons but the main one is that it includes a death that shocks me more than any 'serious' film - R.I.P. Marge #stillhurts

Rob Wainfur: *Jaws 2* had the unfortunate task of following a perfect movie. It's like following Queen at Live Aid. However *Jaws 2* did a fantastic job. A worthy sequel

Neil Blackshaw – Manchester, UK: *Jaws 2* is a tense, action packed thriller with some frightening, action sequences. Good, solid, performances from the cast and a stunning score by John Williams.

Tommy Francis – Scotland, UK: *Jaws 2* has the look and feel of the first film in terms of photography and music. And another great turn from Roy Scheider.

Christopher Stefanic – Los Angeles, California: *Jaws 2* is a masterfully crafted thriller, commercially and artistically, and stands as the epitome as to how a "money" sequel should be made

Steve Nelson: Love *Jaws 2* - it brought a fresh new teenage scream theme presence, which made it subconsciously even more fearful for beach loving youth, we also got to see the original cast members give real emotional depth to their characters

Andre Dursin – Wakefield, Rhode Island: Growing up I gravitated towards *Jaws 2* because it was one of the earliest ABC Sunday Night at the Movies I remember seeing. From John Williams' score to the kids on the open sea, the movie captures a particular time and place in my childhood and will always be special to me for that reason.

Matthew Drinnenberg – Bangor, Maine I love *Jaws 2* because it breaks from the typical copycat sequel and gives you a completely different spin with its casting and story. It is as much its own entity as *Jaws* is which, for a sequel, is quite refreshing.

Pauly Tee: I love *Jaws 2* because it had that feel of the original but with a totally different storyline with great action sequences and a fantastic soundtrack

Bill Boswell – Isle of Wight, UK: A great sequel to the best film ever made, so thanks for giving us the behind the scenes story.

Ted Swift: *Jaws 2* was the first movie I simply couldn't wait to see. For 3 pre- internet years I scoured newspapers and magazines for any news of pre-production, re-writes, fired directors, malfunctioning sharks, ratings battles and anything else I could find to hold me over until June 16, 1978. I loved the movie as a 15 year old, and I love it now.

Chris Lucente – Putnam Valley, New York: I love *Jaws 2* as it is the first movie I became happily obsessed with. I was 11 years old in that magical summer of 1978 and I saw the film every weekend that summer, pretending that I was Sean Brody.

John Carroll – Atlanta, Georgia: A sequel is rarely spoken of in the same breath as the original. *Jaws 2* is a well-deserved exception to that.

Michael McCormack: *Jaws 2* is an underappreciated classic that still delivers the goods thanks in part to a strong performance by Roy Scheider and an excellent music score by John Williams. It still provides great entertainment and deserves a book of its own.

316

Dassy Pauly – Middlesbrough, UK: *Jaws 2* was a part of *Jaws*. I never saw it that way as separate films just the other half of the movie that I grew up with and love so much.

Howard William Mattis-Sprouse Jr. – Petersburg, Virginia: I love *Jaws 2* because of the many shark scenes...plus when the shark attacked those kids on the boats and they are falling in the water and the music score while it was happening...also Jackie was my favorite of the teens...."Jaws 2" is and always will be my favorite movie

Kevin Flynn – North Arlington, New Jersey: I love *Jaws 2* for the suspense. Only the audience and Chief Brody knew what was happening but nobody else did, until it was too late. The music is also amazing

Jay Shinn – Burleson, Texas: I love *Jaws 2* because of the contributions from Roy Scheider and John Williams!

Helen Browne – Chester, UK: I love *Jaws 2* even more than the first movie because of the mix of interesting and relatable characters. Coupled with the beauty and horror of one of the oceans most amazing creatures, it creates a gripping adventure movie

George Hadjipateras – London, UK: Despite the undoubted genius of *Jaws*, the makers of the sequel had a tough challenge and they succeeded by making the story about the shark hunting the kids rather than in the original where the hunters were chasing the shark .

Frank Sparks – High Desert, California: The look on the faces of the bait.

Paul Newbery – UK: I thought it was very well cast and although there were a lot of cast they all carved their characters out well, the shark was technically better and I agree about the soundtrack, the underwater ballet for divers track is beautifully written and the score is underrated. It was probably a very difficult shoot but the comradery shines through

Daniel Garceau: I love the sailing scenes. They are well done. Learning how much went into the training of the teenagers makes the scenes that much more impressive to me. Plus seeing the shark early and often has this shark obsessed guy favoring it over the original.

AW Ratliff – Crestview, Florida: Reinforcing our fears to never get back into the water, *Jaws 2* did what no other movie had done before. Daring to challenge the status quo and send its audience on one more thrill ride. *Jaws 2* broke the barriers and changed our movie experience forever. If you've ever enjoyed watching a part 2, then you can thank "*Jaws 2* - the birth of the sequel.

Russell Buckley – Wales: I loved *Jaws 2* - It is a sequel which remains true to the origins of 'the' original summer blockbuster and continues to thrill its audience as a tour de force

John Maher – Northampton, UK: I love *Jaws 2* because of its great story line - an attack on a group of teenagers - which in reality could happen.

Kalanos Kalmanitas – Haiko-Eupen, Belgium: Having seen *Jaws 2* on the big screen as a teenager it was great to relate to a character in the movie that was my age at the time. Other than that, Roy Scheider, Bruce and John Williams' score made it a must-see sequel!

Chris Heath – Newfoundland, Canada: I've loved *Jaws 2* since childhood and still do to this day. A very worthy sequel to a timeless masterpiece that both fascinated me, and terrified me from swimming in the ocean...and I live on an island

Eric Rendon – Minnesota: As a kid I always grew up wanting to be in the water. *Jaws 2* instantly made me want to never set foot in the ocean.

Steven Bayman – UK: A film that was far more technically ambitious than the first, a film that deserves far greater respect as a stand-alone film and remains one of the greatest sequels ever made

Victor Mirabelli - Toronto, Canada: I love *Jaws 2* MORE than the original *Jaws* because even with No Shaw, No Dreyfuss No Spielberg, it's still a great product.

Paul Colman – The North UK: I love *Jaws 2* because it has some amazing shark bites in it such as the helicopter scene and when the girl is trying to help Sean on to the boat, and also another amazing score by John Williams that really sets the tension again.

Dave Golowski – Pennsylvania: I love that it was like seeking revenge from *Jaws*.

Danny Foster – Atascadero, California: The sequel acts as the perfect bookend to its shark filled predecessor.

Peter DeVincent – Rhode Island: I absolutely love *Jaws 2* and hold it right up there with the first one. Whenever I see that image of the shark popping up behind the water skier from the original poster, it brings me right back to being 8 years old and seeing the movie the first time. And I just started collecting the original Topps cards again. I'm 44 now.

Ed Rodriguez – Albany, New York: I liked *Jaws 2* for the returning original cast, the score and the Sunset teaser and Water Skier release posters.

John Konrardy – Dubuque, Iowa: I LOVE *Jaws 2*. Saw it opening day and was not disappointed a bit. First off, I think it is Johnny Williams best score to date. Melodic and beautiful. The film is so bright and vibrant. Seeing the original cast back is great

Stuart John Richardson – Isle of Man, British Isles: I love *Jaws 2* - visually it's an amazing movie! And the soundtrack is one of John Williams' best EVER!

Paul Knoop – The Netherlands: "A fun and action filled sequel to one of the most mesmerizing movies in blockbuster history"

Robin Cavey – Chillicothe, Ohio: *Jaws 2* is the only sequel I like.

Gary D Wheeler – San Diego, California: A well-defined continuation of the story. With all the action, drama and heart of the original.

Nathan Swank – Kansas City, Missouri: One of my many favorite scenes in *Jaws 2* is when one of the teenagers is being dipped in and out of the water by a bungee pulley system between sails and gets stuck briefly in the water

Veoletta Williams Goodeye: Personally I loved *Jaws 2*. Not as good as *Jaws* but still scared the heck out of me.

Rich Toombs – UK: Coz it's the only *Jaws* sequel with bite.

Ian Maloney – North West of Ye Olde England: That opening scene, the rope, than the wreck of the Orca with a musical nod to the original movie. Cracking sequel.

John Fulcher – Leland, North Carolina: It scared the heck out of me at age 12 back in '78 and the score by John Williams is one of the best film scores ever! *Brody Misunderstood* is a gorgeous piece of music

Andrew Mcgarvey – UK: *Jaws 2* is a great sequel to the single greatest movie of all time.

Vince Ashjornsen: I was 7 when I saw *Jaws 2* in 1978. I loved it as a kid, and because I grew up in Pensacola, saw the "shark," the lighthouse and the destroyed boat on the beach. So, because of that, I loved it more.

319

Tony Jones: I loved *Jaws* 2 because of the fact that Roy Scheider returned and the attack on the kids sailing, made it an awesome sequel.

Mark Ames – Greenfield, Massachusetts: What I liked about *Jaws* 2 was we see more of Chief Brody doing his job. The fact that he once again proved that there was a shark and wasn't going crazy.

Edward Viveiros: *Jaws* 2 was the first *Jaws* I encountered when it was first broadcast on network TV. Marge's death scene haunted me due to how sympathetic a character she was & it still holds up well even after all this time. A+++

Dusty Jay: *Jaws* 2 is a wonderful addition to the *Jaws* franchise! Can't wait for this book! I'm going to need a bigger bookcase!

Paul Ezzard – UK: I love *Jaws* 2 because-- SAY AHHHHHHHH!

Lucas Boger – Greensboro, North Carolina: Saw this way too young (before I was introduced to the first one) and it kept me out of the ocean for most of my childhood - a testament to the quality of horror in this film!

Lee Ferrier – UK: It kept what worked in the original and added enough to keep it fresh and exciting. One good bite deserves another!

Jennifer Cahill – North Carolina: I have loved *Jaws* 2 since I was a child. It had a great plot, lovable characters, and awesome action scenes

Becky Blackwell Birks – UK: "Sssssssssshhhhhhaark!!!!"..........That's why I love *Jaws* 2.

Paul Whittleton – UK: Roy Scheider, John Williams and a Big Shark. What more would you want from a sequel?

John Cantwell – Hollywood, California: I love *Jaws* 2 because of Ann Dusenberry's beach naturalness, beauty queen realness & terrified acting during & especially after the attack on "Tina's Joy". She is amazing.

Steven Nixon – Troy, Michigan: I LOVE *Jaws* 2! Jeannot Szwarc brilliantly and beautifully mastered a sequel that most would have found impossible to achieve. He recaptured the magic of the original

Marty Milner – Flowery Branch, Georgia: Well since I worked on *Jaws* when they returned to the Island we agreed I should work in a minor way in this movie too. It was fun to see some of the old gang again

Al Daugherty – Knoxville, Tennessee: Dorsal fin POV camera angles and John William's score!

John Russell Stiefvater – Winchester, Virginia: Scary, adventurous nostalgic childhood memories! That is why *Jaws 2* sticks with me to this day. It's still a lot of fun

Leo Dean: Saw this in theatre when I was 10, just clicked for me on every level. The fantastic poster with the water skier!! Fantastic!! And the teaser trailer was awesome as well.

Colin Scrowther – UK: I love *Jaws 2* for... 'I'm telling everyone, that's a shark. And I know what a shark looks like because I've seen one up close. And you better do something about this one because I don't intend to go through that hell again.

Robert Wayne Luxford: *Jaws 2* is one of those rare sequels that live up to the original. It continues Brody's arc forward rather than rehashing the original story.

David Leckey- Belfast, Ireland: I love *Jaws 2* because... Being a kid growing up in the 80's watching *Jaws 2* on television along with the original film it cemented my love of the *Jaws 2* movies. Today I consider it an underrated classic among the sequel genre.

Jonathan Wade – Suffolk, England: More shark - More suspense - More terror.

Joe Kenney – Marietta, Georgia: I love *Jaws 2* because we got to visit the town of Amity and its residents one more time. And then watch them get eaten!

Gerard Paulov – Clifton, New Jersey: The terror carries on well in the sequel, but the film has a wonderful tone and pace that distinguishes it from the original. Like the classic first part, it's always a must watch.

Ross Eisenberg – Berlin, Ohio: "Saw it when it first came out. My Dad took me to see the first one and he pulled me out of school to see *Jaws 2* as a surprise!

Mickey Miller: Because the scene where Brody sees the photo being developed that reveals the shark eye creeps me out.

Tina Henry Dawson – Ontario, Canada: I'll admit it ......I wanted Jackie to be eaten! Yep I was rooting for the shark!

David Hickey: because it's *Friday the 13th* on the water! It was my first 'A' certificate movie, I was 12 and it terrified me and my friend. We left the cinema with our nerves in shreds! Awesome!

Ryan Hall- North Wales, UK: I CAN'T GET UP!!! I CAN'T GET UP!!! Poor Marge. That kind of stayed with me, proving that this sequel is a very worthy follow up to the first film.

Edward McCormack – Liverpool, UK: "An enjoyable sequel to the greatest movie ever was never going to be an easy stunt to pull off, but they did it." Sir Ed.

Amy Berrios – Pennsylvania: *Jaws 2*. Great sequel to follow the best movie of all time. Still gonna need a bigger boat.

David Pecchia – Attleboro, Massachusetts *Jaws 2* had an eerie feel and score. Bringing back most of the original cast made the film that much better.

Kathleen Cherry – the Jersey Shore: The young teens in the movie remind me of the joy and fun I had when I was their age, hanging out with friends, going to the beach and just having good clean fun.

Shaun Adair – Long Beach, California: An exciting and well-made sequel.

Debbie Penland Lawrence – Winston-Salem, North Carolina: Loved *Jaws* sooo much, looked so forward to *Jaws 2* and it didn't disappoint!!!

Paul Neighbours Jr – Hendersonville, Tennessee: To recapture the intensity and realism from the original movie is not a common thing in sequels. They caught lightning in a bottle TWICE!

Maynard Maynard – Kapfenberg, Austria: *Jaws 2* was the very first good movie-sequel I'd ever seen. I must have been 11 or 12 years old, and I clearly remember telling my fellow schoolmates (who weren't allowed to see it) for weeks and weeks how awesome it was to see a shark 'eating' a whole helicopter

John Powers: The poster and the tagline says it all.

"Just when you thought it was safe to go back in the water"

Andy Soltysiak – Farnborough Hampshire, UK: It's a roller coaster ride of tension, shocks, and excitement and a shark bigger and badder than the first.

Karl Lovelace – North Carolina: "That's a shark. I know because I've seen one up close. And you better do something about this one because I'm not going through that hell again. Excellent acknowledgement of the first film.

Ryan Patufka – The Poconos, Pennsylvania: I love *Jaws 2* because once again Brody needs to do the right thing. Only this time before he confronts the shark, he must confront paranoia from himself and skepticism from everyone else

Tim Ritter: Great musical score, Chief Brody back in action, cool characters, and breathtaking ocean attack scenes! Also one of the first great sequels ever made.

Benita Harris – Fairhope, Alabama: I've watch *Jaws, Jaws 2* and *Jaws 3* over 40 times. My favorite movie of all times.

Robert Wayne Luxford – Sydney, Australia: His new fears are warranted given his past experience. Even though his authority has been elevated there is still strong opposition to his actions. It is his journey to overcome his fear that we applaud. Saw it when it first came out at the State theatre.

Ian Dunn – Derby, UK: It's the best sequel to the best film - ever!

Michael Olson – St. Petersburg, Florida: My Dad was taking me to a Pittsburgh Pirate game. It got rained out. I was young and upset, he took me to see *Jaws 2* instead. Great memory, great sequel.

Charlie Brigden – Caldicot, Wales, UK" I love *Jaws 2* because it's a great proto-slasher movie. And the John Williams score is just incredible.

Roberto Knippels – the Netherlands: *Jaws 2* had it all, great cast, good action, a great soundtrack and a big ass scary shark!! For me it is one of the greatest sequels ever made.

Russell Wagus – Westland, Michigan: I wasn't able to see the original in the theater. But I did with the sequel. It is a very enjoyable film. One of the better sequels out there.

Duncan Campbell: *Jaws 2* did the impossible - a worthy sequel to the best movie ever made.

Ron Wilson – Montgomery, New York: SWIM EDDIE, SWIM !!! I love *Jaws 2* because it is a beautifully filmed and well-cast movie that becomes a rollercoaster of terror and suspense. It's unfortunate that today's filmmakers don't (and can't) make films like this anymore.

Mark Chapman-Coombs – BC, Canada: *Jaws 2* is a pulsating teen slasher movie... with bite!

Craig Moonen- Edmonton, Canada: After all these years the coolest thing about *Jaws 2* for me is that they used that shark finale to inspire the Universal Studios Orlando ride! RIP

Gaz Evans: My earliest ever film memory is seeing Roy Scheider hanging onto the electric cable. It's fascinated me ever since. Meaner shark. Faster pace. Holds up to the original.

Richard – Quebec, Canada: Who doesn't feel a chill when the fin rises up like a knife—with John Williams' pulse-pounding music—behind the water skier? Brilliantly orchestrated attack sequences that grab you every time!

Terry Lewis – Dansville, New York: I like *Jaws 2* because it's the best sequel ever made, and to the best movie ever made!!!

Kevin Davis: This shark looks scarier because of the burns and the scar. BEST JAWS SEQUEL.

Brian Kirwin: To this day, I remember being nine years old in a packed theater with everyone cheering Brody when they figured out his plan with the cable. Audiences don't cheer like that anymore.

Carolyn Thomas O'Daly: Because Tom Dunlop was in it, of course!

Steve Hicks – Spartanburg, South Carolina: What can I say? I love everything about *Jaws 2*! Best movie ever!

Stu Rankin: Roy Scheider is boss!

John Konrardy's "Jaws 2" shark

Young fan David Leckey's artwork

UPDATED/EXPANDED
SECTION

The voice of the movies – Mr. Percy Rodrigues
(image from *The Shark is Still Working*)

PREFACE:
BUT WAIT, THERE'S MORE!

To PARAPHRASE THE GREAT Percy Rodrigues from the original trailer for
Jaws 2, "in all the vast and unknown depths of Hollywood…how could
there have been only one?"

If you grew up in the 1970s and 80s, Mr. Rodrigues was the
soundtrack of your movie-going life. His voice enhanced many a trailer,
making even the most mundane of films look like true "must sees." One
of my proudest *Jaws* accomplishments was informing the filmmakers of
The Shark is Still Working (2007), a brilliant documentary detailing the
making of the movie *Jaws*, of the existence of Mr. Rodrigues. They were
able to interview him for the film and even got him to narrate a trailer for

their film. They also very kindly thanked me during their commentary track, an honor I'm proud to have.

Which brings me to this point. After the original release of this book in September 2015, we learned that there were, in the vast and unknown depths of Hollywood, more stories to be told and, most excitedly, more photos to be seen. For the last eighteen months we have strived to leave no stone unturned in our attempt to tell the whole story about the making of one of the first, and certainly most influential, film sequels of all time.

As with all things, nothing comes easy. The majority of these new interviews came about because of a random email or comment, asking me why we hadn't talked with so-and-so. Our explanation was that either we were turned down politely (Susan Ford and Sarah Holcomb) or were not able to make our schedules work (Richard Zanuck, who sadly passed away before we could speak). Some people (Kevin Pike and Frank Sparks among them) got lost in the shuffle while completing the first book and graciously spoke to us for this edition. I must also thank Kevin Pike for his keen memory. I had a very large collection of on-set photos with crew members I could not identify. I sent them to him and he was able to put a name to several of them, many of them now included in the book.

Now sit back, relax and take a walk through the doorway into the continuing adventures of "Jaws 2: The Making of the Hollywood Sequel."

PROLOGUE

Hello dear friends, fans and readers. Michael here. With Lou's gracious acquiescence I have decided to tackle the updated/extended version of the book you are about to read. But first some background on how the book originally came to be.

On July 1, 2011, Lou, myself and other close Jaws friends gathered on Martha's Vineyard to help our friends Matt Taylor and Jim Beller celebrate the release of their book "Jaws: Memories from Martha's Vineyard." Not only was it a great way to support our friends, but it also gave us a chance to snag some autographs we hadn't had the opportunity to get, including Jonathan Filley, who played Cassidy, the young man who falls asleep on the beach while the beautiful Chrissie Watkins is being attacked in the opening scene of *Jaws*. Jonathan went on to a successful career as a production and location manager for such filmmakers as Woody Allen, Spike Lee and Steven Spielberg and worked his way up to becoming the co-producer/producer of such films as *Big Night* (1996), *The Siege* (1998), *Inside Man* (2006) and *American Gangster* (2007). He also produced the television programs "Elementary," "Seven Seconds" and served as the Executive Producer of "The Blacklist." Despite over four decades in the industry, his only on-screen appearance remains Jaws. I guess he knew he couldn't improve on perfect!

Earlier in the day, Lou and I were speaking with Matt and Jim, who told us that they had received a lot of requests about them doing a book detailing the making of *Jaws 2*. However, having just invested the last six years of their lives into their current tome, they declared that they had no interest in a sequel about a sequel. Jim knew that both Lou and I had an interest and background in writing, so he commented that Lou and I should tackle the subject. We laughed. Later that day, Lou and I were standing on Main Street talking to Tom Dunlop. Tom had played Timmy in *Jaws 2* as a teenager and was now a successful author (you can find a listing of Tom's books in the original "Catching Up" chapter of this book). Tom also has the distinction of being the only Amity Kid to also appear in *Jaws*.

We had both met Tom at the 2005 JAWSFest and were proud to think of him as a friend. We told Tom about what Jim had suggested and he began to laugh. "No one," he said, "would want to read a book about the making of *Jaws 2*." Lou and I explained to him how the book would not only talk about the making of the film but how Hollywood had become "sequelized" (my word) over the past 30-years. Tom continued to chuckle and suggested that maybe a couple people would be interested if we made it an E-book. As wise as he is, Tom did not know that when you tell two strong-willed Italian guys they can't do something, they're pretty much going to do it. Seeing we were serious, Tom gave us his blessing. He even told us that, if he could see we were serious, he would do what he could to help us locate and speak with people. And he kept his word.

Knowing Tom Dunlop the way I do today, I'm sure I would embarrass him if I went into detail on how much he helped us. I will say that he had answers and suggestions for every question we asked him and was very instrumental in putting us in contact with cast and crew members Lou and I had spent months trying to get ahold of with no success. If there is a patron saint of literature it is Tom Dunlop. Actually, the internet says the patron saint of literature is St. Helena, but since I've never met her, I'm sticking with Tom.

Tom Dunlop – the only Amity kid to appear in *Jaws*

Since the release of the book in September 2015, both Lou and I have made some great friends. Book signing events kept us busy and allowed us to rub elbows with members of the cast and crew. People we only knew from their work on-screen became our friends. The most humbling thing that happened to me occurred in July 2017 at the Westin Hotel in Los Angeles. While walking into the lobby I noticed Carl Gottlieb speaking with some gentlemen and walked over to say hello. Before I could say anything, Carl pointed at me and said to his associates, "This is my friend, Michael Smith."

This updated and expanded edition is due in great part to the cast and crew of the film that we either couldn't locate (but sought us out after the book came out) or people we were unaware of. Even with the internet, this film is now 40-years old and cast and crew members who were in their late 20s/early 30s have since retired. Sadly, many of them have passed away. But we heard from enough people to make this updated/ expanded edition feasible. More stories. More photos. Enough of both that we hope if you purchased the first edition of the book you'll feel your money was well spent to double-dip. If this is your first time reading it, welcome aboard.

Now sit back, relax and turn the pages.

Michael Smith
5/2018

IN MEMORY OF...

SADLY, SINCE THE BOOK'S original release, we have lost several members of the production. I asked their families to send me a few photos that they felt really represented their loved ones and I am proud to include them here.

Ellen Demmy

Ellen was the beloved sailing instructor to the Amity kids on the film. Her love for the water was infectious and she was so loved by the teenage cast that they lobbied to get her a small part in the film (she is the waitress that Gary Springer informs works in "the only place in town where the garbage man delivers.") I was unaware of the extent of Ellen's illness (nor should I have been) when getting information for the book. Her husband, George, was very instrumental in making sure my questions

337

were answered and for that I thank him. To quote George, Ellen "set sail for the last time" on December 16, 2015 from breast cancer. She was 75.

Ellen Demmy in *Jaws 2*

Ellen Demmy

Gary Dubin

Gary played Eddie Marchand in the film. He had been sick for some time. He was supposed to be a part of a book signing event I did in Los Angeles in November 2015 but was too ill to attend. I did get to speak with him on the phone that trip and he was pleased with the book, which was most important to me. Gary passed away on October 8, 2016 after a long, brave battle with bone cancer. He was 57.

Gary Dubin   The cover of Gary's Memorial Program

April Gilpin

The sister of Marc Gilpin, who played Sean Brody in the film, April was pulled into duty at the last minute and cast as the little girl who befuddles the big shots by not only asking why Brody is in the shark tower but knowing that it actually IS a shark tower. April sadly left us far too soon, passing away on July 30, 2017 due to natural causes. She was 38.

April Gilpin

April Gilpin and her brother, Marc

Joseph Mascolo
As Len Petersen, everyone's favorite land developer, Mr. Mascolo gave the shark a run for its money as the biggest villain in the film. Mr. Mascolo passed away on December 8, 2016 due to complications from Alzheimer's disease. He was 87.

Joseph Mascolo

Sol Negrin

Mr. Negrin was the cinematographer who oversaw the re-shoots necessary on Martha's Vineyard. He passed away on March 20, 2017 at the age of 88.

Sol Negrin

I can't thank these people enough for their contributions to the book. Each one had a story to tell, from their own unique viewpoint, and I am so proud that I was able to speak with them and include their memories. One of the reviews I read of the original book complained that it included TOO MANY interviews. I'm sure if you read the memories shared by Ellen, Gary, April, Joseph or Sol, you will certainly disagree.

AND ONE VERY SPECIAL FAN
Howard William Mattis-Sprouse, Jr. - "Will"

No sooner had we announced the book on Facebook then we began getting messages from *Jaws 2* fan Will Mattis-Sprouse, Jr. He had been able to meet some of the cast – he treasured Donna Wilkes – and was as almost as enthusiastic about the project as Lou and I were. As the book began to take shape, Will would comment "can't wait to read this book." Sadly, right before the book came out, Will suffered a stroke. He was recuperating in the hospital when I received a note from his husband, Duone, who had ordered a copy of the book for Will. I told Duone that I would be attending a book signing event in Los Angeles with many members of the cast and crew in a few weeks and would have them all sign a book for him. Duone thought this would cheer Will up immensely. Sadly, Will passed away on September 21, 2015. He was 47. The book Duone ordered for him arrived the next day. When I heard the news of his passing I was devastated. Here was a person I had never met yet was so supportive of our work. Duone did share that Donna Wilkes called Will at the hospital and spoke with him before he passed, and that her words made him smile. I'm sure he's smiling down on us now. God bless you, Will.

Will Mattis-Sprouse, Jr.

343

PROLOGUE (PART 2)

BEFORE WE BEGIN I want to address two things that fans commented the most on after the book's release.

THE HANCOCK VERSION

Fans were shocked to discover how dark and brooding director John Hancock planned to make the film. They went back and re-read the novelization of the film, which was based on Howard Sackler and Dorothy Tristan's original script, and marveled at what could have been. Several of them contacted us, curious if Universal would ever do what Warner Bros. had recently done, which was release the "Richard Donner" cut of *Superman II* (1981). A quick note: to save money, director Richard Donner filmed both *Superman the Movie* (1978) and parts of *Superman II* at the same time. After the success of the first film, Donner and the producers parted ways and Richard Lester, who was best known for directing the Beatles in *A Hard Day's Night* (1964), took over and finished *Superman II*. Thirty-five years later, Warner Bros., with the help of Richard Donner and film editor Michael Thau, compiled what would have been Donner's version of the film. Would Universal ever release the "John Hancock" cut of *Jaws 2*?

Unfortunately, there is no footage remaining from the Hancock period. Actress Lenora May, one of the original Amity Kids, remembers requesting, and being shown, some of her footage after she was let go. I contacted Universal while researching the book and was given a list of all of the *Jaws 2* footage in the vaults. Sadly, it consisted mostly of test footage of the shark. In the past year or so, some of the footage has made its way to the Internet so if you want to see a lot of fins going left and right, feel free to search for it.

John Hancock on the set with Roy Scheider

Dorothy Tristan

Only two scenes supervised by John Hancock are in the finished print. The first, is the fin slipping through the harbor at the beginning of the film. The second is the scene of the kids playing on the parachute/ sail thing (my term).

The shark slips into the harbor – directed by John Hancock

347

The second surviving scene directed by John Hancock

As mentioned earlier in the book, Hancock only filmed on Martha's Vineyard. Constantly on set was photographer Edith Blake, whose photos – along with some studio released images – are really the only record of the Hancock era. With Edie's kind permission, we were able to reproduce some of her slides, which you saw near the front of the book. She had donated most of her negatives – of all of her work, not just the films – to the Martha's Vineyard Museum but sadly, many of the ones connected to the films were stolen (most have since been returned by the thief). Sadly, the negatives for *Jaws 2* have never been found. However, they did have some contact sheets of some of the negatives and we've done our best to reproduce the images here.

Roy Scheider getting a cup of coffee (this collection of "on location" photos are courtesy of Edith Blake)

Roy Scheider as Police Chief Martin Brody

Preparing the shark to set out to sea

Roy Scheider in front of the Amity Police Station

Towing the shark out to sea

A production car

The town dock

Setting up a shot with the Amity P.D. vehicle

Shooting in "Amity"

"Camera ready?"

In November 2013 I traveled to Indiana to speak with John Hancock and Dorothy Tristan about their experiences on the film. I visited them at their home and they were more than gracious hosts. I can't imagine having to speak with a stranger about a chapter of my life that didn't go as planned and for their kindness and, most importantly, openness, I offer my sincere thanks. Over the years we've kept in touch. When John wanted to screen his latest film before a test audience I arranged for a screening in Kansas City, coincidentally the town where John was born. After the screening, while I drove he, Dorothy and film editor Dennis O'Connor back to their hotel, I listened as the three of them discussed possible changes to the film, some of them only requiring the loss of a couple of frames of film. I told John later that it was like going to film school. As I noted earlier, I've made some new friends due to this project, and I'm very proud to include John and Dorothy among them.

John Hancock and Dorothy Tristan at their home

Ricky Schroder as Sean Brody

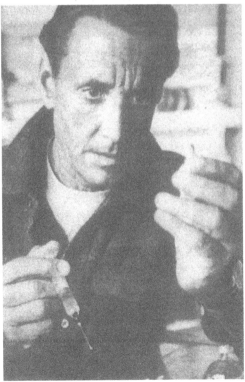

Roy Scheider readies cyanide bullets – from the John Hancock period

The shark on Martha's Vineyard

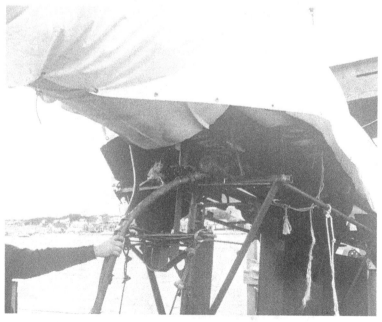

Inspecting the shark (photos courtesy of Rene Ben David)

Under wraps

Under wraps

Islander Arthur Ben David with the shark

THE "IRISH" VERSION

Early in the book, while speaking with Martha Swatek, Marc Gilpin and others, I commented that, according to legend (and the Internet), a very special version of *Jaws 2* ran on Irish television – and ONLY on Irish television. In this version, after the character Marge is taken while saving Sean Brody, there is a shot showing her in the jaws of the shark. This would be commented on often on various *Jaws* message boards and I made it a point to ask Swatek, Gilpin, director Jeannot Szwarc and anyone else who may have been on set if such a shot existed or was even filmed. I was told "no" by everyone. I've met Martha Swatek. She is a teacher and I'm pretty sure smart enough to remember if she had ever been inside the jaws of a mechanical shark.

Still, the rumor persists. After the book came out, there was a discussion on our Facebook page that lasted weeks, with literally hundreds of people chiming in. People from Ireland still insist they've seen it. And they list the following reasons why it's possible:

1. John Hancock filmed the scene, so Jeannot wouldn't have known about it.

2. As second unit director and associate producer, among his many other duties, Joe Alves took a crew off to the side one day and filmed it, not telling Jeannot.

3. Universal had someone else film it and had it edited into the Irish television print to test it.

One person went so far as to produce the footage in question, which turned out to be a very badly edited clip that appears to show a shark eating something quickly. Like the person who complained that we interviewed TOO MANY people, or the person who gave the book a bad review on Amazon.com because, even though he hadn't read the book, his opinion was that the movie sucked so any book about it must also suck, the person with the "deleted scene" footage is a few sandwiches short of a picnic.

For years, there was an urban legend regarding the old television show "The Newlywed Game." Rumor had it that on one episode, host Bob Eubanks asked a woman "what was the weirdest place that you ever got the urge to make whoopee?" The woman thinks for a moment, then replies, rather sheepishly, "in the ass?" For years, Eubanks swore that it had never happened, even going so far as to offer $10,000 to the person that could provide the footage. Well, years later the footage showed up. I'm not sure if Eubanks paid off the 10K but if anyone can find me the footage of Marge in the shark's mouth, there may be a few bucks in it for you.

MORE STORIES, MORE PHOTOS

BEFORE WE BEGIN, I must tip my hat to ANYONE that wrote a book before 1995 when, instead of having the Internet at your fingertips, you had to spend years doing research at the library or make hundreds of telephone calls to track down someone for an interview. Even with the magic of the Internet, Lou and I spent FOUR YEARS compiling the original edition of this book and I've spent a good 18-months on this expanded edition. A true labor of love, but labor none the less.

One of the many questions I was asked when the book first appeared was "why didn't you interview (insert name here)." Except for Roy Scheider, who passed away in 2008, we tried our best to talk to everyone and anyone we could find that was part of the production. I mention Roy only because I did receive an email from a reader who complained that, while we spent all of our time talking to the "little people" we "apparently made no efforts to speak to Roy Scheider." I emailed the writer back, explaining that, sadly, Roy had passed away three years before we began the book and, if I was going to speak with him, I'd no doubt need the assistance of Whoopi Goldberg! Well, guess what dear readers. I've done the next best thing. I found a cassette tape of an interview done with Roy for his fan club from July 1980. Among the discussions of him doing Broadway and his gratitude to Bob Fosse about being cast in *All That Jazz*, he talked a little bit about *Jaws 2*. I am happy to include his comments in this edition of the book.

For the curious, here are the people we contacted but were not able to speak with:

Roy Arbogast: Mr. Arbogast worked on the special effects teams for both *Jaws* and *Jaws 2*. In fact, of all of the people that worked on the effects for *Jaws 2*, only he and Bob Mattey received on-screen credit for their labor. I hadn't been able to track Mr. Arbogast down while working on the original edition of the book but did manage to find him right after beginning the expanded version. We spoke on the phone and he agreed to be interviewed. I offered to send him a copy of the existing book so he could see what we had already done and he accepted. I put the book in the mail and called him on the day we were scheduled to talk. He was not happy with me. There is a line in the book where one of the crew comments on how they shouldn't have made the shark out of steel, because it constantly rusted. Mr. Arbogast took that comment as a slam against Bob Mattey. I explained to him that it was just one person's opinion and that it certainly wasn't mine. Anyway, he decided not to speak with me..

In July 2017 I was a celebrity guest at the Hollywood Show in Los Angeles, along with several of the "Amity Kids" and Richard Dreyfuss (this is where our "interview" took place). Also at the show were Joe

Alves, Carl Gottlieb, Ted Grossman and Mr. Arbogast. I had brought with me a binder containing many of the new photos I had received for this new edition and dropped it off for Joe, Carl and the others to look at. After a while, Mr. Arbogast brought the photos back and commented that there were a couple he'd like copies of. "Not a problem," I told him. I also told him that I hoped he would reconsider speaking with me. I explained that I had just quoted someone, that I personally had no grudge against Bob Mattey and that there were many instances of people praising Bob Mattey – they do the same in this edition – throughout the book..

I sent him the photos he wanted, along with a very apologetic letter, again asking him to reconsider. I did call him a couple times, but never got an answer. I left a couple of messages but I never heard back from him. As much as I can understand his feelings, I'm sorry that you – by way of me – won't get to hear what I can only imagine are some great stories. Again, Mr. Arbogast, my sincere apologies.

Richard Dreyfuss: Matt Hooper appears in *Jaws 2* when Brody attempts to contact him, only to discover that he is out on the research vessel "Aurora" and out of radio range. But I knew in reading original drafts of the script that there was a part written for Hooper and that Richard Dreyfuss was contacted. Obviously he said no. I tried for seven years to speak with him, going through his representatives. Like the others listed below, they never said "NO," only that they would do their best. I did have the chance to speak with Mr. Dreyfuss at a function in Los Angeles and I told him I'd been trying to track him down for a conversation about *Jaws 2*. Here is the extent of his comments: "I wasn't in *Jaws 2*." When asked his opinion of the film, he replied, "I didn't see *Jaws 2*." Not sure if this counts as an exclusive interview but I'm proud to include it in the book.

Steven Spielberg: Though I tried and tried I was never able to speak with Mr. Spielberg. What's funny is that, when I first commented to a Universal Studio rep about writing the book they asked me if "Mr.

Spielberg had approved the project?" I explained to them that Mr. Spielberg was not involved in the production of *Jaws 2*. There was a pause on the phone and then the rep replied, "We prefer it if Mr. Spielberg approves everything."

A quick call to Dreamworks, who also told me that Spielberg had nothing to do with *Jaws 2*. When I explained to them Universal's position they laughed. Spielberg is represented in the book via quotes he made to other sources regarding sequels. I explained this in my requests and commented that, with a series of Indiana Jones and Jurassic Park sequels under his belt, perhaps he changed his mind and wanted to say so.

John Williams: Does this man ever stop working? Despite repeated attempts to speak with him, including multiple phone calls and emails with his representative, he could never find the time to speak with us. His score for *Jaws 2* is beautiful and many fans consider it better than the one he wrote for the original film. He recently received his 51st Academy Award nomination so at least it's obvious he is putting his time to good use.

Richard D. Zanuck: Mr. Zanuck was one of the first people we contacted for an interview. Sadly, before anything could be finalized he passed away.

You can't say we didn't try!

I hope you enjoy these new stories (and photos) and are as happy as I was to hear (and see) them.

Von Babasin (Craft Service/Special Effects)

Von is the son of famed jazz musician Harry Babasin. The acclaimed bass player, nicknamed "The Bear," played on nearly 1,500 recordings, including ones with Charlie Parker, Chet Baker and Al Haig. Von also had a passion for music, taking up the bass at age 15. But there was also a Hollywood connection in the family. His grandfather, Russell Schoengarth, was a film editor for forty-years with such films as *My Man Godfrey* (1936), *The Egg and I* (1947) and several of the Abbott and

Costello comedies of the 1950s. In a nice coincidence, Von's father was the bass player in Benny Goodman's orchestra and his grandfather later edited *The Benny Goodman Story* (1956).

"I was hired on the Universal lot as a Craft Service man in August 1976. It was a busy time. All of the soundstages were busy and they even had to rent spaces off the lot to handle all of their projects. My first job was on the greens crew of "Rich Man, Poor Man." We had to go out to some big mansion in Pasadena and spray paint the lawn green. We did everything we had to to make this mansion presentable to the cameras. After a few weeks of work, I was sent to the home of the Craft Service people - the scene docks. Just about every wall of every shooting production at Universal is kept at the scene docks. If they needed to recreate a room for an existing show they would call down to the scene docks and we would pull out the walls needed, load them on a tractor and they would be dragged down to the soundstage. That was our home and we would hang out there until we were called for a specific purpose on a specific production. I was sent to Stage 27 to assist a special effects crew on the first day of shooting for *Airport '77*. The coordinator on that film was Frank Brendel, who had recently won a Special Achievement Academy Award for the special effects for *Earthquake* (1974). I spent five months on that set. And the rest is history (laughs)

The shark in PreFab – l-r: Mike Wood, Roy Arbogast and Von Babasin
(Photos courtesy of Von Babasin)

365

Von Babasin with the shark skeleton and platform

A pristine shark before shooting began, hanging in dry dock in the effects shop.

The shark out to sea on its platform

Roger Lifsey working inside the shark body.

Craft Service people are a small, elite crew who are assigned to specifically assist special effects crews. My foreman' name was Joe Palmowski and he ran the special effects show in the mill at Universal and sent out members of his crew when they were needed by crews on stages.

I had made a name for myself on the *Airport* crew and as soon as that movie wrapped, I was requested by name to join the *Jaws 2* crew. They worked down in PreFab and it was next to Stage 27 where we had the *Airport* main stage. They saw me kicking butt for Bob Warner, the effects foreman, and they wanted me on their crew when I was available. This really set my reputation as Joe's main man. We spent 6 months working pre-fab putting the sharks together. We built everything, loaded it up on trucks and waved goodbye when they left for Martha's Vineyard. When the *Jaws 2* crew left for location on Martha's Vineyard they left me on the lot. They didn't need me. I was kind of bummed but I went back into the effects shop and found work in the steel/welding shop. I was the ONLY guy they could get to work there. It was very demanding working with structural steel…no craft service person would work there. But, I did and I thrived.

One of the three explosions Von set at the wrap of location shooting

Roger Lifsey in the sand blowing up those last explosions

Roy Arbogast

James Nash Jr. – "Jimbo" - he ran the staff shop

Mike Wood, Special Effects team

Jimmy Guest, local hire

Guy Faria, Special Effects team

Cindy Grover takes a break on the set

Von Babasin fiber-glassing a mold for a boat. This photo was taken through the helicopter.

Von Babasin and local crew worker, Carl, clowning around on the helicopter.

Special Effects team member Richard Beck, inside the shark's head.

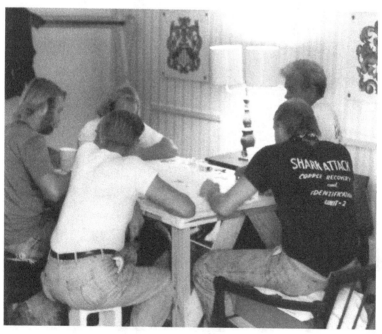

Break time. L-r: Roger Lifsey, Frank and Frank Jr. (local hires), Richard Beck
(in SHARK ATTACK t-shirt) and "Jimbo" Nash

When *Jaws 2* went to Florida, they discovered they needed one representative from the Craft Service union to come from Hollywood so I was again personally requested to be flown out to Florida. I was literally sweeping the shop floor at 3 o'clock in the afternoon when my boss came in and asked me if I wanted to go to Florida. I asked if I could have a day to think about it and he told me no. So I left - THAT NIGHT. He told me to pack for two weeks and I ended up working seven months of location on *Jaws 2*. I became legendary in craft service lore (laughs). By union contract you have to have 8 hours between jobs. I signed out that day at 3:30 p.m. At exactly 11:30 p.m. that night a stretch limo pulled up to my house in Pacoima to pick me up. I was shuttled off to the airport and flew out that night. Kevin Pike picked me up at the airport and that was it.

Another thing that took place on *Jaws 2* was that I crossed over to Propmaker, became a certified diver, and worked on the shark as an actual member of the effects crew. I worked about three months of the seven months I was there as a Propmaker, mostly on the crew of the sea sled shark. I was also the key man. I was the first one on set in the morning and the last man out every single day. One week I had a check for 40 straight-time hours and 60 overtime hours.

The tug boat that sank in one of the storms.

375

The Frances Candies pulls the tug boat back to shore

The deck of the boat that pulled the Sea Sled Shark. The deck is full of pressure tanks and air compressors and hoses and cables of all sizes that come together and lead out to the shark to control it and pull it

A postcard from the Holiday Inn

The Amity Kids hang out on Cable Junction waiting for cameras to roll

Sundown at Shalimar putting the boats to bed for the night

Sundown at Bayou Chico

Gigi Vorgan getting a cup of coffee

A shot with most of the kids' sailboats to the left in a row and two of the water
ski boats, sitting at Shalimar. This is, of course, pre-shark.

The phone in Vons room. I include it here because I wonder how many people looking at this photo ever used a rotary phone?

Room #210 at the Holiday Inn. Vons home for six months

The view from the balcony of room #210

Sunset

Setting up for the first shark burn. Jimmy Guest and Mike Wood below the diver's flag.

Going out in a blaze of glory!

387

Charles Burke (Picture Boat Crew)

An afternoon's recreation changed Mr. Burke's life. "I was fishing when a man named Bill Badalato came up to me and asked what I knew about the waters around here. I told him I fished there a lot so he asked me if I wanted to work for a couple of days. And that's how I got hired to be a part of the picture boat crew. After Frank Sparks left the film I got promoted and I became the department head all of a sudden.

I was in charge of everything you saw. All of the sailboats. I think there were 40 because I had five sets of boats. If you saw a Boston Whaler it was Freddie Zendars but the majority of the boats you see on film were mine. We had multiples of the same boats for various scenes. We knew they were going to wreck at the very end so we had to be able to combine them all together for when the shark bites the cable. We shot some of that in the parking lot of the Holiday Inn and I remember one day in the dailies you could actually see the markings of a parking spot."

Mr. Burke sheds some light on a tragic incident that Bill Badalato briefly mentioned when I spoke with him – the suicide of one of the crewmember's girlfriends. Mark Gruner also commented on this incident during our conversations but I decided not to use it as he didn't have a lot of details. I also learned that it was a well-kept secret from many in the cast and crew. Most of the "Kids" I spoke with had no idea the event had even happened. According to Gruner, he only knew about it because the young lady he was out with that night was a friend of the young woman and he accompanied her to the site of the tragedy. Out of respect to the crewmember in question I will not reveal their name. "We had a lot of unusual things happen on set. We actually had a girl kill herself. She had come in from California to visit her boyfriend. There was a group of apartments next to the Holiday Inn and she shot herself there one night. We had been sitting with her at the bar at the Holiday Inn about a half-hour before she did it. It was very sad."

You can also spot a member of Mr. Burke's family in the film – his son Chris, who appears as the happy hotdog kid (the young man happily eating a hotdog on the beach before the "bluefish" panic). He also served as Marc Gilpin's double, being pulled into duty when they shot from a distance or did a sailboat shot where Sean Brody's face wouldn't be seen. Mr. Burke even has a little screen time, though you never see his face. The shots of the waterskis moving across the water weren't wobbling from fear. "They had a world champion water skier playing the part. But when you see the skis from underneath the water and they look wobbly, it's because that's me and I wasn't very good at waterskiing. They pulled me around behind a boat in Catalina and it took quite a few takes to do that. The reason they shake isn't because "she" was making all kinds of movements. It's because I was trying to stay up. I was the only one they could pull slow enough so that the camera could catch up because I only weighed about 120 pounds."

But it wasn't always work on location. "For Thanksgiving 1977, my wife, son and I got together with Bill Badalato, his wife and son as well as

David Brown and his wife, Helen Gurley Brown, to celebrate the holiday and have dinner together. My wife was all excited to meet Helen Gurley Brown. I didn't even know who she was."

John Kretchmer (Assistant Director Trainee)

Though he anticipated a career in show business, John Kretchmer's career took a turn.

"My plan after graduating Amherst College was to become a theater producer, but after working in a minor capacity in a small theater in Chicago, I discovered that audiences were not really interested in the type of theater I was. So, after some encouragement from a fellow Amherst graduate, I moved to Los Angeles with the hopes of becoming involved in the film industry. I spent nine months attempting to break into a low-level job, and, through a variety of coincidences, was hired by Universal Studios as a craft serviceman, whose responsibilities ranged from providing the crew with coffee and doughnuts to working as a laborer with the special effects department, digging holes for their explosions. In the course of working on *Rollercoaster* (1977) I met Eddie Milkovitch, who was the Assistant Director Trainee on that project. He told me that I could apply to the program, and, if accepted, after 400 working days I could become a member of the Directors Guild of America as a Second Assistant Director. This seemed to me to be my best option, inasmuch as I knew no one in the business that could get me a more prestigious position. I applied, took the test, was interviewed, and, in June, 1977, was accepted into the program.

I was working on "Kojak" when I learned that there were some personnel changes on *Jaws 2*. I was called into the office of the person who supervised all the Trainees at Universal and asked if I wanted to fly to Florida to work on the movie. Of course, there was no hesitation and within 3 days I was on a plane to Pensacola to join the crew. This was in August of 1977. I joined the production after they had started filming in Florida, soon after Jeannot Szwarc had been hired to replace John

390

Hancock as director. Coincidentally, I had met Jeannot a year previously at a party where we discussed the French historian, Marc Bloch. But I digress.

November 12, 1977. John Kretchmer on the support boat Flexifloat.
He is smiling as this is the first time he's seen the shark.

Scott Maitland was the First Assistant Director when I arrived, but injured his back badly soon after and Don Zepfel, who was the 2nd Assistant Director, took over. The trainee, Katy Emde, was moved up to 2nd Assistant Director.

As a Trainee, I was in charge of getting the cast through makeup and hair every morning and getting them onto a Boston Whaler boat that would take them from shore to the support boats on the ocean. I remained on shore to serve as a liaison to all shore-bound departments and I remember one of my big jobs was to give a constant supply of dry towels to the shooting company. At the end of the day I was responsible for signing the cast out and to loading the crew into vans that would return them to the hotel. If the company was shooting on land, I shared the responsibility with Katy to help place the extras and give them business so that they looked natural. At the end of the day, I helped Katy in filling out the daily production report. So, basically, I served in a supporting role to the other AD's, but it provided me with very good training to work as a Second Assistant Director and, eventually, a First Assistant Director: Don and Katy were superb mentors."

Did anyone ever talk to him about why John Hancock had been released from the film? "All I gleaned was that the producers and the studio were not happy with the film they saw, and that the company was falling behind schedule. But I was not present at the firing and have no first-hand knowledge of what really went down."

As the new kid in town, every day was an adventure for Mr. Kretchmer. "This production was at the beginning of my career and so every day was exciting for me. I adored Jeannot - I could sense his talent, and he had a wonderful sense of humor, especially when things were going poorly which, it seemed to me, they usually were. Living in Navarre Beach and working up to seven days a week did get a little grating, especially as we approached Christmas, but I maintained my enthusiasm all the way to the end of shooting which was in early February, 1978, if memory serves me.

I also enjoyed several of the cast members who were my age: David Elliot, Gigi Vorgan, Ben Marley, Gary Springer, Ann Dusenberry, and Billy Van Zandt come to mind. I think I was probably closest to Jeffrey Kramer, only because we could make each other laugh. I recently got in touch with Keith Gordon, who, like myself, has gone on to directing. And I became friendly with Lorraine Gary, who was married to Sid Sheinberg, head of the studio, for whom I later directed a film.

And I made many friends on the crew. Aside from Katy and Don, I am still friendly with Tom Joyner. I thought Bill Badalato, the line producer, was spectacular, and I became close to Don MacDonald, who was Jeannot's assistant. I had a crush (as did every other male on the

392

show) on Max Manlove, our production coordinator. I became close with Jerry Moss, who was the dive master. Jerry went on to become a prop master, and I worked with him again on *Jurassic Park* (1993). Sadly, Jerry died much too young. I liked Roy Arbogast so much that I recommended him to work on *The Naked Gun 2 ½* (1991). On top of all of this, I was able to meet and work with David Brown and Dick Zanuck, two of the greatest producers of the decade."

Production Manager Tom Joyner (standing on right/glasses and beard)

Mike Wood in hat, Kevin Pike in light colored shirt

393

Gary Seybert – Art Department

l-r – foreground - Andy Evans (Special Effects), Tom Joyner and
cinematographer Michael Butler

l-r – Effects workers Greg Landers, Stan Parks, Elpidio Cobian, Andy Evans;
Production Manager Tom Joyner and DP Michael Butler

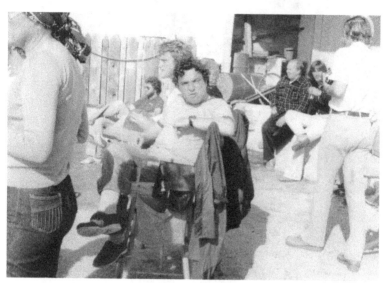

Center – Michael Butler and director Jeannot Szwarc

l-r – foreground – Michael Butler, Jeannot Szwarc and Andy Evans

l-r – seated – Producer David Brown, Michael Butler

Center – Katy Emde, 2nd Assistant Director

Asked if he has any favorite stories to share, Mr. Kretchmer cites two.

"Filming on the ocean with sailboats is extremely hard. You have to anchor the boats with at least two anchor lines, and if you have many boats in the shot, this can take hours. By the time you have anchored them, the sun has moved and the tides have changed, and you often have to start from scratch. One morning, Jeannot arrived on the set and described a complicated shot which involved the Terminal Island set (which was free floating and enormous), every young cast member, and a crane on a camera barge. John Black, the sardonic key grip, said to Jeannot, 'Jeannot, there is no way we can get that shot.' Jeannot said with a smile, 'The spit of the frog will not soil the wings of the white dove.'

Well, the divers, the grips, and the effects guys spent at least 9 hours attempting to get the shot, to no avail. We had to call a wrap without accomplishing any work that day. John Black turned to Jeannot and said, 'Frogs – 1, Doves - 0.'

The other wonderful memory I had involved Gene Barragy, who had worked on *Psycho* (1960) with Hitchcock, and whose job was "marine grip," meaning he built all the special camera boats, including the wonderful catamaran which had a diving bell for the camera. This served as the shark's point-of-view. It was a remarkable piece of engineering because the bell could be raised from below the surface to above the surface while the boat was moving, which made for a very exciting shot. Anyway, Geno was not shy about voicing his displeasure with his assignment as chief mechanic and designer for all things marine.

One evening, I was in our office and saw Geno sitting in a chair, rifling through an issue of "Sail" magazine. I started to laugh and asked 'Geno, what are you doing?' He said, 'I'm thinking of buying a sailboat.' I said, 'Geno, what are you talking about? You hate sailboats.' He replied, 'Well, I'm going to buy one…and then I'm going to sink the sonofabitch!'"

Mr. Kretchmer ended out conversation with some final thoughts. "I must emphasize that I had but a very minor role in the making of *Jaws 2*, but many of the people I worked with I later went on to work with again when I became a director, among them Roy Scheider. I should also emphasize how hard Jeannot worked on this film; he dedicated so much time and effort to pulling it off. He was faced with obstacles at every turn, but always maintained his enthusiasm and his sense of humor. And he treated everyone on the crew, from Mr. Brown, to CB, our craft serviceman, with equal respect. I have run into him occasionally over the years, and I know that every crew he has worked with since then feels the same way about him that I still do."

Scott Maitland (First Assistant Director)

Scott Maitland came aboard *Jaws 2* very early. In fact, some on the crew may have thought TOO early. "I was working on *MacArthur* (1977) for Zanuck/Brown. David Brown told me they were going to do *Jaws 2* and he wanted me to work on it. It became an uncomfortable situation because I was hired before either the director (John Hancock) or the production manager (Tom Joyner) had committed. It was an awkward situation for me in the beginning. It also was awkward when John got let go...I became part of the Dorothy and John situation."

Off the record, Mr. Maitland and I discussed a couple of off-set incidents that may have hastened John Hancock and Dorothy Tristan's departure. "The day they let John go, everybody on the crew was watching Zanuck and Brown, who had me walking up and down in the park on Martha's Vineyard. I think they both got themselves caught up in the enormity of the production. They almost destroyed Ricky Schroder. They were filming him having a temper-tantrum on the dock – he wanted to go out in the boat and they wouldn't let him – and John and Dorothy were laughing so much about something that they weren't sure if they got the shot or not. So they had him do it again. And again. The number of takes reached into the twenties and you could see it almost destroyed the kid, who I think was six years old at the time (Schroder had actually just turned seven in April 1977).

My wife, Carol, and I were kind of the pseudo-parents for the kids

399

while they were on the Vineyard and learning to sail. Most of their parents had signed a disclosure/release that stated that we were their parents, disciplinarians and teachers – all at the same time. It was a great time later but initially the experience destroyed a few of the kids, who never made it down to Florida."

Sadly, once the crew got to Florida, Mr. Maitland was involved in an accident on set. "If you remember the scene where the Sizzlers are coming in, they were being pulled by two 100 horsepower engines. They're going 40 miles per hour and are heading right towards the cameras, with the cameramen right down on the water. We were rolling camera when the wind picked up the sail on one of them and flipped it. I jumped and put my feet on the blade across the front. It tore my equipment off, flipped me over the camera barge and I ended up in the Gulf of Mexico. I ended up breaking the second, third and fourth lumbar vertebrae in my back."

Despite his injury, Mr. Maitland has some fond memories of the Florida shoot. "The Holiday Inn treated us just wonderfully. And on Saturday nights they reaped the rewards because we would spend Saturday nights partying in the bar. We all had a good time. And the kids were fabulous. Annie Dusenberry and the kids were out of this world. They were all super, they really were. And the crew was a good crew. The people of the area were phenomenal. Jeff Sligh, God rest his soul, he was just terrific. He controlled all of the rental prices. He made money on them but, all things considered, if we were in a bind he always seemed to come through and get us something if we needed it."

When asked about Ricky Schroder's hair turning green, he notes that it wasn't due to anything the crew did, but to the chlorine in the Holiday Inn swimming pool. When reminded that it was in young Schroder's contract that his naturally blonde hair had to be restored when he left the shoot, he notes something he observed about Schroder's mother, Diane. "She was a stickler. We were surprised when she made us his guardian. We were actually guardians of he and his sister, Dawn, when she went back up to New York. She was a taskmaster. She probably played the contractual card better than anybody. Out of all of the parents she was easily the toughest. She protected her brood. And they were both beautiful kids. They were well behaved so I can't begrudge her."

Mr. Maitland also comments on the unfortunate death of a crewmember's girlfriend. "Unfortunately one of our crew's girlfriends did herself in. He was devoted to his job and she wanted his attention 24/7 and he couldn't give it. We were working 12-14-16 hour days and he didn't have the time for her. She just became more and more obsessed until finally… He (the crewmember) was really a good person and a very, very conscientious worker. And he had that weight on him for the rest of the shoot, which didn't do him any good. But all things considered, it was a great time and it was a really super group of people."

Mr. Maitland is proud of his part in the contribution the Jaws 2 crew made to the community of Catalina, California. "When the shoot was over we put a boat down off of Catalina for fish to live and for people who dive to explore. We sank the boat and it's still there."

I asked him if he had anything special he wanted to share. "I just want to say that Zanuck and Brown were really super to everybody, God rest their souls. David Brown was something else. I thought I was in trouble one day after I broke my back when he called and asked to talk to Carol. When she asked him what was wrong, he said, 'I'm really upset with Bear (Mr. Maitland's nickname). Now that he's hurt I have to stay on the set all the time. I never had to be here when he was here.' It was a nice compliment. I was truly blessed to be able to work for them."

Kevin Pike (Special Effects Foreman)

There's a lot to be said for being in the right place at the right time. Kevin Pike will certainly agree with that. In December 1973, he was a busboy at a restaurant on Martha's Vineyard. One evening, one of the members of his party walked out of the restaurant and left their briefcase behind. Pike chased him down and returned it to the grateful man. The man in question was Joe Alves, and he and his party had been on the island scouting locations. He mentioned to Pike that he would be back on the island the next summer, gave him a business card and told him to look him up if he wanted a job. He did and an amazing career was born.

"I had worked on the first *Jaws*, and a lot of the same crewmembers had worked on *Close Encounters*. I was working in the shop at Universal when Joe Alves came through and confirmed to me that they were going ahead with *Jaws 2* and he asked me to come on board.

On this film I was really an assistant to Bob Mattey in every way. I was his right hand man. I was the special effects office coordinator. I took care of all the paperwork and all the time cards and all the petty cash; cut checks and purchase orders; shopping for supplies and making sure that everything hummed along as far as the executing of the special effects."

Mr. Pike was part of the crew from the beginning. "I was part of the build. I was working in a section of the Universal lot called the Prefab, which was a building down behind the prop shop and effects shop. And I worked there for several months before we loaded up and moved everything to Pensacola, Florida."

Asked if he had any stories to share, he replies, "I have many stories. We were there for 10 ½ months. We almost forgot where we lived when it finally came time to go home. I remember one storm that came in and trashed our shark carriers, which were moored out at sea. That's still a vivid memory. We had to send people out to cut loose what was getting beat up so it could free-float away. We had a lot of gear. And we spent a lot of money to get everything right.

Another time I was working on the barge and David Brown came out to see the shark work. I began to apologize to him because it was taking so long. He said to me, 'Don't worry. The shark WILL work. We'll take a picture of it and we'll make the movie. And we'll keep on making these movies, just like the James Bond franchise.' And when I heard that everything began to set in.

We had to make a mock-up of the helicopter that gets attacked by the shark and pulled under water. And we had to have an engine for it. One of the challenges of the shoot was that we were so far away from the city of Pensacola that, to get any equipment, took a long time. We would have to go to town, shop and come back. It took at least a half-a-day to run to town, get a nut and bolt and come back. But I remember we had to get an engine and we didn't have the time to shopping in junk yards when I found someone that had a Volkswagen motor. I needed them delivered to Navarre Beach. I offered him $200 to deliver them – remember this was 1977 - $200 in cash. He kept trying to tell me that the engine didn't run but I told him if he could get it to us we'd deal with that later."

Joel Salisbury (Super Fan)

There are a lot of people, myself included, who have incorporated the word JAWS somewhere on their license plates. But not Joel Salisbury. Joel's love belongs to *Jaws 2*, as his Rhode Island license plate clearly reads. Ironically, years before the idea of this book was even born, someone posted a photo of a car with a JAWS 2 license plate courtesy of the Ocean State. Many fans, myself included, assumed the car belonged to Jim Beller, known to fans world-over as "JimmyJaws" and a resident of Rhode Island. But it wasn't. The proud fan was Joel.

"I grew up in New Orleans and every August my family would stay at the Holiday Inn on Navarre Beach in the early-70s. Our family became friends with all of the general managers, including Daryl LaPointe, who became the GM in 1971 and was there when they began filming *Jaws 2* in 1977. My sister and I were asked to come back later in the year to be extras in the film. I was going into the 4th grade and my sister was going into the 1st. But they wanted us to come back in October, and my parents blew it off because we would already be back in school.

While we were there that August we were brought down to the sets and got to see the mechanical shark and Cable Junction."

What was it about *Jaws 2* that intrigued Joel so? "I was a big fan of the original *Jaws*, even though my parents wouldn't let me go see it. They waited until *Jaws 2* to let us see sharks. They didn't want us to see a movie about a beach and a killer shark, since we were always on the beach or in the water. Even as a kid I was intrigued. I read about the making of *Jaws* and learned that it had been filmed on Martha's Vineyard and that the Vineyard was a part of New England. I went to college in New England because of *Jaws*."

Joel soon began working at the Holiday Inn when he got older.

"I was a lifeguard there in 1985. And then from 1998 through 2004, we had *Jaws 2* parties. Every Labor Day weekend the general manager would let me take over the outside pool area from 4:00 to 10:00 p.m.

Joel Salisbury and his classic license plate!

We would have an open bar, serve food and we watched *Jaws 2* on the big screen, advertised as a "jump in" movie. The food and beverage guy was kind of skeptical that we could get anyone to show up but we packed the house. We ended up with over 100 people out there. He was amazed. We came up with a drink called the "Shark Attack," which had grenadine to look like blood. We had buttons made. And t-shirts. (One of Joel's t-shirts can be found on page 291).

We had a band. Did t-shirt giveaways and had a lot of stuff for kids. It was really a fun evening for the entire family."

Roy Scheider relaxes between takes on the set of *Jaws 2*

Roy Scheider (Chief Martin Brody)

In September 1977, I was given permission from Roy Scheider to start his official fan club. As a seventeen-year old boy I felt pretty cool having

405

a movie star for a friend. Roy loved his fans, and for the eight years the fan club existed he would take time to drop a short note or give ME a phone call to fill myself and the fans in on what he was doing next. I still remember his phone call from December 1977 when he told me he had just gotten done killing the shark – he forgot to say SPOILER ALERT! – and was heading back to New York City.

Roy's letter authorizing his official fan club.

Over the years we would do "interviews," either through the mail or, with a clumsy cassette recorder, over the phone. The following comes from an interview conducted on July 3, 1980. If you weren't a member of the fan club, then this will be brand new to you. It is my honor to be able to share his words with you. This part of the conversation begins after he was asked if he felt like his next role would be his most important.

"When I start it, it will be the most important part of my life. That's the only way to look at it. No matter what the reasons. I did not want to do *Jaws 2*. I owed the studio a movie. And I did not like the idea of doing a sequel to it. But once I started it, I had to say to myself, 'OK, you signed the contract to do the movie. Here you are, you're making the movie. There's only one way to attack it, and that's to attack it as if it was the most important movie you ever did in your life.' And that's the way I went at it. Because if you don't, then what's the use of getting up? I mean, you may not like it, but in the end, no one forced you to be there. You're there because you put yourself there. Nobody "did" it to you...you did it to yourself. So, if you accept the responsibilities of where you are, then what's wrong with it? You can't blame it on anybody. You can't say "they" did it to me."

Roy was asked why he was under contract for additional films at Universal and Richard Dreyfuss wasn't.

"Because mine was the key role. The most important part. It's the part that represents the audience. I am the audience. It's the role that the entire film is based around. So, when Spielberg began casting the film, he went to the studio and told them that he wanted Brody to be a New York cop who was a fish out of water himself. He suggested me to the studio boss - and he was an old-time studio boss - who said, 'Yes, you can have him. But he has to agree to do two more studio films. That his next movies will be for us. Or that he will guarantee us a second *Jaws* film at such-and-such a price.' In other words, if the actor's career takes off because of the picture they've got you for the next one. And they've got you for less than they would get you if you had to renegotiate." (NOTE: Ned Tannen was the boss in question. He started in the mail room of Universal in 1954 and by the early 1970s he was the head of the studio's Motion Picture division.)

"Spielberg came to me and said, 'Look, I really want you to play the part. I know what the studio is offering you is a lousy deal but I think it's a terrific part. I think you'll be terrific in it and I think it will be good for your career. Will you do it?' I thought about it and I said, 'OK, I'll do it. I know I'm getting screwed but I'll do it.' So, I agreed to do it. And I knew, sooner or later, that they would come calling. So, I did my best to distance myself from *Jaws*. I snuck in *Marathon Man* and *Sorcerer* back to back before I finally did *Jaws 2*."

As a bonus treat for you fine readers, Roy was asked what actress he most wanted to work with. His answer: Barbra Streisand.

Arthur Schmidt (Film Editor)

The editing of *Jaws 2* was credited to Neal Travis, an Emmy Award winner for his work on the mini-series "Roots." He would also go on to win an Academy Award for the film *Dances with Wolves* (1991). Mr. Travis passed away in 2012. He was assisted on the film by film editors Steve Potter, who I could not locate, and Arthur Schmidt, who I could.

The son of two-time Academy Award nominated film editor Arthur P. Schmidt (*Sunset Boulevard* (1950), *Sayonara* (1957)), who spent over three decades at RKO and Paramount. Some of his other films include *When Worlds Collide* (1951), *Sabrina* (1954) and *Some Like It Hot* (1959). The son didn't fall too far from the tree. "When I was younger, my father often took me to the studio with him. The magic of film making intrigued me, to say the least. When I was a kid in the 1940s I spent most of my weekends watching double-bills of movies at my neighborhood theatres in North Hollywood. But my father always advised me not to get into "the business" because it was too hard and insecure."

Not feeling suited for business, science or engineering, Mr. Schmidt became an English Major at the University of Santa Clara, hoping to become the next Ernest Hemingway. Then he began traveling. "To avoid a second stint with the Air National Guard during the Vietnam War, I took off for Spain. While there I got a job teaching English in Ronda, a beautiful mountain town in Andalusia. One day I got a telegram telling me that my father had died of a heart attack. I left Spain and came home for the funeral. Two weeks after the funeral two of my father's former assistants called and told me there was a job open as an apprentice editor at Paramount. I took the job, telling myself that I would work until I got back on my feet financially. If I liked the work, I would stay on. If not I would find something else or return to Spain. Obviously I liked editing and I stayed.

I was an assistant for almost ten years. I was working on a film called *Bogart Slept Here* with two of my idols - Mike Nichols, with whom I had worked as an assistant on *The Fortune* (1975), and Dede Allen, the legendary film editor with whom I worked on *Little Big Man* (1970). But two weeks into filming, the film stopped shooting because Mike and the leading man didn't agree on what was funny. (NOTE: *Bogart Slept Here* was a film written by Neil Simon that concerned the exploits of an up and coming actor named Elliot Garfield. Somewhere in my collection of memorabilia I have an industry booklet from Columbia Pictures announcing the film going into production. The actor in question was Robert DeNiro and, rather than try to recast, the production was shut down. Not one to give up easily, Simon took the character and wrote a film detailing his beginnings in New York City. That film became *The Goodbye Girl* (1977). Richard Dreyfuss would go on to win the Best Actor Academy Award for his portrayal of Elliot Garfield). I was out of a job and desperate. I got a copy of the Daily "Variety" and looked up "Films in the Future" and saw *Marathon Man* with an impressive line-up of actors and film makers, among whom was the film editor, Jim Clark. I had been a big fan of Jim's work for years. He was one of my idols. I called Jim in London and asked if I could be his assistant when the film came to Los Angeles for final shooting and editing and he hired me.

He gave me some scenes to cut, liked what I had done and gave me an Associate Editors credit. When he went back to England he went to work for Marty Feldman who was directing his first film, *The Last Remake of Beau Geste* (1977). Marty had just fired his first editor and was having a terrible time. Jim called me and asked me come and help him rescue the film. I flew to London where we worked on a first cut which we then brought to Universal. We screened it for the studio and

Verna Fields, who was head of editorial, and they didn't like what they saw. Jim and I worked with Verna, trying to make a better film out of not very good material. We did our best but the film died a quick death at the box-office.

Shortly afterwards, Verna called me about going to work on *Jaws 2*, which was in trouble. Universal had fired the first director, John Hancock, and hired Jeannot Szwarc, a protégé of Verna's, to replace him. It was cold and chaotic in New England and Universal decided to move the location from Martha's Vineyard to near Pensacola, Florida where it was warmer and calmer. I had known Neil Travis since my early days at Paramount when he was an assistant and I was an apprentice. My job on *Jaws 2* was to go through all the underwater shark material shot in New England, which no-one had kept very good records of, and put together the shark scenes as best I could and tell the director and second unit filmmakers what they still needed to shoot in order for the scenes to work effectively . So that is basically what I did. I often edited the shark scenes to John Williams' score from the first *Jaws*, thinking that his brilliant score would help make anything work and help disguise the deficiencies of the material. It certainly helped but couldn't disguise the fact that additional filming was necessary and could make the scenes better. Sometimes they would just shoot the entire scene over if Jeannot was not happy with what he saw. Occasionally Neil would give me a non-shark related event to cut. At the end of filming in Pensacola we came back to Universal to finish the first cut. I think I worked for another month or two when Neil and Verna thought the film was in good enough shape and I was laid off. At the cast and crew screening I was amazed at what a wonderful job Neil had done in pulling together a very difficult film."

Rick Sharp (Makeup Department Head)
Rick Sharp apprenticed in the makeup department at Universal Studios

for three years, beginning in 1965. He remained on the Universal staff until 1980 and was assigned to work on *Jaws 2* in 1977.

Rick was on set while John Hancock was in the director's chair and, while he never heard anything official, he did offer his thoughts as to why Hancock was replaced. "As for the problems the studio had with him, just from my observation, he had trouble finishing a day's work. I was at dinner with my wife, son and other crew members one Saturday night when Roy Scheider came by our table and broke the news that Hancock was being replaced. The following Monday we flew back to Los Angeles to wait for the hiring of the new director. From there we went to Florida to resume filming. Not only was John Hancock replaced but Ricky Schroder, who had been playing one of Roy's sons, was also replaced."

Rick Sharp working with Paul Newman on *Slap Shot*

Many of the stories we've learned include a part about Roy Scheider and his constant tanning. Was there any problem in dealing with Scheider's makeup because of the constant sun? "There weren't any problems with Roy's tanning in regards to his makeup. It was a beach movie and he always looked the same. Not a problem on our end. My duties as the department head were keeping continuity in the looks of the cast, things like their haircuts and coloring. I also made sure we had enough extra help when needed. Ron Snyder and I covered the cast pretty much on our own."

When asked if he enjoyed his time on the set, Sharp replies, "It was a long shoot, due to the unusual working conditions. Sometimes the shark would not cooperate, but the production crew and the cast were great to work with."

Rick Sharp and Julie Andrews on the set of *Little Miss Marker*

Ron Snyder (Makeup)

Makeup must have been in the Snyder family blood. Mr. Snyder's father, Allan "Whitey" Snyder, was one of the best makeup men in Hollywood for 40-years, where he served as Marilyn Monroe's personal makeup artist for her entire career. He also had the sad duty of making up the actress for her funeral and served as a pallbearer. Coincidentally, Gary Springer's father represented Ms. Monroe, which gives this book a very cool "Six Degrees of Kevin Bacon"-type association with the actress.

Besides the eleven films he worked on with Ms. Monroe (twelve if you count *Something's Got to Give*, a film she was dismissed from and was never completed), he also performed makeup duties on movies like: *Viva Zapata* (1952), *South Pacific* (1958), *Rosemary's Baby* (1968) and *The Poseidon Adventure* (1972).

Ron Snyder began his adult life as an athlete. California born, at age 25 he was short-listed to be a member of the United States Volleyball team that competed in the 1964 Olympics in Tokyo. In 1969 he began his makeup career working on the popular television program "Love, American Style." He also worked on various "made for television" films, including "The Hatfields and the McCoys," "Sherlock Holmes in New York" and "Arthur Hailey's 'The Moneychangers'." His first feature work came on Brian De Palma's *Carrie* (1976). He describes how he came to work on *Jaws 2*:

"I got hired to do Jaws 2 by telling the studio I had no interest in working on the picture when they first contacted me. I already lived at Malibu Beach, and grew up as a beach kid, so the seaside allure wasn't a persuading factor. With most of the bigger pictures, when you turn them down they come back at you with a better offer. It's like 'how dare you say no to us at Universal?' Next thing I knew, I was off to Martha's Vineyard."

As Roy Scheider's personal makeup man, Snyder spent a lot of time with the star, both on set and off. "I had rented a house in Fort Walton Beach, Florida and I would have Monday Night Football parties with Roy, Teddy Grossman, some of the cast and some local talent. One Monday, after losing a bet to me, Roy had Maine Lobster flown in from his area of the East coast for the party which began an argument about which lobster is better, Maine or Australian, an argument that Roy and myself continued for the length of the shoot. He was easy to get along with." When asked if there were any problems with Scheider's incessant tanning, he replies, "Roy wasn't a problem for me. He stayed tanned for the entire year. My sole job was evening out his sun-bleached eyebrows

413

and staying handy. I also did a lot of the kids, though there really wasn't much to do with them either"

Besides working on Scheider, Snyder worked on the scene following the death of Eddie Marchand. "It was what I called my "shocked" makeup, which I applied to her (Ann Dusenberry) as her boyfriend was attacked by "our" shark. I later used a similar style while working on John Frankenheimer's film, *Prophecy* (1979) on a character that had witnessed a bear attack."

Frank Sparks (Stunts/ORCA Diver)

Many *Jaws* fans are unaware that *Jaws 2* wasn't the first time they had seen Frank Sparks on film.

"I was the stunt/photo double for Richard Dreyfuss under the water. He couldn't dive and I could. The gal who got me into the first film, as well as *Jaws 2*, was Verna Fields. I grew up and competed in gymnastics with her son, Kenny. I went into the Navy, where I was a Navy Seal for four years. When I got out of the service I came back to the Valley, where I lived, and I went over to see Verna. She was working on *Jaws* at the time. She had just gotten back from Martha's Vineyard and had discovered they needed some footage of Hooper underwater. They needed a photo double because Dreyfuss had an ear infection at the time. Also, he didn't know how to dive."

Mr. Sparks filled in for the actor and appears in two of the film's most terrifying scenes. "I'm the one that finds the tooth in the bottom of the boat. Also I'm the one in the shark cage when the shark is attacking and smacking at it. I'm the one that takes the bang stick out to stab the shark with the poison. And, after he damages the cage, before he kills Quint, I escape from the cage and swim to the bottom of the ocean to get away from him and watch the shark explode from an underwater point of view."

Mr. Sparks was on the film while John Hancock was the director. "I got over to Martha's Vineyard and was there for about a month of John

Hancock and his wife being there. Then Jeannot came on board. I didn't do a lot of stunt work on the Vineyard but I was also a boat master for all of the small boat craft. I was the small boat coordinator. They kept me close in case they needed me for a stunt. I'm small so I could double a lot of the kids."

He talks about the film's opening scene. "In *Jaws* we filmed both in a studio tank and the ocean. In *Jaws 2* it was all done in the ocean. I'm the first guy you see, the one with the camera who's taking pictures of the other guy posing on the ship. I'm taking pictures of the other guy and I get wiped out. That was filmed completely in the ocean off Catalina. When I was in Florida my job was to get the little Catamaran boats from here to there. I worked quite a bit with David Owsley. We were buddies and we palled around a lot in Florida. He's a super-good guy and one hell of a sailor."

Frank Sparks as the doomed diver in *Jaws 2*

A lot of his memories involve the many storms that hit during filming. "It was fun when the storms came because most of the people on the set had never really lived ON the water or worked on the water, including the directors. Some of the things they wanted to do during different situations when Mother Nature wouldn't let them do it were pretty interesting. They would want to launch a boat in one direction when the wind was blowing in another. You'd have to explain that it's physically impossible to do what they wanted. And you surely couldn't do it with the sail up in the air. Those poor kids were getting bounced around all the time. Trying to get them used to the water and swimming was hard. Some of them couldn't swim that well. It was always fun when I had to be their lifeguard. David Owsley and his sister, Susan, were great in the water. On the other end, Donna Wilkes was a little weak."

Gene Starzenski (Set Paramedic)

Mr. Starzenski had just started working at Universal when he got the call for *Jaws 2*.

"I'd been working at Universal since 1976. You had to get 30-days of work in and when you did you could join the union. You have to go through a lot of testing. And in 1977 I became a member of the Studio Medics union. One of the shows I worked on was "The Rockford Files." After they fired the director they brought everyone back from Martha's Vineyard. They asked me if I could go down to Florida for two weeks to help with the construction. It was a Friday afternoon and they told me there would be a ticket waiting for me at the airport on Monday morning. That's how fast they wanted someone there. I was married at the time and I had to go home and tell my wife I was leaving and would be back in three weeks. When I got down there they found out I was a paramedic. They needed a nurse. I guess on the first *Jaws* they had a very heavy-set nurse that no one was very happy with. So, when they found out I was a paramedic they decided to keep me. As long as they weren't shooting they didn't need a medic so on my days off I helped with the construction. It was chaos and confusion. So many things were going on on that show. They would start something, then they would shut down. They were still trying to find a director. They tried to get a DGA card for Verna Fields. We were in "stall" mode. I went to the local hospital in Pensacola and met with the nurses and doctors there. I learned they had a helicopter and I talked to the hospital. I explained to them that we would be shooting out on the ocean and that I hoped they could support me. Rather than sit at the hospital, maybe they could sit on shore. Obviously if they had an emergency they could leave. But otherwise we had them for free.

Gene Starzenski, in his *Jaws 2* crew shirt, on the set of the television show "Mother, Juggs and Speed" with Joanne Nail and Joe Penny.

Our schedule was almost always the same. They would pick us up in the morning at the hotel and they we'd drive to 7/Eleven to pick up whatever food we were going to eat for the whole day. Because once we were on set, there was no place to go. So, we'd buy our day's groceries. I'd buy whatever I wanted for breakfast. Then for lunch I'd by some Dinty Moore stew in the little cans. I used to bury them in the sand so that when it was time for lunch the stew would be warm."

So, did he stay longer than the originally planned two or three weeks?

"I was down there from June through December of 1977. It was probably the biggest project most of the people on it had ever been on. I can remember having to deal with Ricky Schroder and having to give him his allergy shots. Roy Scheider was great. I used to take care of Roy all the time. He used to come to my office and I'd clean his eyes out. He was a runner. He ran every day out in the sun. Then he got banged up on one of the boats and cracked four ribs. He was as lean as could be. A real super guy who never said a lot. He was always nice to me. He never looked down on you. I hung out a lot with Jeff Kramer too. He was under contract to Universal and he would get mad because, with my overtime and everything, I was making more money than he was. I was working constantly. The special effects shop was in the parking lot right outside my office so I was out there a lot. There were so many people in so many different places that I called back to Hollywood and told them I needed a few more medics out here but they never sent them. So, I would hire retired nurses to work in different units. And if anything big was going on out on the water I would be the one that went out there. If I had the time, I would get a nurse to watch the office and I would ride to Pensacola to pick up stuff. I'd go to buy medical stuff but I'd always get a list of other things the production needed. I could go to a store and drop $500 with no trouble."

How about the Amity Kids? Did he have to deal with a lot of sunburns and sprains during the shoot?

"Definitely. But it wasn't just that. I dealt with a lot of different things." He lowers his voice and whispers, "Someone got the crabs. They came to my room and knocked on my door and said, 'I have these things.' I knew right away what they meant. 'Do you want to see?' I didn't want to see. I told them I'd have something for them tomorrow. (NOTE: Out of respect to the actor in question I will neither reveal their name or gender). I ended up getting a case of RID because I knew where there was one case there would be more. Somehow word got to our transportation coordinator, Mel Bingham, that someone had the crabs.

He came down to my office and said, 'Gene, I want to know who has the crabs.' I told him I couldn't tell him. I didn't know how word got out and then I realized that they must have slept with somebody on the crew and told them about the situation. Next thing I knew I was dealing with another crew member. Mel would keep bugging me about it. One day I went down to the water and picked up five blue crabs. I put them into a paper bag and went to Mel's office. I tell him, 'Mel, I know who has the crabs!' He looks up from his desk and asks, 'Who?' I dump the bag on his desk and yell at him, 'You do!' He was so mad he chased me down to the ocean."

Eddie Surkin (Special Effects Crew)

Mr. Surkin was another veteran of *Jaws* that joined the *Jaws 2* crew.

"I was in charge of the same shark on both movies, which was the "sea sled" shark. The shark that came between the boats of the kids. The shark that grabbed Robert Shaw and took him down. We used that shark for most of the movie. The other sharks – the right side shark and the left side shark – had so many problems with their carriage systems. On *Jaws 2* we got caught up in a very bad storm which sunk the shark platform before we even got a chance to use it. So consequently, the sea sled shark had to do a lot more work than it was originally scheduled to do."

Eddie Surkin peeks out of the shark's mouth (photos courtesy of Eddie Surkin)

Mr. Surkin also did a lot of diving during the production. "I had always been the diver for Universal Studios for any show they did on the water. Any time they had a show on the water they called me because I was well known as a diver as well as an underwater mechanic, which is something I still do, by the way. So as soon as they started mounting up for *Jaws 2* they called me up. I had just gotten done working on *King Kong* (1976) and I got on the production right from the get go. Building the sharks. Making the mechanical parts. The electronics and pneumatics. I knew which shark I was going to be in charge of and I remember I had plenty of arguments with Bob Mattey and Roy Arbogast over it. They weren't the ones that had to go underwater to fix it if something happened. I was. I wanted to make sure that the valves were accessible. That I could float it. Because on *Jaws* we didn't know better. Every time I would have to do work underwater, maybe 40-feet down, I would have to take my oxygen tank off and slide it inside the shark's belly and then swing behind it with the mouthpiece so I could breathe. The shark couldn't fit both myself and the tank but it could take me "following" the tank. It was pretty dangerous stuff. The tank could get stuck. I could get stuck. The hose could get wrapped. It was a dangerous thing.

When I was putting the sea sled shark together at the Universal Studios Prefab area, I put most of the sharks on the exterior and everybody started bitching about the aerodynamics. I said, 'don't worry, I'm going to build a shroud around it.' That way we could take it off when we had to perform maintenance deep under water. Many times the shark would catch itself on somebodies anchor line. It could be the sound department or the camera department, but it would catch and then slide right down to the bottom of the ocean. It was very complex. We might be able to do two shots a day because it would always get caught on an anchor line. Always. And then I would have to go down and deal with it.

We shipped the sharks to Martha's Vineyard but then the director got laid off. So, we all went down to Florida to work on other entities.

420

I got called back to California to do a job for the company and then I flew back to Florida. I was re-reading the script when some guy tapped me on the back. I turned around and he asked what I was reading. I told him I was reading the script for *Jaws 2* and he said, 'meet your new director. My name is Jeannot Szwarc.' Jeannot and I became very, very close friends. Both on the movie and afterwards. We worked together on many, many projects."

Because of the weather, the sea sled shark was required to do things it wasn't built for. "It took 20 semi-trucks to ship the sharks from Universal to Florida and no sooner had we built everything when we took a big hit from a hurricane. A big hit. And it sunk. I don't know if it hit the bottom upside down or right side up. But Roy Arbogast came up to me and said that now my shark would have to do things it wasn't intended to. When I asked what, he mentioned it having to come up in the middle of a flotilla of children. And I told him that the shark wasn't designed to do that. So, he told me to design something new.

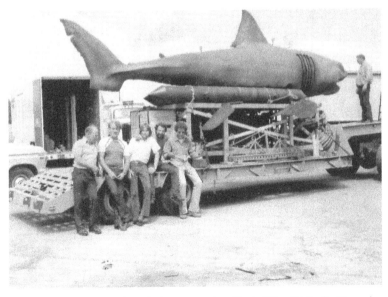

l-r – Bob Mattey, unidentified crew member, Kevin Pike, Eddie Surkin and Roy Arbogast. Stan Mahoney is on the platform with the shark

421

I remember having to call Universal's special effects department and request a really big winch. And in the right instance we could winch the bottom off the armature up so it would change the angle of the shark moving forward towards the boat. I know it sounds crazy as hell but we were able to achieve shots we never thought we'd be able to do."

As for the burns the shark received, did they design a special shark? 'No, it was the same shark. We built the head of the burnt shark. It was just the shark head and the gills behind it. We never destroyed a whole shark. Never.   Roy Arbogast did that. He was in charge of all of the skins and the rubbers. Mike Woods ran the machines. And I was with the shark. It was my baby. I also ran the diving team."

Eddie Surkin (left) and helpers wrestle one of the shark's pneumatic hoses

Mr. Surkin had a true birds-eye view of the action. "When I was steering the shark I was in a boat – in the crow's nest. I was probably 30-feet high so I could see what I was doing when I ran the controls. I had a lot of switches I had to operate. Electric switches that ran pneumatic valves. Very complex. And very tough to keep dry. The main

Filming the end

thing was trying to keep the shark and the kids together in the same shot. Sometimes we succeeded perfect. Sometimes we succeeded half-ass perfect. (laughs). One night on Martha's Vineyard I was woken up around midnight by a crewman who told me that 'we have a problem.' I asked what the problem was and he said, 'we have to go get the shark.' It seems that while towing it in Captain Murphy had a few drinks. He took a left when he should have taken a right and the shark sank to the bottom of the ocean. He had anchored his boat where it happened and when I got out there the water was running several knots and running out. So, they make a ring with the boats, make it as bright as possible and I have to go look for the shark. It was really spooky because there was nobody else in the water but me. I found the shark about 30-feet down. I had to look for the eyehooks and then attach cables. The idea was to do it without tearing up the shark more than it already had been.

The first time I jumped in the water I ended up in Timbuktu, as the water was just rushing me away. They had to send a boat to get me. I couldn't swim back to the boats because the currents were way too fast. The next time I jumped in I took a big weight. I could feel the hoses under water but I couldn't see shit. I couldn't see anything. Then you'd really look and wonder to yourself 'is that MY shark?' (laughs) It was really spooky. I could hear my heart beating. I finally climbed onto the shark. I had to hold on tight because otherwise the water would sweep me away. The water was rushing, like I was inside a big pipe. I learned that the water is either rushing IN or rushing OUT of Chappaquiddick. There is only a 10-minute lull twice a day. So you're always fighting it. I finally got a plug out, got an eye bolt in and attached a rope. I shimmied my way up the hoses back to the boat. It was freezing cold. They got more crew members out there and got the shark back up. I went back to the hotel and went back to sleep. It was five o'clock in the morning at that point. As they hauled the shark back up, Murphy was arrested and put in jail. Of course, they couldn't keep him in jail because we needed him to pull the boat. He was a maniac." (laughs)

Among his fondest memories are the Saturday night cast parties at the Holiday Inn. "I never had clothes on for the parties. I was always in my Speedos. Everybody thought I was ridiculous. They used to call me Tarzan. I looked like Tarzan. I was pretty well built. I was definitely in good shape." I remark that he and Roy Scheider were probably the only two men there confident enough to wear Speedos. "You're right. You're absolutely right. I remember kidding Roy about it. He was an awesome, awesome dude. I spent lots of time talking to him."

Signs at Universal announced that *Jaws 2* was "coming sooner than you think"

THE ART OF JAWS 2

THE FILM POSTER FOR *JAWS*, designed by Roger Kastell, remains today one of the most iconic of all time. During the film's heyday the style was often used in everything from political cartoons to book covers. Which meant that the *Jaws 2* poster had a high bar to live up to.

In late 1976, posters went up at Universal Studios trumpeting *Jaws 2*. These posters announced the return of Roy Schedier and Lorraine Gary, as well as returning producers Richard Zanuck and David Brown. The poster also noted that the film would be "directed by John Hancock from a screenplay by Howard Sackler and Dorothy Tristan."

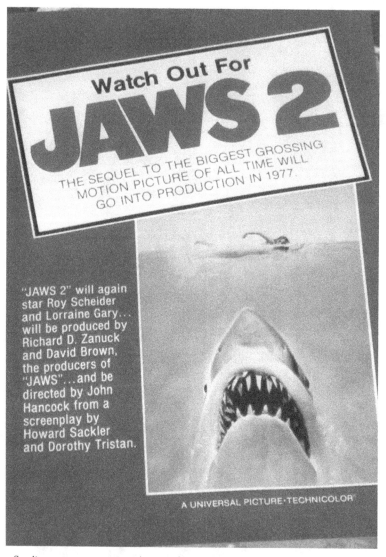

Studio poster announcing the new film with John Hancock as director (from the collection of Jim Beller)

The bar was reached, and maybe even cleared, by the next poster, which was released in late 1977. A striking red poster, featuring a beautiful sunset and an ominous fin announced the upcoming film. It also included one of the most imitated and parodied taglines in history, "Just when you thought it was safe to go back in the water..." The tagline is thought to have been written by Andrew J. Kuehn, who created many of the great trailers of the 70s and 80s. I was able to find a copy of the trailer's script in the archives of the Academy of Motion Picture Arts and Sciences, but there was no writer credited.

The poster went on to inform the looker that the ALL NEW *Jaws 2* would be in theatres on June 16, 1978.

This poster was designed by Jack Leynnwood, an artist best known for his hundreds of paintings that came on the boxes of model kits released by the Revell Company. A one-time child actor and saxophone prodigy, Leynnwood learned to fly as a child and spent World War II training Air Force fighter pilots. After the war, Leynnwood studied commercial illustration at Art Center College of Design in Los Angeles on the GI Bill.

Besides his amazing model kit paintings, he also designed other movie posters, including *Hell's Angels* (1930), *Airport '77* (1977), *Gray Lady Down* (1978) and *Great White* (1981).

Mr. Leynnwood passed away in 1999, but I was able to talk to his protégé', artist Mike Boss, about how he met Mr. Leynnwood , whose work he had admired as a fan for many years, and how he came to do the *Jaws 2* poster.

"I was taking a history course at Colby (Kansas) Junior College and there was a teacher there from Germany whose name was Horst Chaftenger. For some reason he liked me and he pulled me aside one day. He knew I hated academia. He said, 'I don't care if you want to be an orchestrator or an illustrator but you need to write your hero a letter. If they're worth their salt as a human being they will answer you.' And I did.

429

I wrote to Phil Lang in New York and, after speaking to him for about an hour, decided that wasn't the path I wanted to go. And then later on I called Jack. I called Jack at home and he told me to send him out whatever I had and he would give me his honest opinion of them. I still have every letter or note or card that I ever got from Jack. What he saw in the artwork I sent him, I don't have a clue."

Mr. Boss relates how he learned about the poster. "I called him up one day and after we talked for a while I asked him what he was working on. He said, 'I'm working on the biggest piece of shit I've ever done in my life and I'm getting paid damn well for it!' That was Jack."

Jack Leynnwood's original art (image courtesy of Mike Boss)

The release poster, which hit theatres in early May 1978, was designed by artist Lou Feck. Mr. Feck was a well-known artist who made his living creating the covers of paperback novels. Among his most iconic are the early novelizations in the "Star Trek" series as well as the cover paintings for both "The Deep" and "Black Sunday." Sadly, Mr. Feck passed away in 1981, but I was able to chat with his son, Mark, who was 16 when his father passed. He shared some great stories about his father and the original painting.

One of the best movie posters EVER – the *Jaws 2* advance poster

Mike Boss (left) with Jack Leynnwood

"My dad went to the Pratt Institute but even before that he knew he wanted to be an artist. He knew it before he went to high school. He had that rare thing that we all wish we had in that he knew what he wanted to do at an early age. He went to Pratt and then became an artist for Bantam/Doubleday/Dell. He won several awards for his work. He was named "Illustrator of the Year" more than once.

Besides "Jaws 2" he did the covers for "Black Sunday" and "The Deep." If you remember the painting for "The Deep," that's my half-sister Faith on the painting. I came home one day to find my sister on the floor and my father above her on a ladder. She's got scuba gear on. That's what was going on at my house. (laughs). I walked by, shook my head and just kept going to do my homework. That's what I remember best about my father. Things like that."

So, did he do a book cover or a movie poster?

"When a book is published it comes out as a hardcover. If it's really popular the publishers decide to release it as a paperback. Bantam would

432

then have him do the covers. Sometimes they note whether or not the book is going to be a movie. If that happens, sometimes that same artwork will be used for the film poster."

Lou Feck's original art

The release poster for *Jaws 2*

The image first appeared on the cover of the novelization of the film, which was released on April 19, 1978. If you have an original printing of the book you will notice one big difference from the movie poster: the water skier is nowhere to be seen.

"It was something the publisher did, and I think this was the only time they did it. They had him do the painting with the water skier present, then asked him to re-do it with the water skier missing. So he did two versions. I've seen both paperback versions. You can obviously see the wake the water skier leaves on the poster featuring her. But if you look closely, the skier's wake remains in the version without her. It's so well done that if you didn't know this you would never be able to tell.

My father used to work out our basement and most of the time he was cranking out one painting a week. That's tough. He needed to be undisturbed. I didn't spend a lot of time down there with him because he was working. That being said, I do have an interesting story about that painting. While my father was in the process of painting the poster, my cousin Rick came up from Tulsa, Oklahoma. He was enamored of my father's work and so proud of him. He would brag at school about his uncle. So, my father, with both of us in front of him, decided to include us in the painting. The paint was still wet when he put two small dots next to his signature. He said that one of them was for Rick and the other one was for me. He told us this way, when we saw the poster, we could tell people he did it and that he had added the two dots to the artwork just for us."

Lou Feck (image used with permission of Mark Feck)

Jaws 2 Sharkfacts poster

Alternate release poster – this art was later used elsewhere

Mexican release poster

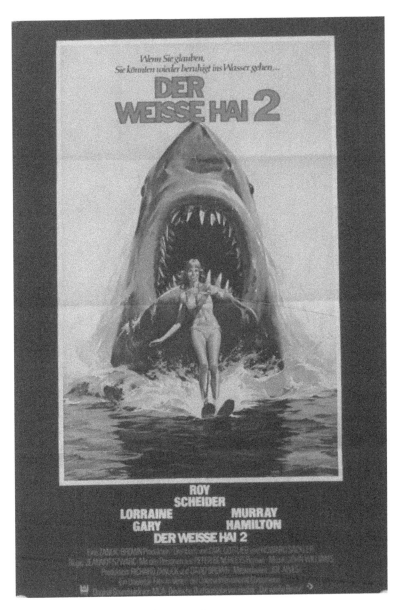

German release poster

Polish release poster

1981 Re-issue poster

2017 MONDO *Jaws 2* poster

Record album

Marvel Comic Book Adaptation

443

MAD Magazine had some fun with the image

As did CRAZY

Collect enough cards and you could make your own poster. Funny, I never once had a person come up to me and say "I'll trade you two Marge's for a rare non-screaming Jackie."

Or you could color your own

"Starts Tomorrow" ad from the Tampa Tribune. My friends and I were first in line the next day at the Britton Cinema

As you can see, there was a lot of *Jaws 2* art going around. But what about the fans? I did feature a few fan drawings in the original edition, drawn by fans with some talent. And then I found the motherlode.

Federico Alain

Some of the most amazing art work I've ever seen has been created by this gentleman. An unconditional fan of *Jaws*, he has created over one-hundred original digital paintings, including the cover of this book, based on scenes from Jaws and its sequels, sharing them with fans all over the world by posting them on the Jaws 2 Group Facebook page administrated by Paul Tastanis. He is also an art teacher and has a Master of Arts in Visual Communication.

447

"Brody Shooting"

"The Last Shot"

"The Attack"

"The Burn"

"Keep Off – High Voltage"

"Bob's Death"

Check him out at: http://fa57579.wixsite.com/artwork-of-fredain

Lee Hartnup

Another friend and fan whose work I admire is Lee Hartnup. Lee loves all things horror and enjoys writing, drawing, sculpting and playing musical instruments. His images are so impressive that seven time Academy Award winning makeup maestro Rick Baker is a fan. I'm sure once you see his work you will be too. Lee lives on the south coast of England with his wife, two children. a dog and a Venus fly trap!

Poster

"Unaware"

"Before the Burn!"

"Bullets at the Beach"

"Bob Taken"

You can contact Lee at: https://www.facebook.com/lee.hartnup.

Mike and Cathy Schultz

Art is much more than pen and ink to paper. My friend Mike Schultz and his wife, Cathy, have decided that every home needs their own *Jaws 2* shark. Here are two of the ScarFace Bruce sharks that they sell.

The first is an All New MASSIVE 1:6 Scale Cable-Chomping ScarFace Shark Bust. Released in June 2017, the product run is limited to the life of the original molds only. The bust is approximately one-foot tall [30.48cm] by 13-inches wide with removable cable [33.02cm].

Next up is a bust that is just being released as this edition goes to print. This All New Full-length Epic Class ScarFace Bruce Shark measures an impressive 25-inches long [63.5cm]. Again, the product run is limited to the life of the original molds only. This shark comes with a Fincredible Mechanical Arm Style Display Stand.

Both sharks are made with a Pure Resin Construction and come with Free Paint and Gore customization and a Signed Certificate of Authenticity from Industry Practical FX artists Mike and Cathy Schultz.

For more information on these amazing items, and many more *Jaws* themed busts, visit: http://www.sharkcityozark.com/index.html.

FROM THE ARCHIVES

IN THE PAST TWO YEARS, I've learned that, as large as my personal collection of *Jaws* and *Jaws 2* memorabilia is, there are a lot of people that have some great items. Props. Costumes. Toys. Thanks to cast, crew and friends, here is a peek at some of the memorabilia of *Jaws 2*.

This is as good a time as any for me to thank Chris Kiszka for his assistance in putting this book together. Chris has the largest collection of screen-used props from *Jaws* and *Jaws 2* then anyone I know. If you were lucky to attend the first JAWSFest in 2005 you probably saw some of his collection, which was one of the featured displays at the event.

Chris Kiszka with a friend (the man has his own Quint)

Roy Scheider's Amity PD Uniform Shirt (from the collection of Chris Kiszka)

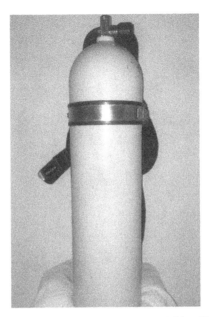

Scuba diver's tank (from the collection of Chris Kiszka)

Diver's Camera (from the collection of Chris Kiszka) I learned after the first edition came out that I had published the photo of the camera upside down.

Crew Jacket (from the collection of Chris Kiszka)

Another collector is my friend Peter Spadetti. I've sat down in some pretty comfortable chairs in my lifetime but none of them made me as happy as when I sat in a chair at Peter's house. The reason: it was the fighting chair that Quint sits in on the deck of the ORCA in *Jaws*. It is now Pete's chair, as well as the rod and reel. And a few more items.

Peter Spadetti and the Tow Fin (from the collection of Peter Spadetti – photo credit - Allison Courtemanche)

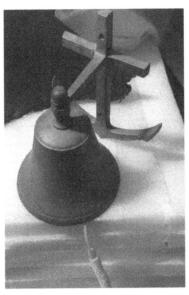

A bell from one of the boats used in the film (from the collection of Peter Spadetti – photo credit - Allison Courtemanche)

Proposed Roy Scheider's Amity PD uniform tops from the John Hancock era. These were used in costume tests prior to the beginning of filming. Note the different color AMITY PD patches (from the collection of Peter Spadetti – photo credit - Allison Courtemanche)

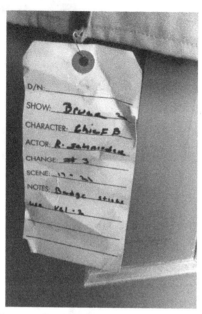

147. SHOW: Bruce 2. CHARACTER: Chief B. ACTOR: R. Schneider (really wardrobe person – Schneider?). AND his badge sticks! (from the collection of Peter Spadetti – photo credit - Allison Courtemanche)

The author in Quint's fighting chair. Thank you, Pete!

460

Christopher Lord is a friend whose job took him to the backlot of Universal Studios in California. While there he noticed something that looked familiar. Could it be? Yes, indeed, Chris had stumbled onto the resting place of "Tina's Joy," the boat used by Ann Dusenberry and Gary Dubin in *Jaws 2*.

"Tina's Joy" abandoned on the back lot (photos courtesy Christopher Lord)

Missing the piece torn off by Eddie during the attack

461

The rear of the boat

If you look hard enough, you will see where the letters J-O-Y have been
removed

Capt. Daves on the Gulf isn't just a great place to eat. It also served as one of the main location spots during the production of *Jaws 2*. Many a morning cast and crew would sail off to work from their docks. The restaurant also makes a few appearances in the film, most notably right after the diver suffers the embolism and Brody and Ellen rush to the scene. While the film is celebrating its 40th Anniversary in 2018, Capt. Daves is celebrating their 50th.

They very kindly shared some of their photos for your enjoyment.

Roy Scheider and Lorraine Gary run past Capt. Daves in *Jaws 2*

Filming off the dock

Filming off the dock

Roy Scheider

The sign means YOU, kid

Capt. Daves boat, the AQUANAUT, was also featured in the film

This 3-dimensional billboard once greeted visitors to Destin.

For more information, hop on line and head to http://www.captdavesonthegulf.com/. Tell them the *Jaws 2* book guy sent you.

Verna Fields

Jean Coulter burns the shark (photos courtesy of Jean Coulter)

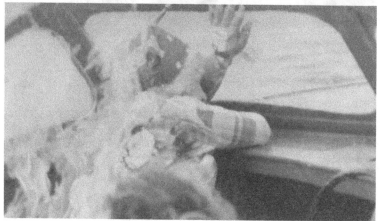

Donna Wilkes

Jeff Kramer mans the slate

Carl Gottlieb and Jeannot Szwarc plot the day's adventures

Deleted scene, featuring Tom Dunlop, Keith Gordon and Billy Van Zandt.
Notice Billy's hat?

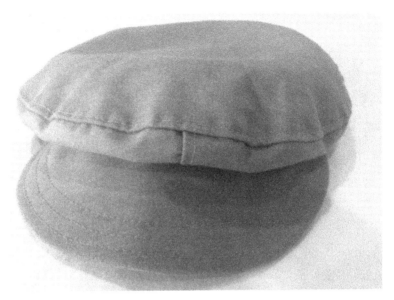

Billy's hat! (courtesy of Billy Van Zandt)

Roy Scheider gave Billy Van Zandt this Farrah Fawcett puzzle for his birthday.
(courtesy of Billy Van Zandt)

Deleted scene – the death of Bob – an alternate view

Tom Dunlop and Gigi Vorgan (photo courtesy Tom Dunlop)

Original teeth from the *Jaws 2* shark

Los Angeles book signing at Dark Delicacies – (l-r) Carl Gottlieb, Gigi Vorgan, Ann Dusenberry, Joe Alves, Jeff Kramer, Martha Swatek, Donna Wilkes, David Elliot, Lenora May, the author. Many thanks to Del Howison for inviting us to his store.

I love the fact that young fans love this film. (l-r) Kyle Foster, Riley Foster, the author

The Foster boys with Joe Alves and Carl Gottlieb

Riley, Ann Dusenberry, Kyle and Gigi Vorgan

Lenora May, Kyle, Donna Wilkes, Riley

Chicago book signing with Karen Corboy

Florida book signing at the Magnolia Grill – (l-r) Bobbie Chasarik, Captain Jerry Baxter, the author, Ben Anderson

Bobbie Chasarik, holding a photo of her father

While in Florida, the book visited the bar of the Hog's Breath Saloon, where the Amity Kids used to hang out

Some nice press for the book

Back to Los Angeles – (l-r) Ben Marley, Tom Dunlop, Martha Swatek,
the author, Billy Van Zandt

(l-r) the Shark, Tom Dunlop, Martha Swatek, Donna Wilkes, Ben Marley,
Gigi Vorgan and Billy Van Zandt

479

CATCHING UP

AGAIN, MY SINCERE THANKS to everyone that shared their stories. Here's a look at what they've done after their *Jaws 2* adventures.

Von Babasin

While at Universal, Von worked on the entire productions of *Airport '77*, *The Incredible Shrinking Woman* (1981) and John Carpenter's *The Thing* (1982). He also worked on the sets of *The Blues Brothers* (1980), *Where the Buffalo Roam* (1980) and, due to his familiarity with the round set used for the airplane barrel rolls, he spent some time on *The Concorde...Airport*

'79 (1979). For television, his work includes "Battlestar Galactica," "Buck Rogers in the 25th Century," "The Rockford Files," "Baa Baa Black Sheep," "Knightrider" and "BJ and the Bear." He also provided his feet to make plaster castings used for the Incredible Hulk's feet. After leaving Universal he worked on several independently made films, including *Big Bad Mama II* (1987), which starred Angie Dickinson and Robert Culp, *Steele Justice* (1987) with Martin Kove and Sela Ward and *Phantasm 2* (1988). He also served as a grip on Luis Valdez' *La Bamba* (1987). He did multiple duties both on and behind the camera for the film *Forever* (1992), which starred Sean Young, Keith Coogan and Diane Ladd. Not only did he handle the special effects, Foley and sound effects, he wrote the music for the film and appeared on screen with his band, the R H Factor.

Von Babasin (left) with his band, the RH Factor

Von lives in Los Angeles, where he continues to play his music and is currently producing and directing a documentary about his father. He also has a Facebook page dedicated to his father and the music of the era. You can check it out at: http://www.facebook.com/jazzinhollywood.

Von Babasin

Charles Burke

Mr. Burke is retired and lives in Florida.

John Kretchmer

After completing his assignment on *Jaws 2*, John Kretchmer worked for the next 15 years as an assistant director on films as diverse as *The In-Laws* (1979), *The Naked Gun* (1988) and *The Naked Gun: 2 ½* , *Flatliners* (1990) and, ultimately, *Jurassic Park*. Through his association with Steven Spielberg and Kathleen Kennedy, he began his directing career on their television show "seaQuest DSV." Since that time, he has directed over 160 hours of episodic television (including several episodes of Matt Nix's "Burn Notice" and "The Good Guys"), and has directed more episodes of "Special Unit 2," "Veronica Mars," "Charmed," "The Twilight Zone" (the 2002-2003 version), "Army Wives," "White Collar" and "iZombie" than any other director.

John Kretchmer and Roy Scheider on the set of "seaQuest DSV"

In addition to his work as a director, Kretchmer has worked as a producer/director on "Push," "Special Unit 2," "Army Wives," "Forever," "Frequency" and "Life Sentence." He has written several screenplays, one of which was a finalist at the Sundance Lab and a comedic play, "Shh! Art!," which received staged readings at the CAST Theater, the Williamstown Theater Festival and the Pasadena Playhouse, among other places.

John loves to put *Citizen Kane* (1939) on his resume just to see if anyone is paying attention.

When not on location for work, Kretchmer lives in Los Angeles, where he is tolerated by his sainted wife, Wendy, and three of his four children. The fourth child lives in Brussels, Belgium, where he works for Apple. It is still unknown if this child tolerates him.

Scott Maitland

After Jaws 2, Scott Maitland continued as an assistant director on both television - the "Centennial" mini-series, "Hawaii Five-O" - and film - *The King of Comedy* (1983), *Jaws 3-D* and *Unforgiven* (1992). He also served as Production Manager on over twenty television films and series, including "Walker: Texas Ranger" and "Without a Trace." Now retired, he lives with his wife in California.

Scott Maitland and his wife, Carol

Kevin Pike

Following *Jaws 2*, Mr. Pike worked on the special effects teams for such films as *1941* (1979), *Escape from New York* (1981), *Star Trek II: The Wrath of Khan* (1982) and *Star Wars: Episode VI – Return of the Jedi* (1983). He served as the Special Effects Supervisor on *Back to the Future* (1985), which netted him a BAFTA nomination.

He has continued to work in both film – *Hook* (1992), *Jurassic Park*, *Ed Wood* (1994) – and television – "Cold Case," "Star Trek: Enterprise" and "Earth 2," for which he won an Emmy for Special Visual Effects.

Kevin Pike

Mr. Pike is also a member of the Directors Guild, the Screen Actors Guild and serves on the Special Visual Effects Committees for both the Oscar and Emmy Academies. He is president of Filmtrix, Inc. which he started in 1983. He resides in Sherman Oaks, CA.

Arthur Schmidt

Mr. Schmidt's first film after *Jaws 2* was *Coal Miner's Daughter* (1980), which earned him his first Academy Award nomination. Other films in the early part of the decade include *The Idolmaker* (1980), *The Buddy System* (1984) and *Fandango* (1985). Then fate took charge. As Mr. Schmidt explains, "I was very lucky that Bob Zemeckis walked into my cutting room one day and asked me to cut the first *Back to the Future* (1985)." That collaboration led to seven more films and two Oscars, for *Who Framed Roger Rabbit* (1988) and *Forrest Gump* (1994). "Bob

486

Zemeckis is a brilliant director and his material is a gift to any film editor."

Other films cut by Mr. Schmidt include *The Last of the Mohicans* (1992), *The Birdcage* (1996) and *Primary Colors* (1998), the last two films directed by Mike Nichols.

Arthur Schmidt

Rick Sharp

Now semi-retired, with 101 films to his credit, Sharp spent the next four decades after *Jaws 2* working on some of the most popular films of all time. He did six more films for Universal, including *Walk Proud* (1979), *Little Miss Marker* (1980) and *Xanadu* (1980).

He met actress Julie Andrews on the set of *Little Miss Marker* and the two began a long professional relationship. In fact, Sharp was the makeup artist on seven films directed by Andrews' husband, Blake Edwards, including *S.O.B.* (1981), *Micki and Maude* (1984) and *Blind Date* (1987) and continues to serve as Ms. Andrews' personal makeup artist. He has also worked extensively with Tom Cruise on such films as

Top Gun (1986), *Cocktail* (1988), *Rainman* (1988) and *Born on the Fourth of July* (1989), where he served as Cruise's personal makeup artist.

Rick Sharp, with Tom Cruise, on the set of *Days of Thunder*

His other films include *Grumpy Old Men* (1993) and its sequel, *Grumpier Old Men* (1995), *Forrest Gump* (1994), *That Thing You Do* (1996), *Bowfinger* (1999), *Charlie Wilson's War* (2007) and *Get Smart* (2008).

Ron Snyder

Following Jaws 2, Mr. Snyder continued what would become a 46-year career with work on films like *Goldengirl* (1979), *Bustin' Loose* (1981) and *Hard Country* (1981), the first of several films featuring Kim Basinger, who he had married in October 1980. They divorced in 1989. Other films include *Three Kings* (1999), *The Road to Perdition* (2002) and *The Last Samurai* (2003). In 2006 he returned to television, where he received two Emmy Awards for his work on the series "Deadwood." He also worked on "John from Cincinnati," "Swingtown" and "Hung." In

1998 he published the book "Kim Basinger: Longer than Forever" under the name Ron Britton.

Frank Sparks

After *Jaws 2*, Frank Sparks spent the next two decades risking his life while doing stunts for such films as *Star Trek III: The Search for Spock* (1984), *Commando* (1985), *Ghostbusters II* (1989), *Hook* (1992) and *Sphere* (1998). He is now retired and lives in California.

Gene Starzenski

Following *Jaws 2*, Gene continued to take care of the casts and crews on the sets of such films as *Wanda Nevada* (1979), *Megaforce* (1982), *The Doors* (1991), *Cool World* (1992), *Swordfish* (2001), *Mr. & Mrs. Smith* (2005) and *The Dark Knight Rises* (2012). He currently resides in California.

Gene Starzenski

Eddie Surkin

After his work on Jaws 2, Eddie Surkin went on to work on the special effects crews of such films as *Escape from New York*, *To Die For* (1988), *Single White Female* (1992) and *The Jungle Book* (1995). He also worked on such diverse television programs as "Scarecrow and Mrs. King," "Reno 911" and the "Alien Nation" films. He is now retired and living in California.

Eddie Surkin

EPILOGUE

So, WHAT HAVE WE LEARNED? On June 16, 1978, *Jaws 2* changed Hollywood in a way that few films before or after ever would. It showed the industry that people would turn out for more of a good thing.

Jaws 2 was the first film to put the numeral "2" in the title. But whether it's "2" or "II" or 3,4 or 5 for that matter, it's apparent that it's the name in front of the numbers that matters most.

If you remember, in the Prologue we listed the ten highest grossing films at the time we started writing. They were:

1. *Avatar*
2. *Titanic*
3. *The Avengers*
4. *Harry Potter and the Deathly Hallows – Part 2*

5. *Frozen*
6. *Iron Man 3*
7. *Transformers: Dark of the Moon*
8. *The Lord of the Rings: The Return of the King*
9. *Skyfall*
10. *The Dark Knight Rises*

As we finish, let's once again check out *Box Office Mojo.com* and see what they are now:

1. *Avatar*
2. *Titanic*
3. *The Avengers*
4. *Furious 7* (2015)
5. *The Avengers: Age of Ultron* (2015)
6. *Harry Potter and the Deathly Hollows – Part 2*
7. *Frozen*
8. *Jurassic World* (2015)
9. *Iron Man 3*
10. *Transformers: Dark of the Moon*

Notice anything? In the time it took us to write this book, three films have moved into the top ten. What did they all have in common? It's ok, you can say it. THEY WERE SEQUELS. And we should also note that Disney has announced they will be making a sequel to "Frozen." Finally, as we finish up, "Jurassic World" has only just opened so it may be even higher on the list by the time you read this.

At press time there are currently twenty-nine sequels/remakes slated for 2016. That's more than one every two-weeks. Are we heading toward a time when the only movies made are sequels? Hopefully not. With the ease and in-expense it is today to pick up a video camera, hopefully there are still people out there with an original idea that they want to share. It's just a matter of getting people to see them. Of course, if they're successful, you can always look forward to the sequel!

ENDNOTES
AND THANK YOUS

[1] Carl Gottlieb, introduction by Peter Benchley, The Jaws Log © 1975 & 2001, Newmarket Press for It Books, HarperCollins, New York, 217 pp, 2012. Available online wherever books are sold, in a variety of editions.

[2] Ray Lloynd, The Jaws 2 Log (New York City: Dell, 1978) 21

[3] Lloynd, The Jaws 2 Log, 25

[4] Joseph McBride, Steven Spielberg: A Biography (2nd Edition) (University Press of Mississippi, 2011) 247

[5] McBride, Steven Spielberg: A Biography (2nd Edition) 248

Well, we did it. We made it through, hopefully without any papercuts, and we learned some more about the sequel that started it all.

And, on that note, let's see how the sequel has affected the list of the Top 10 Highest Grossing films of all time.

When we were last together, these films were at the top of that list:

1. *Avatar*
2. *Titanic*
3. *The Avengers*
4. *Furious 7*
5. *The Avengers: The Age of Ultron*
6. *Harry Potter and the Deathly Hollows – Part 2*
7. *Frozen*
8. *Jurassic World*
9. *Iron Man 3*
10. *Transformers: Dark of the Moon*

As we closed the original edition of this book we noted that *Jurassic World* had only recently opened and would surely climb higher on the charts. That being said, as I publish the latest list I will note that *The Avengers: Infiniti Wars*, just opened this weekend so, by the time you read this, it may be well on its way up the list. Here is the latest Top 10 Highest Grossing films of all time as of May 1, 2018:

1. *Avatar*
2. *Titanic*
3. *Star Wars: The Force Awakens* (2015)
4. *Jurassic World*
5. *The Avengers*
6. *Furious 7*
7. *The Avengers: The Age of Ultron*
8. *Harry Potter and the Deathly Hollows – Part 2*
9. *Star Wars: The Last Jedi* (2017)
10. *Black Panther* (2018)

It's a sequel world and we're all just a small part of it!

THANK YOUS

There are many people to thank for their participation and support of this project. First off I'd like to thank Lou Pisano, whose support and assistance during the production of this expanded edition was greatly appreciated. Much thanks also to the following for their help in obtaining interrviews and/or photos: Edith Blake, Von Babisin, Jim Beller, Mike Boss, John Carroll, Corey Castellano, Jean Coulter, Bobbie Chasarik, Capt. Daves on the Gulf in Destin, Florida, Rene Ben David, Mark Feck, Alain Federico, Lee Gambin, Chris Kiszka, Jeffrey Kramer, Christopher Lord, Edward McCormack, Kevin Pike, A.W. Ratliff, Tom Rice, Peter Spadetti, Gene Starzenski, Eddie Surkin, Pauly Tee, Jackie Blue and the staff of the Ramada Inn in Destin, Florida, Bow Van Riper of the Martha's Vineyard Museum, Kathy Marler Blue of the Destin History and Fishing Museum, Jessica at Scott E. Thomas and Daughter Photography in Lee's Summit, Missouri – she worked miracles with the Edith Blake contact sheets, the Federal Express Office in Lee's Summit, Missouri (especially Tabitha) and Chad Godfrey at Summit Video Services in Lee's Summit, Missouri.

I'd also like to thank someone we didn't thank in the original edition and that is our publisher, Ben Ohmart. From our first email detailing our project to today he has been nothing but supportive of what we were attempting to do. And if you are holding a "color" edition of this book, thank him as well for listening to the fans. Also, much thanks to Allan Duffin of Duffin Creative, who worked under a demanding deadline to get this published on time.

Speaking of the fans, my sincere thanks to every one of you that supported this project, be it from Day 1 or just by purchasing this book. This truly was a labor of love and I hope you all feel the same rush I did when you hear a story or see a photo for the first time. For those of you I have chatted with, either via email or in-person, I know I speak for Lou when I say it was an honor to undertake this project and your kind words for our work are most humbling.

A special thank you to the family members that sent in photos of the special people we lost over the past two years: George Demmy, Jeff Dubin, Marc Gilpin, Michael Negrin and Duone Mattis-Sprouse. Unfortunately I couldn't locate any of Joseph Mascolo's family (both the phone number and email address I had were no longer valid) so I picked one of him that I liked and I hope they agree with my decision.

Finally, I'd like to thank my family, including my son Phillip and his family. But most of all I'd like to thank my beautiful and patient wife, Juanita. We just celebrated our 10th Wedding Anniversary and she has put up with everything *Jaws*-related with good humor. The other night we were at a Kansas City Royals baseball game when, for no obvious reason, the stadium P.A. began playing the *Jaws* theme. As soon as she heard it, Juanita turned to me and said, "I just can't get away from it." Thank you for your love, dear. Without you in my life all of my endeavors would feel empty.

ABOUT THE AUTHOR

Michael A. Smith is STILL a member of the governing board, as well as secretary, of the Kansas City Film Critics Circle, the second oldest film critic group in the country, and his reviews and commentary can be found on a website he co-founded with fellow *Jaws* pal Mike Gencarelli, Media Mikes.com. He is also the co-host, with Jeremy Werner and Loey Lockerby, of "Behind the Mikes," a Podcast produced by Media Mikes. com.

In June 2016, he became a grandfather again of future Major League Baseball player Hudson Smith. Together with his granddaughter, Harper, they are among the most beautiful gifts God could have ever given him. He still lives with THE most beautiful gift he's ever received, his wife Juanita, in Lee's Summit, Missouri.

The author, staying far away from the water.

INDEX

9 781629 333298